Festival
Planning Guide

Creating Community Events
with Big Hearts and Small Budgets

Written and illustrated by

Betty Lucke

Published by Spearmint Books

Festival planning guide © 2013 Betty L. Lucke

Published by Spearmint Books, Vacaville, CA .
Printed in the United States of America

For more resources for planners, visit www.festivalplanningguide.com

Publisher's Cataloging-in-Publication
Lucke, Betty.
Festival planning guide : creating community events with big hearts and small budgets / written and illustrated by Betty Lucke. -- 1st ed.
p. cm.
Includes bibliographical references and index.
ISBN 978-0-9884631-8-9
1. Special events--Planning--Handbooks, manuals, etc.
2. Special events--Management--Handbooks, manuals, etc.
I. Title.
GT3405.L83 2013   394.2
QBI 12-600241

Cover design by Tara Baumann
Ink drawings by Betty Lucke.
The footprint icon and the puzzle piece are from Microsoft Word clip art.

Some event forms have been based on the Medieval Fantasy Festival, hosted by the Downtown Vacaville Business Improvement District in Vacaville, CA. Permission for their use has been granted.

Acknowledgements

My heartfelt gratitude goes to the dedicated, persevering Medieval Fantasy Festival committee members, without whose enthusiasm and hard work there would not have been a festival. For their challenge and assistance I would like to extend my thanks to the Downtown Vacaville Business Improvement District, former Executive Director, Steve McKay, present Executive Director, Bob Vollmer, and the board members with whom I served.

Special thanks go to Shirley McGowan and Ellen Simonin for their cooperation and support on each event we have worked on together. Special thanks go to my focus group members, Shauna Manina, Bev Morlock, Phil Venable, and Shelley Dally. Not only did they help on events, but they also gave me valuable insight and input as I completed the book-writing process.

For their support and encouragement, many thanks go to the Town Square Library Get Published Group and Writing Groups.

I would like to thank these folks for sharing their expertise with me:
- Art contests, silent auctions, and décor—Dotty Schenk
- Brainstorming and creative ideas—Shauna Manina and Bev Morlock
- Chamber of Commerce insights—Alex Hall
- Computer gurus—Ted Harding, Amy Mason, Joseph Whitson
- Document chaser, *par excellence*—Judy St. George
- Entertainment—Bryn Tucker, Live Music Center
- Festival of Trees—Bonnie Rodda
- Grant writing—Bev Morlock
- Program and ad creation—Lenore Chancellor
- Proofreading and editing—Deni Harding and Bev Morlock
- School events—Shelley Dally and Mark Stevenson
- T-shirt printing—Sean Sandahl
- Venues and logistics—Phil Venable
- Website—Brian Irwin

A huge thank you goes to my husband, Rick. With much grace, he put up with my spending countless hours—dreaming, scheming, sitting in front of the computer, and meeting with folks. His support has been invaluable.

Table of Contents

Preface

Festival Planning Guide

This book is for those who care about the quality of life where they live. They want to help their community, school, or nonprofit organization put on an event in which frugality and making-do are key facts of life. It is for those who work with volunteers instead of salaried folks. It is for real, creative people with big hearts and small budgets who learn new skills along the way, form new friendships, and know the satisfaction of a job well done. It is about a community working together.

Do not underestimate the power of dedicated leaders and volunteers. Hired experts may put on a spectacular event, but the volunteers have the advantage with their passion, love for their community, and roots that go deep. Long after the hired professionals have moved on, the effects of the home-town workers will remain.

I fell into the world of special-event management through an idea for an event in my city's downtown where I owned a business. My husband and I had read aloud to each other *The Lord of the Rings* by J.R.R. Tolkien. My soul was touched by watching Peter Jackson's movie trilogy version of Tolkien's epic about leaders with great integrity and little people—hobbits who did great things. I had a vision of a festival that could fulfill several goals for our downtown as well as celebrate this inspiring story.

I was intimidated, never having been in charge of anything like this before, but very determined. This vision morphed into the Medieval Fantasy Festival which had a glorious seven-year run.

To guide my initial steps in planning I turned first to the library and the bookstores. I couldn't find much help there for planning an event. There were books about planning conventions, corporate meetings, and charity luncheons, but not much for a grass-roots community event. I found a book which listed and commented on many different types of festivals in the United States. Just by studying that lengthy annotated list, I discovered that most successful festivals had the same five components in common:

- Food
- Music
- Entertainment
- Vendors (art, crafts, and other merchandise)
- Children's activities

My friends who had worked on festivals gave me some checklists for events—mostly logistical items. Over lunches and coffee, my ideas were batted back and forth; this input from others helped my vision take on a more realistic shape. As our festival took shape and grew, I visited many events, observed, and learned. Surfing the net gave me a much wider insight into a broad range of events. I volunteered to be on event committees for different organizations. I saw a great need for a helpful, step-by-step guide for others who were intimidated by the same process I was going through. There is no need for everyone to re-invent the wheel when a guide can show you the way and instill confidence in your ability.

Putting on an event is like doing a giant, living, moving jigsaw puzzle. Chapters in this guide describe the puzzle pieces you need to successfully complete the whole puzzle.

When you put together an event, you will find that doing it properly will require a lot of initiative, passion, and time. If you love what you are doing, you are already proceeding in the right direction. This guide will help you utilize your time in the most profitable way.

Author's Note:
I have tried to use non-sexist language throughout, knowing that good workers come in both sexes. Often I tied myself in knots grammatically. I ask the reader's forgiveness for my use of the pronoun 'they' to refer to a singular he or she.

Sample Festival

A mythical festival has been created to give you ideas and to show you how things work. This is the Third Annual **Green Festival: An Eco-friendly Future Fair,** held in the make-believe location of Opswatch, IZ, and hosted by the Downtown Opswatch Business Association. It will be a one-day event held on Saturday, April 18, 2015, at Old Town Square, a park in the center of Opswatch, surrounded by shops and businesses. Some sample forms from this event are included in the text, and some are found in the Appendix. Use them for templates to draft your own forms.

Event plans include:

- Craft vendors, vendors of eco-friendly products and services, nonprofit groups, and food vendors will have booths on the closed-off streets surrounding the square.
- Classes and workshops will be in the Carnegie Library and Community Center and at Old First Church, which face the park. There will be a presentation from a local nursery: "Water-Wise Gardening and Landscaping"; a forum by the Master Gardeners: "Four Seasons Color in Your Garden"; and a class: "Return of the Victory Garden". Caren Marsh, editor of the *Opswatch Through the Seasons Cookbook,* will speak on planning meals with locally-produced food.
- Children's and intergenerational activities will be sponsored and run by the 4-H club, FFA, FHA, local scout troops, Home Hardware, the Women's Association of Old First Church, local cycling clubs, the Opswatch Valley Audubon Club, and the Carnegie Library Friends.
- Musical Entertainment will be provided by a John Denver Tribute Group (specializing in folk songs and acoustic music), a Native American drum, flute, dance group, and the Opswatch Elementary School Chorus with a program of patriotism, peace, and growing things.
- Food vendors will be challenged to serve at least one dish with food ingredients that have traveled no more than 300 miles.

Icons and Tip Boxes

I don't know where all of the little rodents came from. It began with the rat and the trebuchet, inspired by the Medieval Fantasy Festival and the Ratapult. That little fellow invited his friends, they multiplied, and before I knew it there were rodents throughout the book. They just hustled out of my brain, moved through my arm and hand, and came out through my pencil. Some of them even had attitudes! It is a puzzle!

TIP - Good ideas from experience!

Warning! It is important not to overlook this information.

Take note. More wisdom from experience.

Stories from the Medieval Fantasy Festival.

Greening Your Event. These tips help your event reduce its carbon footprint.

Story from the mythical, sample Green Festival   .

Learning from other events.

Introduction to the Planning Process

Putting together a special event or festival is mostly done with good, old-fashioned common sense. Don't be put off by seeing the whole mountain of work. Rough out the big picture and then just chip away at it one piece at a time. You may not have chaired an event committee before, but you *have* organized events—be they birthday parties, canoe trips, a wedding, or a church family night.

My version of the **Planning Process** uses four steps:

I.	Vision (You get the idea.)
II.	Planning (Laying the groundwork.)
III.	Execution / Celebration (Delivering the goods.)
IV.	Evaluation (How did you do?)

These are not isolated steps. They are interwoven, twined about each other like a living organism. They merge into one another until you aren't sure what step you are in. They nourish each other in a positive sense. To neglect or to forget one diminishes the whole.

This book will give you ideas to inspire your own event vision, checklists to make sure that details are covered, and templates for letters, applications, and other event forms. It will give you some confidence in your ability to create a fun, worthwhile event. Along the way, treat others as you wish to be treated. That philosophy goes a long way toward success.

Being a festival coordinator is a little like spinning a dozen jacks. Take a game of ball and jacks. Discard the ball, and choose a smooth, wide surface. Now get all the jacks spinning at once. Some fall over before you can even start others. Sometimes one collides with another and several are wiped out. Life is like that! Expect it.

 TIP   This might sound strange, but skim through Chapter 21 *"Why Events Fail: To Fix or To Move On"* very early in your reading and planning. Keep those thoughts in your mind. If you know what might happen, you will be able to avoid many problems altogether.

Part I
The Vision Comes First

See a need and a way to meet it.

**You get the idea
and map out the big picture, setting your goals.**

Chapters

1. Vision, Theme, Goals

If you have picked up this book, you must have thought about planning a festival. You might even have a wonderful idea for an event in mind. You may have bounced ideas around with your friends and colleagues. This guide will clarify your thoughts on *why* you want a festival, *what* you will want it to accomplish, *who* you will want to come, *where* will it be, *when* it will happen, *how* you will pull it off, and *what* you want to happen at the festival.

In short, you have begun to think about the five Ws and the H which will come up again and again in this guide. This group of words has been linked for centuries. Whenever you plan, or tell someone about your plan, these letters will help organize your thoughts and communicate to your audience. Rudyard Kipling's little poem, "The Elephant's Child," is a good way of remembering them:

> I keep six honest serving men
> (They taught me all I knew);
> Their names are What and Why and When
> And How and Where and Who.

(Source: *The Complete Just So Stories* by Rudyard Kipling, Viking, Penguin,1993.)

Why Have the Event?

Throughout history communities have come together to celebrate with song, with dance, and with feasts. Many of the ancient festivals revolved around the seasons, the patterns of life. Spring celebrations brought rejoicing for the light and warmth of the returning sun and new growth sprouting after long and dreary winters. Harvest seasons celebrated in thanksgiving for bounteous crops. These events broke the pattern of daily toil with festivities out of the ordinary.

These communities also celebrated rites of passage and goals reached—the birth of a child, the coming of age, a marriage, the marking of new achievements, and gains in status or leadership. Even a funeral—for a good life remembered and a passing into the afterlife—all mark an occasion of celebration and festivity.

Adopting and adapting the ancient festivals, the Christian Church celebrated a year of seasons beginning with Christmas, the birth of Christ – hope, and Epiphany, the coming of the Wise Men. Mardi Gras, while seen as secular, has its roots in the Christian year—the last big bash before the contemplative, austere journey of Lent. Lent gives way to Easter with glad rejoicing and to baptism with new beginning, continuing to Pentecost with its gifts of the Holy Spirit needed for the mission ahead. The circle is complete with Advent, preparing for the coming of the Christ child.

The ancient celebrations were not strangers to "fundraising" events. Look at the market days where goods and crafts were traded. Whoever their event planners were then, they knew that they would attract even bigger crowds for their market with jugglers, feats of skill, and tournaments.

> We celebrate events in community because we need to remember the past, enjoy a break from our daily routines, and bring hope to our future.
>
> Also, a little fundraising doesn't hurt.

There is an educational component to these festivities, too. Children learn history from celebrating it. They learn about great leaders and their legacies as the community retells the stories, in word, song, dance, and pageantry. Nations, too, celebrate—their beginnings, their accomplishments, and the truly great leaders that have inspired them.

Against this grand panorama of history, even our own festivals and special events find a place. We celebrate because we need the hope, the reward, and the break from the daily patterns. We need to keep important memories alive. We need to raise funds for projects near and dear to us. We relish the entertainment and having fun together.

 I grew up in Elbow Lake, a small town in Minnesota settled predominantly by folks of Scandinavian heritage. Three sides of the town were bordered by a body of water called Worm Lake, the unappealing repository of the burn-and-bulldoze town dump.

In the decades since my childhood, the city fathers and mothers have cleaned up the town, and have worked to improve the ambience of the community. The lake has been renamed Flekkefjord. A festival was begun called the Flekkefest.

The civic groups, businesses, churches, and other organizations worked together and made this a true community event. It has become a "homecoming" happening with the population of the town probably doubling during the festival, providing a needed influx of cash. This is one instance where a festival, properly planned, has been instrumental in aiding the health of a community in a major way.

Think about what you want to accomplish with your event.
You might wish to:
1. Celebrate a milestone or a heritage:
- Mark a centennial, a 50-year anniversary of your organization, or reaching a long-sought goal.
- Honor your community's ethnic heritage, or historical roots.
- Instill or enhance a sense of community pride and identity.

2. Promote a food crop that your area is well known for, a local historical event, or a natural phenomenon on which your community prides itself:
- Stockton Asparagus Festival, California
- Pony Express extravaganza or a founders' day
- St. Paul Winter Carnival, Minnesota

3. Celebrate a seasonal or holiday event:
- Mardi Gras
- Midsummer's Eve or Summer Solstice
- Festival of Trees for Christmas

4. Raise money for your organization:
- Money for school sports or music program
- Income needed to continue the mission of your organization
- Money for scholarships or for supporting a worthwhile cause

5. Infuse money into your community and increase the health of your retail and tourism businesses:
- Promote the downtown area with unique mom-and-pop businesses that find themselves in competition with the big box stores.
- Bring visitors to spend money in your community.
- Bring related businesses together to promote an event with shared interest, for example, a bridal fair.

 TIP   The success of an event is not measured only by the money that it takes in. Not all events have the goal of making money. Some will bring awareness of a need, some will bring visibility to a company and its products, and some will demonstrate the charm of an area. An organization that hosts a Halloween stroll in a downtown will lose money doing it. An event showcasing nonprofits harvests volunteers and increases the awareness of opportunities a community has to offer. Some events raise funds. Some make friends, and that's okay!

---

6. Educate folks about an idea, or bring awareness to a cause:
- Raise awareness for health and fitness, for fighting a certain disease, for supporting performing arts, fine arts, and sports in the local schools.
- Educate for life style change—promote a green, eco-friendly way of life.

7. Celebrate an historical period:
- Renaissance or medieval fair, or Civil War re-enactment.
- The 1950s with vintage cars and rock and roll music.
- Recreate the Colonial Days or the Victorian era.

8. Celebrate music, one of the fine arts, or creativity in general:
- A music type, such as jazz, Bach, Celtic, bluegrass.
- Theater or other performing arts. Ashland, Oregon, has put itself on the map with a widely-known, high-quality Shakespeare Festival.
- Painting, sculpting, or crafts such as needlework, leatherwork, or jewelry.
- Film festival or storytelling fair.
- A science fair or maker fair. (See an example of a maker fair at www.makerfaire.com.)

9. Bring the community together for work on a project needing many hands:
- Build a playground in a park.
- Clean up a creek bed or a shoreline.
- Plant a rose garden in a park or create a community garden space.

10. Foster an event:
- Where the community unites
- Where families re-unite
- Where the community just has fun!

Setting Goals and Objectives

Answering questions about why you want an event leads you to the next level of planning. Now you are ready to set goals and objectives. You are ready to think about more detail. Festival planning begins with an idea, either your own, or one that has been created through group think or brainstorming. What will be your theme?

What are your goals? Goals are the big ideas that will guide you. They are the foundation, the mission statements, the underpinnings that support your event. They are the answers to the question, "What are you trying to do?" The goals might go through some revision, but they will remain fairly constant throughout the years for the life of the event. Objectives are more the little pieces that make up your event. Usually measurable, they may change often as your planning and evaluation dictate.

> **TIP**   Don't get all huffy about the difference between goals and objectives. I have attended many meetings on the planning process, and they are enough to make your eyes glaze over and send you into a different dimension. Get the goals and objectives down on paper, get them into your mind as part of the process, put them where they make logical sense to you, get over it, and get on with it.

For an example of the difference between goals and objectives, let's look at the mythical Green Festival of Opswatch, IZ, a community which might be like yours. One of the **goals** of this Green Festival is to highlight awareness of alternative energy. One **objective** that might help reach this goal is to feature three electric car vendors, one hydrogen cell vehicle, and one compressed natural gas vehicle.

I wrote the goals on the following page for the proposal for the first Medieval Fantasy Festival in Vacaville, California. As time passed, experience and input from committee folks helped to fine tune them.

Frankly, these goals were not much in public view, even among the committee folks. They were more of a mind-set, a framework upon which we could hang the festival components. They were brought out from time to time to guide us. They were shared when we sought to convince sponsors that we deserved their support. They helped us through the evaluation process.

Goals of the Medieval Fantasy Festival Committee

♥   To provide an outstanding event that will attract   people to the historic downtown area, highlight the variety and excellence of businesses, and showcase the charm and ambience of the downtown.

♥   To provide a wholesome, affordable, fun-for-the-whole-family event. There will be no admission charge, and most activities will be free.

♥   To provide an opportunity for retail stores, restaurants, and other downtown businesses, the theater, the libraries, and area churches and schools to work together as a community and create a homegrown event, and in doing so, to prosper themselves.

♥   To raise money to support the programs of the Downtown Vacaville Business Improvement District.

♥   To encourage participation in performing arts by including local talent for the staged and walkabout performances.

♥   To promote awareness of good literature and the joy of reading by soliciting displays from students highlighting various fantasy authors, holding book-related contests that are fun, and by providing forums and discussions on the themes of fantasy and Earth Day.

♥   To celebrate fantasy authors whose heroes are ethical role models.

♥   To encourage quality arts and crafts by inviting local and regional vendors to participate. To encourage participation by local art organizations and school art departments.

♥   To promote appreciation of old-time arts and work skills from the past that continue to enrich our life today.

♥   To foster awareness of the ecological themes of fantasy authors who speak to our life style choices, and by having a vendor section devoted to green, eco-friendly products and services.

The **goals of a chamber of commerce event** might include the following:

- Creating community—interacting with the public, forming relationships, and making the community a better place in which to live and do business
- Forging connections with nonprofit groups and establishing good public relationships
- Networking—making new contacts so that businesses will prosper, building relationships that may be mutually beneficial in the future
- Providing opportunity for members to show off what they do
- Raising funds for chamber projects

You will want to put your goals down on paper. Follow each with objectives that help you reach those goals. When you choose what goals you want to guide your event, don't just think of fundraising. Draw the complete picture:

- Make money for your cause.
- Raise the profile of your group.
- Have fun and learn something.
- Build community; make new friends..
- Enjoy an activity as a family.
- Support the arts.
- Appreciate history and the skills that come from an earlier time.

For Whom Is the Event?

You will need to identify your target audience early on in the process. This will determine event location choices, how and where you promote the event, and the activities you choose to have at the event.

Ask yourself questions like these:

- Is it a fundraiser for a cause that would benefit from the widest possible participation? Will it become a regional draw?
- Is it going to be for families, or for teenagers, or single adults, or for a specific family reunion?
- Is it going to be for your school and the families related to your school only, or be open to the general public?
- Is it targeted to a specific segment of people, for example, employees and their families of a large corporation, a class reunion, or members of one civic organization?

What Activities Would You Like at Your Event?

Will there be:
- Activities, hands-on projects, or games for children?
- An educational aspect? Will there be speakers, exhibits, or classes?
- Beer or wine sales?
- Contests, a car show, or an athletic activity (like a fun run)?
- Dance, theater production, beauty pageant, talent contest, or other entertainment?
- Food? Who will provide it? What type of food will suit your event best?
- Music? What kind? Will there be professional music groups, local groups, or an amateur talent contest?
- People in costume?
- Relaxation and conversation, a formal program, a worship service, an art show, demonstrations of skill, or a parade?
- Vendors? What type?

I have included an extensive list of possibilities to choose from in later chapters. See Chapters 15 (Smorgasbord of Activities), 16 (Children's Games and Activities) and 17 (Fundraising Activities and Merchandise) to begin thinking about what activities to include. Add your imagination to these ideas, stir the pot with the help of your committee, and come up with entertaining solutions tailor-made for your event.

Consider more questions about what you might like to have happen at your event:
- How do you want the event to grow? What do you want the event to look like in five years?
- How will it be paid for? What will the funds you raise be used for?
- How will you get people to come?
- When will it happen, and how long will it last?
- Where will it be? A park, a lake, a rented hall, a field, a parking lot, a community or senior center, or your local school?
- Who will help put it all together?

Building a Vision – an Example

Say you are from a little town, far from any Kodak-approved picture point of natural beauty. There is no special agricultural crop; there is no general ethnic makeup of the citizens. You don't have a large base of musicians clamoring for a blues or a Bach festival. You are sitting on your front porch one day watching the wind blow a tumbleweed down the road. Aha! What you do have is wind.

You start to imagine a festival on the theme of wind, and dream of:

- A beauty contest with the winner being crowned, Queen of the Wind. Her scepter is a pinwheel.
- A character with a marvelous costume. He is called Windy Willy and will entertain the children.
- A contest of kites: the highest flier, the most beautiful, or one that can carry a stuffed animal payload from point A to point B.
- A flag or a pinwheel contest.
- A race with auctioned-off tumbleweeds, designated by spray paint. Set these up on a starting line and give a prize to the one whose tumbleweed crosses the finish line first.
- An educational booth about weather, forecasting, and storms. This might be a good way to involve the meteorologists from the local or regional TV stations.
- Asking all of the ministers of the churches in your community if they might preach on the Holy Spirit that Sunday. In fact, this event could be held on Pentecost weekend. After all; spirit, wind, and breath are tied together, coming from the same roots in both Greek and Hebrew.
- Contacting a windmill company to see if they can supply the power needed to run your festival and promote alternative energy.
- Master Gardeners talking about plants that make the best windbreaks or that thrive in a windy area.
- No hog calling here, but instead, a competition for who imitates the best wind howling!
- Festival décor with fluttery ribbons, flying flags, and waving banners.
- The set-up of the festival downwind of the popcorn and people just salivating to buy some.
- Vendors with kites, wind chimes, and whirligigs.

How could you take this concept, create a worthwhile event, learn something, have great fun, bring several generations together to work on the same project, bring in tourist dollars, and use it to raise funds for your favorite cause? Notice that this list considers appeal to all ages, to all the senses, activities that pull in a wide number of community groups, and both physically-active and quiet activities.

An event that has caught my attention and earned my admiration is the Woolly Worm Festival in Elk Banner, NC. These imaginative folks have created a festival about the little  black and red-brown caterpillar. This has been going on with great success for more than 30 years. See their website at www.woollyworm.com.

What Will the Event Be Called?

The name you choose for your event and the words that make it up are very important. You will want to consider for your proposed name:

- A name that is easily spelled and remembered.
- Short, catchy, and fun name.
- The name should convey your theme.
- The words you choose for your name will conjure up images for your audience and intrigue them (or not).
- Will the name excite potential vendors to participate?

You want the theme to be understandable to the public. You want to be able to pitch the theme to your target market without lengthy explanations or having folks respond with a glazed look in their eyes.

 TIP   You may choose your event name by committee. Brainstorm all related (even crazy) words that might end up in your name. Write each separately on paper with a marker in letters big enough to be seen by the group. Put them all on the table, move them around, make different combinations. Listen to each person's choices and reasons. come to a consensus. Use remaining key words to create a tag line or subtitle for your event.

When you have agreed on a name, but before you set that name in stone, do some reality checking. You may wish to let the name percolate for a while and ask others who weren't at that meeting for their feedback.

You will want to ask these questions:

- Does the name have strong key words that would bring it up easily on an internet search?
- Would the name appeal to potential sponsors?
- Would the name fit well with your community and the people you are trying to bring in as volunteers and customers?
- Does the name lend itself to a variety of activities? Would the name allow the event to be fresh each year?
- Is the name already in use on the internet? In what context?
- Does it bring up any connotations, either positive or negative? Will it lend itself to crass jokes or crude re-naming? If you abbreviate the name or use its acronym (the first letter in each word), do you end up with an unhappy choice? The last thing you need is to create a Wind Festival and have people bring to mind winding down (as in running out of steam) or breaking wind (as in you don't want to go there.)

TIP   A word of caution. If you are thinking about basing your event on a book, movie, song, or other copyrighted material, you should be very careful. Companies and individuals are very jealous and protective of their creations and rightly so. These licensing organizations don't take kindly to someone's using their images, names, and intellectual property, even if the intent is to support a very good cause. They have well-paid lawyers. If you want to publicize your event at all or have a website presence, they will find you and contact you, at the very minimum, with a cease-and-desist order. You don't need litigation and fines. Any naming or branding that you have done up to that point will have to be changed if they feel it infringes on their property. If this happens, you will have to backtrack in the progress of your event. My advice is not to mess with them or tempt fate.

Event Design—Practice What You Preach

With your goals in mind, start to put the design of the event together. Bring all the pieces together into one complete puzzle. There are several things you might think about. These will help your event to make a statement without sending mixed messages.

For example, you may think about greening your event, making it more eco-friendly.

Take one event element—food:

If you wish to consciously reduce your carbon footprint (see glossary), think about your choices of food, where and how the food is grown, and how it will be served.

- Where you have choices of food vendors, choose ones that fit your standards.
- Request that caterers and food vendors avoid the little individual packages of ketchup, mustard, and sugar. Don't serve coffee in foam cups. Since product presentation is part of the footprint, avoid items that are packaged to the nth degree. Consider ways to reduce the amount of trash your event will produce.
- Take the footprint a step further and think about how the food is grown and how much energy it took to grow it. Rather than use the eight-ounce beef steak, you might choose chicken. Rather than using a large piece of

meat, think about dishes with a smaller amount of meat with other ingredients. Or you could choose to have vegetarian meals.

- You may also think about organic food as opposed to food grown using pesticides and antibiotics. If your region has community-supported agriculture, consider using that network of farms.

- Choose food that is in season and grown locally, if possible. The carbon footprint of food also includes the energy that it takes to get it to you. Having fresh grapes and strawberries in February probably means they are flown in from the southern hemisphere. Lots of miles, bigger footprint.

- If your event is celebrating the growing popularity of "made in the USA" to support manufacturing and jobs, your food choices may follow suit. Your message will be more clear.

- Some foods, such as bananas and coffee, are not available in the continental US as in-season and local choices at all. That doesn't mean you should exclude them. There is another level of ethical choices to consider as well as the footprint. What you can do is purchase these and other foods fair trade. (Fair trade goods are those grown by people who earn a minimum wage and have high health and safety standards.)

- While we are thinking about ethics, think twice about scheduling that hot-dog-eating contest where individuals compete for eating the most in a given period of time. In our increasingly weight-conscious world, is gluttony something we want to promote?

- Be cohesive in your message. On your beautiful buffet table of in-season, local delicacies, and vegetarian wonders, do not display a creation of flowers flown in from Timbuktu.

- Are your sponsors in sync with your message? Does what they manufacture conflict with your goals? Don't make an obvious faux pas like asking the jelly donut company to sponsor a weight-loss event.

- Make arrangements with your caterer or your food vendors ahead of time to donate leftovers to a local organization that feeds the homeless and the hungry. Do not send good food to the landfill.

Let people know why you have made the choices you have. You don't have to be in their face, but subtle education with a program note may make your point.

Take another element—activities
These should also line up with your goals. Is the activity right for your group? Experiences teach. People learn from watching. Do the activities you provide teach the lessons you want folks to take home?

Some thoughts:
- What is entertainment and what do we laugh at? Is it always funny to watch people make idiots out of themselves? Can it be okay sometimes and hurtful at other times?
- Think about beauty pageants. Some are designed to consider the talent, intelligence, personality, and beauty of the contestant. Some pageants, however, encourage attitudes that aren't so healthy. If you wish to have a beauty pageant, what kind of message will yours send? Design it carefully.
- Design your family-friendly event with care. There is much to think about here. Entertainers might be cautioned to choose their language carefully. For example, the patter during a juggler's act in a family-friendly event should not contain lots of innuendo and adult humor.
- What kind of a message does it send to serve alcohol to adults at an event for the purpose of raising money for a sober grad night for seniors? What is the answer? I'm not saying that it would be right or wrong. Just think through all of the ramifications and be able to give your reasons for your decision.

What do your activities say about?
- People working together to solve problems.
- Helping those who are weaker than we are.
- Cooperation and competition.
- Are we part of the solution or the problem in today's world?
- Inclusiveness for people different than ourselves and for people who are disabled.
- If one of your goals is to build community, do your activities foster or hinder the process?

Think about other event elements in this same way. Design your event to practice what it preaches with regard to décor, publicity, entertainment, and fundraising.

Event Design—Cohesive and Compelling

You want your event to look good, feel good, and have some cohesion. The pieces of your puzzle should all fit together. When it all works in unity, the total will be larger than the sum of the individual pieces.

The décor, the entertainment, the signage, the music, the costumes, the ads, and the event program should all feel like they are part of a whole. You can create characters to interact with the audience. Carry out your theme in all of the aspects. Use your logo or mascot wherever you can. If you have chosen special colors for your décor, use them in other elements of the event as well.

You might coordinate your poster to the actual event. If you have a costumed character in the poster, have the character walk around the event as well. It would give a feeling of unity between publicity and event.

Some might say designing an event is like painting a picture. The colors you choose from your palette, the brushstroke style, the subject of the picture, the mood evoked —all make a unit.

In a very real sense what you are doing is theater. You are setting the stage and casting the characters; the audience comes and mingles. A word about theater— think of a grand theatrical happening—the opening ceremony of an Olympics, a half-time performance in a bowl game, or a professional theater production. Movement is exaggerated on a grand scale. It is dramatic and it is effective. There is choreography and intention. Now we are getting to the compelling stage.

In many local festivals the players hit the right notes, but have not yet reached the theater—the drama, the effect, the WOW part. We know our lines; we just haven't given much thought to their delivery. We don't need a bigger budget to do much of this, either—just thought, coaching, and practice. As awareness and confidence grow, the sense of theater should grow as well.

Consider two groups of singers in a parade, both of whom were given battery-operated lanterns. Each group knows the music by memory and each hits all of the right notes. One group, in street clothes, is carrying the lanterns without awareness of what they are doing. Some are swinging them, others have them straight down at their side, and some are holding them in ways that would cause disastrous burns were the lanterns real. They chat with each other between songs.

The other group, in costume, is holding the lanterns high, letting them illumine their path. They move in unison, having thought about the story they are telling. They stay in character, even between songs. The first group is holding props, but doesn't know why. The second group is making a statement and making theater.

2. Special Notes for School Events

Hints for Success

School events deserve some special attention. Successful school events will be educational and fun. They include teachers, children, parents, administrative staff, and maybe the public. They will involve experiences that the classroom probably cannot provide.

You might look to your state standards in education and incorporate some of them in your event plans. Your event will be perceived as more worthwhile and sell better to those with the decision-making power or potential supporters. Create a standards-based festival that is fun and that supports and extends what the school is trying to accomplish. Incorporate literature characters into your event, or portray a part of the history that children are supposed to learn.

Here are some suggestions:
- Build on what has been done before. There is no need to start from scratch. Keep records and pass them on to the next planners.
- Do as much as you can on other people's money by having sponsors and supporters.
- Use your committee's contacts to spread the word, and to find resources. Collectively you have access to an astounding part of the community.

- When you promote the school event, bill it as educational and teacher-friendly. Augment the curriculum. Accentuate the positive.

If possible, involve children in the planning, preparing, helping with logistics, and staffing. Set them up to succeed—with the proper training and guidance. They will learn the valuable process of working on a project from start to finish, a skill they will use as long as they live. They will own the experience more fully. The adults will also see some surprising results as children interact differently than they do sitting in a classroom. Children have skills, talents, and gifts that might never be seen at all in the classroom. Having a new opportunity to shine may earn new respect from adults and classmates.

When you pitch your event vision, have a strong well-understood theme and communicate the potential you see for the event. Include ideas and reasons for doing what you are doing. Allow enough time to get everybody on board. Set up a planning calendar and walk folks through it. Remind them that this is the week we will do this particular task. Don't let the participants wait to the last minute. Thrown-together booths with resentful, too-busy leaders will not help the ambience of the event.

Ask the school district to send out school-wide announcements of the event through their computer network. Be aware that most school districts must approve fliers and ads that may be sent home. Be aware that these are also very costly—just in duplicating the sheer numbers needed. They don't necessarily translate into an increase in attendance, as many never make it home or to their intended recipients.

Set up hints for booth décor. Set up boundaries of what can and can't be done. If vendors from outside your community have booths as part of the event, some of these guidelines might go on the website.

Be aware of—and be instructed by—the rules and regulations of the district. Find out what you can and can't do on school property. Find out about the screening procedures for volunteers in school events. Find out about hours and insurance requirements. Find out about the cultural traditions of the constituent families.

What Kind of Activities?

In a community festival where parents and children walk through as a family unit, group activities such as cooperative games are unlikely to happen. It may be easier to herd cats than to collect two evenly-matched teams for relay races in a community event attended by families. In a school setting children are more likely to be with their classmates. The school setting is likely perceived as a safe environment, and the parents are more willing to let their children wander together. Group activities and games will therefore be easier to do.

Event planners know that performances bring in parents. Try to have activities that will bring in the best attendance.

Successful school events may have booths at which children have fun while they learn. Much thought will be put into the planning of these experiences:

- What do you want the child to take away from this booth?
- What will they have learned? What new skill are they exposed to?
- What is their reward? Is it a new skill, new knowledge, a prize, or something they can make and take home with them?

Limit the activities where a child lobs a beanbag through a hole in a graphic or spins a roulette wheel for a prize. Come up with more creative and satisfying experiences.

 TIP Consider adding vendor booth spaces to enhance an event planned for those who work with children. This works well If the event is targeted to educators, social services workers, and day-care providers whose common denominator of interest is early childhood. There could be speakers and workshops. Set aside an area where vendors (from school supply stores and other businesses and nonprofits relevant to teachers and learning) could be invited to set up booths with related merchandise. The vendors add interest and education for the participants, provide for the purchase of resources, provide raffle prizes for the participants, and make vendor fee income for those putting on the event.

Look at the big picture of activities in chapters 15, 16, and 17. What can you improve and adapt to your school event? Carnivals, auctions, career fairs, and grad nights might benefit from the many possibilities.

You may choose to celebrate or to center your event in an ethnic heritage, possibly ones represented in local classrooms. Make it educational. Planning should be done with respect of the cultural differences. If you do not know how a culture functions, get informed by those who do! For instance, mainstream American culture emphasizes individuality. Some Native American cultures emphasize working as a group. These children will not raise their hands and want to be chosen to answer a question. Find ways of having them respond in a way that respects their culture. People from the culture in focus should be involved in the design. It should grow from the ground up to be the most effective. Emphasize tolerating differences and working together to reach common goals.

Involving Schools in a Non-school Sponsored Event

If you are inviting art students to enter a contest, school bands to perform, or English teachers to solicit essays for your non-school event, you may find cool reception or be totally ignored. Why? First of all, realize that teachers get many requests from well-meaning event planners. Many of these would make very good student projects but the teacher will have to pick and choose. They may even be focused on their own school-created events to augment the dwindling dollars available to the classroom. Don't take it personally if your project is not chosen.

Second, the classroom time is extremely limited. Teachers today face rigorous curriculum scripting and testing-time constraints. They have very little discretionary time. If teachers pitch your proposal to their students, it will take effort and time away from what the teacher is hired to do. You would do better if you can submit your request at the beginning of the year. Possibly then it can become part of the lesson plans and be welcome as an additional activity. If you can, pitch it before the vacation break to be included as an activity when school resumes.

Third, be involved and visible if possible in your community's schools. Be a member of groups that function to raise money for sports, music, and the arts in the schools. Participate in events; volunteer your time. In other words, pay your dues. When you make a pitch for teacher or student involvement, you might be taken more seriously. It can't hurt to increase your knowledge and contact base by being a helpful volunteer.

What is the difference between PTA (Parent Teacher Association) and PTO (Parent Teacher Organization)? PTA is a formally organized group on national, state, and local levels. Members must pay dues to and abide by the rules of national and state levels. The PTA has an annual convention and maintains lobbyists in Washington as advocates for different educational issues.

A PTO, on the other hand, is a more local generic organization. PTOs are most often single-school organizations. They operate under their own by-laws and are concerned primarily with local issues. PTO members are quite pleased to keep the funds they raise for local use and not send off dues to a state or national level.

Learn about—and be sensitive to—the power structure in the particular school. Who is going to be able to help you get the job done? How might the principal, the teachers, the counselors, the PTO, and families whose children attend that school be helpful? Do your homework.

Look for youth-related organizations in the city where you live that will provide networking opportunities, such as Key Clubs or Police Athletic Leagues.

Approach the school counselors. These individuals are good sources for support, although budget cuts have resulted in a heavy work load for them. They have access to all the classrooms and the teachers' ears. They may be able to find good student volunteers for your event. Some schools require community service of their students. Counselors may be able to match students with needs.

Teacher Involvement

A successful school event will involve teachers from the beginning. The event will be better if the power and action grow from the ground up rather than coming as a pronouncement from an administrator.

Planners of both school and non-school events need to be sensitive to the fact that teachers have a life, a family, and obligations outside the classroom. Some are tired, having done this for thirty-some years. Some may be disheartened by budget cuts, more mandates, and a perceived lack of support from administration or parents. More progress will be made if teachers are brought into the project from the beginning. Participation will be better if there is a perceived benefit (like utilizing funds raised for classroom use) rather than an order from on high. If an individual is not happy about being made to participate, they will grumble and the unhappiness will spread.

Begin very early. Do some research and find out how events happen at your particular schools. Who are the ones who can make things happen? Bring people on board at all stages, rather than dumping it on them. Get parents involved. The principal shouldn't do all the work. Have teachers responsible for certain areas. The organizational plan should include a way to check to make sure that stuff is on track and that needed steps are being done.

Goals

Goals for school events will probably include the following:

- Bringing in some of the state standards in education. Ask the principal or the teachers, if you can, about what special standards they would like to emphasize.

- Building community by working together to accomplish goals.
- Raising awareness of school's place in community.
- Ensuring that teachers, students, parents, and the community have a fun, educational, and safe event.
- Growing pride in one's school and gaining satisfaction in a job well done.
- Providing experiences for students that they can't get in the classroom.
- Using more of the senses. Music, people in costume, foods all add to the sensory experience.

 TIP   Be careful. Make a point to know and follow food and health regulations at the local, county, and district level.

- Raising money for a project. Include classrooms and teachers in the money-sharing for better participation from teachers.
- Showcasing students and their talents and skills. Providing new opportunities for children to experience and learn new skills. Having students gain experience by helping set up and run booths.

During the Event

The leadership should check in with the booths or activity leaders. Do they have water, breaks, and enough equipment? If vendors are volunteers, providing an area for breaks and snacks is welcome. Happy participants should translate into more success and also into the willingness to do this again. Express your appreciation vocally.

Carry a recording device or a notepad in your pocket. You will want to note things as you see them so they won't be forgotten. As the event begins and unfolds, you will find yourself starting the evaluation process in your mind:

- Could the activities have been better and more fun?
- Did the participants come up with new ideas that were positive?
- How can you improve the event for next time?
- Were all groups given a chance to participate —parents, teachers, students, families, staff?
- Were any groups over-worked?
- Were opportunities missed for better learning?
- What activities are popular and working well? Which are languishing?
- What could you have done to facilitate better participation?
- What unexpected results will figure into your planning for next time?
- What were the hiccups in your planning?

Part II
Planning: Organizing and Groundwork

You build the foundation, get your plans, committee, and volunteers in order, and get the money to pay for it all.

Chapters

3. The Event Committee and Leadership

Where Do You Find Folks for Your Committee?

The most satisfactory committee member choices are folks that share the passion for the vision and those with whom you enjoy working. Begin with them. It helps if you know the track record of the folks in this initial group. You can always add more to the committee as the work expands, but the initial planning may go more smoothly with a limited group.

Think of influential, hard workers who follow through for certain tasks. Think of folks who will be a good support group for the leadership. Think of folks with good community contacts or who will help you pull in more workers or dollars later in the process. Now is the time to bring them on board.

Here are productive groups you might look within for committee members:

Your parent group

Your event committee will probably be working under an organization that is hosting the event. I refer to this as the parent group. This group is the obvious place to begin looking for workers. These are the folks that have the most invested in the success of the venture. If the host is a downtown board or chamber, look to its members to fill committee chairs and be worker bees. If your host is a church or synagogue, look to your membership. If your host is a school, look to the students, parents, alumni, and the teachers and staff.

The surrounding community

The next level of workers would be others affected by the event. Recruit from the surrounding businesses and stores. If you are hosting a green event, tap those who are in related businesses, clubs or nonprofit groups such as the Master Gardeners, an Audubon club, the regional air quality board, or boards of local wilderness area projects and land trusts. Green events could contact bicycle clubs, hiking clubs, bird-watching clubs, and walking and running groups. If your theme is sport-related, contact related clubs, groups, or gyms.

Your friends, co-workers, your club, or church members

If your extended family, friends, neighbors, co-workers, members of organizations or interest groups that you belong to might be interested, ask them to volunteer. If the host group is a downtown board or chamber, ask your member businesses to suggest or solicit names. Their customers may also be a good source.

Leadership Styles

If you have been tapped to fill the leadership role, reflect on the dynamics of the style that your leadership style brings to the process:

- Are you able to accept criticism and not take it personally when someone approaches a task differently than you would?
- Are you able to make decisions, negotiate, and manage conflict?
- Can you assign tasks that mesh with people's style and gifts?
- Can you convey warmth, enthusiasm, and appreciation to all of your volunteers?
- Can you delegate and let go without the need to micromanage all tasks?
- Can you squash your own ego for the good of the cause?
- Do you know when to prod and when to back off?

When a group of people get together to plan an event, they bring their individual experiences and history with them. They will be acquainted with different leadership styles. These styles are neither good nor bad, they are just individual approaches. It may make for some rough going until people get used to each other's styles and have time to work out the differences. I believe that almost all styles could result in success for the event, especially if there is respect for individuals and if the leaders are able to work with many personalities.

Look at a Few Leadership Styles

The Committee Style

The committee style, which I prefer, is found in some civic, school, and church meetings. For these folks that's how things get done. They meet, hash things out, bounce ideas off each other, come to a consensus, and execute the plan. They have a basic understanding of *Robert's Rules of Order* and operate democratically. They set goals, plan how to accomplish them, find the right people to take on the tasks, do what they need to make things happen, and throw in praise and appreciation. They then look at how it went and how they could improve. It is sometimes a ponderous way of accomplishing things. Getting all of the people together on the same page at one time can be a challenge.

When this system works well, the result is a group of people who are invested in the process, many hands to take on various tasks, and a body of trained people who can carry on. The event won't die if the leader falls off the face of the earth.

Winger

Another leadership style you might find is someone taking a fragment of the task and running with it on his own. Sometimes the results are brilliant, very helpful, and grow into an activity that is hugely popular. Other times this style may result in some decisions that conflict with other activities. Sometimes it leads to resentment, a fragmented group, the budget getting out of whack, and toes getting stepped on. If your committee has leaders like this, learn to work with them and maximize the good while limiting the negative.

Assign and Leave

Another leadership style is to assign good people to a job and let them have at it. They then meet monthly to see how it is going and make sure that what they are doing fits seamlessly with the overall picture of the event. The trouble with this on a new event is that there is no template in place to give them any guidance. There is not the "group think" to give them feedback. If you encounter this style, make certain that the folks assigned to particular areas are committed to the event and share the vision. Choose people who have enough time to devote to the task to do a good, responsible job. Don't just trust or assume that things will be done. You may not want to interfere and barge in, but neither do you want that part of the event falling into the abyss.

Micro Manager

Among other styles you might find is the micro manager, who has to be in charge and has a need to be involved in every step of the process, maybe even with the minutiae. If he or she is an organized person and doesn't leave any of the crucial steps out, this might be a successful style. There are some tasks that demand this kind of attention to detail and would be perfect for this person. There are some volunteers who enjoy working under this type of leadership as well.

Solo Player

The solo players hate meetings and like to keep the process simple. They would like the template for one event to work on the next one as well. They may have some activities down to a science, having done them many times. They often have a lot going on in their life and have to budget their time, juggling lots of roles and hats. They may resent working on a project that is many months away when they have looming deadlines for other activities much sooner. One way of working with the solo player is to give them responsibility for what they do well, feed them information they might find helpful, but let them do their own thing in their own time. Keep in contact with them for updates.

The Movie Director

One style of leadership that I admire tremendously is the one used by Peter Jackson as he directed the movie trilogy of *The Lord of the Rings*. He hired good, creative people, inspired them and trusted them to do their best and produce quality work. He listened to their ideas and often made changes to incorporate those ideas. He respected their gifts and talents and treated them accordingly. He was still definitely in charge, but the collaborative insights produced a better, greater whole. While our events won't have the money and resources that were available to him, we can still look for good people, and not underestimate what they can bring to our events.

General Leadership Notes

Festival volunteers need answers to questions in a timely manner. They need answers for both budget and feasibility questions. On the other hand, volunteers need to be prepared and use time with busy leaders wisely. There needs to be a clear understanding of who is responsible for what and a clear understanding of who should be at what meeting.

Part of the job of the event chairperson is to keep the peace, to see the whole forest as well as individual trees. In the end, it is the committee chairperson who has to bite the bullet and make sure things happen. Sometimes the committee chair just has to make decisions and let the pieces fall where they may. Some people, for good or not-so-good reasons, will flake on the event. The maxim that 20 percent of the people do 80 percent of the work is true in my experience. Expect it.

People will work more happily if they see what needs to be done and the steps that must be taken to accomplish the task. Tasks aren't so daunting if folks can see their way through a little chunk of it. They also need to see where their contribution fits into the whole. Most important, both busy leader and eager volunteers need to feel appreciated for what they do.

A good leader should expect the unexpected. He or she should be flexible and not take it personally when there are different approaches to the problems. At times a leader will be frustrated, but he should not let the frustration get in the way or let it distract the public. He should keep any angry and resentful vibes hidden and work through them out of the public view.

A good leader solves problems diplomatically. In dealing with any unknown individuals or groups, be wise, do your homework, and know that there might be a "little Napoleon" around with whom you may have to tread carefully. They show up in surprising places, maybe among parent board members, city staff, former event staff, or even as volunteers. Leaders will run across other difficult personalities: the very needy individual who is always demanding your attention, the take-charge folks and control freaks, and those who speak a very good line but never follow through. Some understanding of conflict management is very much a plus in a leader. Articulating your expectations and listening to the expectations of individuals and chunk groups (subcommittees) help to avoid problems and smooth out difficulties.

A smart leader does the legwork before meetings. He or she pretty much knows how votes will go and has laid the groundwork. The discussion, and the vote when it comes, will bring more people on board. If you just throw out an idea that needs a decision, you may lose control of what you are trying to do, and set people up on conflicting sides. You don't want to create a non-productive working relationship.

TIP There are many studies done on different personality types. Familiarity with one of these studies may be helpful to you as a leader. Personally, I found it helpful to have a brief understanding of the Enneagram, which is a study of nine different personality types. While we might see traces of all nine in someone's personality, one type will be more dominant. All types can range from healthy to unhealthy. No type is better or worse than another. While my knowledge of the Enneagram is sketchy, it has helped me to appreciate the differences in where people are coming from and how they are "wired". The introduction to the Enneagram has resulted in my not being as frustrated when other people don't think like I do. I am more understanding and more open to insights from a different point of view. This system has been around for a couple of thousand years and is an interesting and fascinating look at what makes us tick. Look in the Appendix for Helen Palmer's book on this topic.

Cultivate your contacts. Become acquainted with those who make decisions in your community, those who have the contacts, the skills, and the resources that would aid your event, and whose who might help during your event. Know and accept that this process is reciprocal—you may need to pay it back. Help in another event to gain experience and connections for your event. You may find genuine friends and solid folks to depend upon as a result.

Makeup of an Event Committee

Every event committee will be different. Basically you want a chair or co-chairs, subcommittee (chunk) chairs for your major components, and then the worker bees that support the whole and do all of the rest that needs to be done.

I have organized the potential personnel of an event committee into seven functions which are listed here. Each function is fleshed out in more detail later in this chapter with mini job descriptions.

1. Administrative

This group includes those who are responsible for the theme, direction, planning, and organizing the whole event. Liaisons from the parent board and the executive director, assistant, and interested board members would be included.

2. Visual Theme

Those in this function will have responsibility for the appearance of any printed material and event décor.

3. Financial

These people will tackle the actual fundraising, grant writing, program ad selling, and getting sponsors and in-kind support.

4. Logistical

All of the logistical tasks that you need to make the event run smoothly behind and in front of the scenes will be handled by these folks.

5. Activities / Main Course

The leaders in this function deal with the entertainment and activities the public will come to see and do.

6. Getting the Word Out

This part of the committee is challenged with letting the public know about the event is such a way that they want to come.

7. It would be nice if we had...

I have listed last as the seventh function those jobs which may not be absolutely essential, but are very good to have. In an organizational chart they would be found under the administrative function.

Job Descriptions for Committee Folks

All event committees will probably need at a minimum people to make sure the first six tasks above are done. Build your committee from there.

The following annotated, brief job-description list for the organization of committee folks is a buffet of possibilities. It is intended to be so exhaustive that you won't overlook important tasks. Depending upon the kind of event, its size and complexity, the type of organization that is hosting the event, and your base of workers, you can combine, add to, or delete some of these functions. These are just ideas; you will put them together in a way that suits you. *Look at each function and decide whether or not it is necessary for your event.* If it is necessary, does it need to have its own person or can it be combined with another task? Some players can wear more than one hat. Pick and choose.

TIP   While theoretically it is possible to do most of the work of the committee with volunteers, in the real world there may be some jobs that require hiring people with needed skills and knowledge. These would depend upon the gifts and talents that you and your volunteers bring. There are some important aspects of a festival that I would hire folks for—including sound technicians, lighting technicians for outdoor night performances, overnight security, and having an attorney check contracts and waiver forms. You know your people and their limitations. Budget accordingly.

1. Administrative – Planning and organizing

Committee Chair or Co-Chair

- o   Coordinates all of the components; oversees the whole event.
- o   Has major input into vision, direction. Makes decisions.
- o   Spreads enthusiasm and encourages volunteers.
- o   Assigns tasks to competent people.
- o   Reports to parent board and keeps them informed and invested.
- o   Keeps all of the players in the loop and updated.
- o   Keeps activities, entertainment, and vendors within the theme.
- o   Thinks about what could possibly go wrong, and then steers the planning and organization to see that it doesn't.
- o   Listens to people and is able to lead diplomatically. Is flexible and can deal with stress.
- o   Has a sense of the whole event as theater.

o   Is the public face of the event, dealing with city special event meetings, the media requests, and so on.

o   Should create and keep current a binder of all of the important information. Sees that nothing is forgotten. The binder should include the budget, timeline, a contact list of committee members and other pertinent names. Copies of the subcommittee timelines and tasks should be included as well. There should be a section for all vendors, entertainers, and others that have been accepted.

 TIP   Build in plans for your own replacement or retirement and the eventual retirement of the chairperson or key visionary personnel. Some events become long-standing tradition and the best way for that to happen is to think about the future as you go. Recruit visionary and dedicated people, give them responsibility, and value their contribution. Most people, if given the proper training, can do the mechanics of a special event well. Finding someone with the spirit, the creativity, and drive to take on the event is challenging but necessary if you want the event to remain vibrant after the present leadership has moved on. Provide training for potential leaders and mentor them. Make sure that the committee is made up of folks of different ages.

Core Committee or Executive Board

This will be made up of the overall chairperson and the chairs of the different chunks or subcommittees. It might just be the major players. It may include those who are being groomed for eventual leadership positions. It should avoid the pitfall of becoming a clique that is resented or viewed with antagonism by others. The functions of this group are:

o   Provide moral support for the committee chair. Being a support group for the leader is an important function.

o   Operates as a sounding board to work out solutions to problems.

o   Sets theme, vision, and direction of event.

o   If your parent board has an executive director or a secretary that will be doing most of the paperwork and credential chasing for you, they should be included on the core committee. Even if they can't come, they should be kept in the loop. They may be your face in meetings with the public, with the city, and with the media. They need to be able to field questions and give accurate, good information. They may take phone calls from the public with questions and concerns about the event. These folks may also take on the tasks of legal matters, insurance, bids and so on.

o   All groups involved in hosting the event (doing the actual work and planning) should be represented on the committee.

o   Drafts budget. Sets up guidelines for handling money. Oversees compliance with their rules.

o   The budget person or treasurer should be included. This person should keep a binder of receipts, invoices, and so on. They may pay bills, make deposits, and obtain cash drawers for the event.

o   Helps set agenda for meetings.

o   May function as clearing house for chunk oversight and progress.

o   Keeps communication flowing up and down the chain of command.

o   May oversee hired workers and 1099 workers.

TIP   You may have hired workers that are not on the committee level. These include those who do the physical set-up and tear-down tasks, if this is not done by volunteers. Under current U.S. tax law, you must submit a *Form 1099* for persons that you pay $600 or more in a year. These are people with whom you entered a contract to perform a service in exchange for valuable consideration—money, goods, services, etc. Check with your accountant.

---

2. Visual Theme

Graphics / Logo Design / Calligrapher

o   Develops the "look". (The business world calls this "branding". Simply put—the look is the unified theme, design, and appearance of the event and all of its parts to the public.)

o   Coordinates overall publicity for uniformity.

o   Should have ability to do designing and graphic arts work.

o   Should have the ability to put things into the appropriate electronic format to deal with the media and those who will print your promotional materials and programs.

o   Deals with logo, poster design, fliers, program, signage, website wizard, T-shirt design, and all other components with graphic design.

o   Works closely with committee chair.

o Does layout for program. Works with the ad chasers (people whose job it is to sell and follow through on program ads) to get ads done properly. Sets up the ad-sell sheet which gives the guidelines for the advertiser.

Décor & Ambience

o Works with the design and vision leaders from the core committee to make the area as festive as possible while spending as little as possible.
o Arranges for volunteers to produce décor, put up, take down, make repairs, and store.
o Makes sure that each spot, stage, or activity has the best décor and signage appropriate to the activity.
o Is familiar with previous year's décor and builds on it.
o Deals with layout of festival, festival decoration and design.

3. Dealing with the financial part

Sponsors and Support

o Seeks out and obtains monetary and in-kind support for the festival.
o Writes letters, does follow-up phone calls, and visits where possible.
o Keeps record of sponsors and their levels.
o Makes sure that the donor gets the credit and goodies due from their level of support.
o Works with the website and program people to credit sponsors properly.
o Writes thank-you letters to supporters after the event.

Grant Writer

o Seeks out appropriate corporations and foundations for application.
o Networks with individuals in corporations and foundations that might be helpful in the application process.
o Drafts the application, runs it by the board or core committee for their approval and accuracy.
o Sends in applications and follows them up.
o Sends thank-you letters and reports to granting institutions.

Ticket Sales

o Is responsible for advanced sales and at-the-door tickets.
o Sets up a system to organize tickets and track their distribution.

- o Deals with promoting, selling, handling charges and Pay Pal™ (if used), checks and cash, getting tickets to purchaser.
- o Responsible for handling lines of people and gate logistics.
- o Assigns seating for performances.
- o Works closely with treasurer.

Prize Person

- o This may be handled by the sponsor / support person or be a job on its own.
- o Solicits raffle prizes and contest prizes from businesses.
- o Keeps records.
- o Sees to it that there are enough prizes.
- o Organizes and labels prizes for all activities that need them.
- o Gets them to where they are needed on time.
- o May be in charge of raffles.
- o If any awards or award ceremonies are to be part of the event, this person may be in charge of ordering awards, seeing that they are properly done, and may even design the ceremony.

Ad Chaser

My experience tells me that this job will be done much better if someone takes it on as a mission. It tends to be an orphan child if left to those who have other major responsibilities. They give it only scraps of time and feel mounting guilt.

- o Solicits ads and support from local businesses.
- o Works with the publicity person, the prize person, the sponsor person, and the design folks.
- o May also be designated to keep merchants (or teachers or parishioners) and businesses informed about all aspects of the event to keep them invested in it.
- o Distributes fliers to keep information and interest current.
- o Needs to be someone who will represent group well.

4. Logistics—Running smoothly behind the scenes

Logistics Chair

The person in charge of overall logistics handles a variety of tasks listed below. They plan for what could possibly go wrong and do as much as possible to see that it doesn't. They get everything in place so that the event runs smoothly. They see to it that all city, school, or church rules are followed. Diplomacy is an important skill for this person as they must deal with different bureaucracies and sometimes with difficult people.

The logistics that this person must oversee include the following:

o **Amenities**

Porta potties, shade, tables, chairs, stages, parking, ice, electricity, greywater tanks and other food vendor needs. Gets things to the right place at the right time.

TIP If your organization does several events a year that need porta potties, or equipment rentals, I suggest that you send all competing companies a bid request. They may give you a deal if they can do all of your events.

o **Security**

Provides daytime or overnight security if needed.

o **Electronic equipment**

- Secures the sound systems and electronic equipment needed for the entertainment areas.
- Secures equipment needed for speakers, PowerPoint® presentation graphics programs, and any recording done.
- Sets up equipment, tests it, and is on call to fix any glitch that may occur during the event.
- Works with the entertainment person to make sure everyone who will use equipment is properly trained.

TIP   Depending on your event, the lighting and sound may make or break the experience for the public. Make certain that the person in charge knows what he or she is doing. It might be the time to hire a professional.

o **Paperwork**

- Secures all needed permits, parade permits, street closure agreements, contracts, permission to do 'thus and so' letters, food vendor applications, inspection papers, business licenses, liquor licenses, insurance—all of the paperwork necessities.
- Keeps all in a binder to show as needed.
- May forward requested documentation to police, health department, sales tax or other government entities.

- o **City Coordination**
  - Takes care of street closures, electricity for vendors and entertainers.
  - Goes to city special event meeting as representative with chairperson.
  - Deals with fire and police departments.
- o **Set-Up / Clean-Up**
  - Responsible for getting all the stuff that is needed to where it belongs on the day of the event.
  - Sets up décor, tables, tents, information booth, etc.
  - Good at organizing volunteers.
  - Able to do very physical labor.
  - May need vehicle and equipment that can handle large items.
  - Responsible for clean up and getting things put away properly.

Street Bosses

You need as many as it takes to cover all the areas / streets/ rooms where your vendors will be located. Street bosses may not be required to come to all meetings, but attendance at your last-minute logistics meeting might be mandatory.

- o Should know what is going on.
- o Meet the vendors as they arrive and begin to set up.
- o Direct vendors where to park.
- o Are able to answer questions and deal with any problems that arise.
- o Distribute programs, evaluation forms, and information to the vendors.
- o Check in periodically with the vendors and make sure they have breaks.
- o Work closely with the hospitality folks.
- o Remain after event until all vendors are packed up and gone.

Beer / Wine Garden Director

- o Sees to the staffing, making sure the pourers, cashiers are properly trained and know the rules regarding the serving of alcohol.
- o Sees that liquor license arrangements have been made.
- o Oversees the perimeter and setup of the area where liquor will be served.

o Organizes cash drawers, instructs staff in handling money, is responsible for getting money to proper person at end of the day.
o Orders supplies, beverages.
o Has the knowledge to run area smoothly and is willing to use authority to make sure that the rules are followed.

 TIP   Alcohol server's training is regulated and mandated by state and local laws. The purpose is to mitigate liability, and to prevent intoxication, underage drinking, and drunk driving. One example of this training and certification is TIPS® Alcohol Training. At least 30 states accept certification from this program. Ask your local police department, your city's special event person, and your state's alcohol beverage control about the procedures needed to have your event in compliance. Your beverage distributer will also have helpful knowledge for you.

Hospitality

Essentially this is taking care of the guests, making them feel welcome and seeing to their needs. This chunk may work with several groups of people, including volunteers and staff, vendors, entertainers, celebrities and VIP guests, those who need overnight facilities either in hotels or campgrounds, and possibly the public.

These may be items for the hospitality committee:
o In an event where there is registration of participants, they may be responsible for that function, name tags, and so on.
o Sets up and staffs information booth.
o Gets hotel and motel information from tourism bureau.
o Prepares list of hotels, campgrounds and RV parking for vendors and visitors.
o Sees to the needs of volunteers, staff, vendors, and entertainers.
o Gives vendors lunch and bathroom breaks if necessary; sees that they have water.
o Works with the vendor chairs and the street bosses.
o Works with the volunteer coordinator and the sponsor person to solicit contributions to cover needs.
o If you have a celebrity or big name band as an attraction, they will expect and/or need security, hotel, limousine service, meals, and other perks. The hospitality person smoothes the way and arranges for needs to be met.
o May welcome visiting chief personnel from other events.

Volunteer Coordinator

- o   Seeks out volunteers from the community and the parent group.
- o   Tries to link their talents and their time to the needs of activities.
- o   Keeps a log and a list of possible resources.
- o   Works with all subcommittees and the chairperson.
- o   Puts together a data base of clubs and groups. Plans how they could be used. Develops contacts.
- o   Seeks cooperation from community groups like schools, churches, service organizations, youth organizations, museums, veterans, athletic teams, civic groups.
- o   Develops fliers or a plan to solicit volunteers and to educate them about their responsibilities.

TIP   This person might have to deal with background checks, identification badges, and other credentials for volunteers. Some communities require a signed release of liability from their volunteers. (A sample is included in the Appendix.) Some city events require their volunteers to wear a wrist band, and show their driver's license or other ID. Some require vendors and volunteers to go through a background check, especially if the event is aimed at children. Knowing the policies ahead of time may prevent a cancelled event because of non-compliance.

---

5. Activities / Main Course

Vendor Chair

- o   Seeks out, solicits vendors that are appropriate.
- o   Develops a database and a vendor-type quota sheet in conjunction with the event chair.
- o   Is part of the vendor jury group. (see Glossary and Chapter 12 for definition)
- o   Sets up a map of the event area and assigns spaces to vendors.
- o   Responsible for communication with vendors about space assignments, missing credentials, and so on.
- o   Gives direction, space assignment lists to street bosses.

Food Vendor Chair

- o   Depending on the total number of vendors, you may need someone to handle just the food vendors. If there aren't that many, one person can handle all vendors.
- o   Does all of the above tasks that are appropriate for the food area.

- o Responsible for dealing with the health department applications, for providing a well-rounded menu, and for dealing with related logistics.
- o Works closely with all vendor persons.

Entertainment Chair

- o Seeks out and solicits good entertainment with appropriate themes.
- o Handles applications, credentials, contracts, and questions.
- o Deals with logistics (stages, sound systems and other electronic equipment, chairs, weather cover, entertainer parking, and so on)
- o Has major input on setting up and coordinating the schedule.
- o Sees that the Master of Ceremonies has needed information.
- o Finds a stage manager and delegates tasks to them.
- o Sits in on scheduling and notes needs for each entertainer.
- o Coordinates with sound system person, may help performers set up equipment.
- o Sees that entertainment goes smoothly.

Speakers, Workshop Leadership

This chunk is responsible for finding quality speakers, workshop leaders, teachers for classes and forum participants when needed. They should prepare any printed handouts necessary and take care of related logistics.

Activity Chairs

Major activities and contests in the event may have their own person in charge. Each should:

- o Be familiar with the goals, design, and theme of the festival.
- o Plan and keep their activities in line with the theme.
- o Seek out new, creative ways to keep activities fresh.
- o Let the chairperson know of needed supplies and signage.
- o Consult with décor folks.
- o Keep a binder with all pertinent information on their activity.
- o Find volunteers to staff activity.

Children's Games and Activities

- o Plans games; is in charge of the game area.
- o Knows what game components the event owns and how they are used. Keeps components in good repair and is responsible for their storage.
- o Seeks sponsors for individual activities.
- o Works closely with committee chair.

o Works to make an attractive, exciting, safe experience for children and families.
o Builds on last year's games, but should include something new each year to keep interest.
o Seeks and trains volunteers to staff the area.

Competitions, Tournaments, and Contests

Each activity might have its own chair, co-chairs, or one person may be in charge of several related activities.

o Responsible for planning, implementing, staffing, running, and evaluating their activity.
o Makes budget and décor suggestions.

Parade

A street parade is a big enough chunk to have its own subcommittee.

o Deals with all of the licenses, permits, city regulations, etc.
o Promotes parade, seeks interesting and varied entries.
o Takes entries, organizes order of entries into a pleasing whole.
o Sets parade route, works to minimize risks, and takes steps to insure safety.
o Deals with street closures and signage.
o Sets up and organizes a staging area where parade entrants await their turn to move out.
o Coordinates and communicates with all segments to keep parade running smoothly.
o Deals with bands, floats, horses, and other units.
o Responsible for providing clean up after the horses pass and after the parade is over.

6. Getting the Word Out

Publicity / Promotion

o Poster distribution, flier and postcard distribution.
o Media coverage. Sees to it that press releases are done in a timely manner and PSA (public service announcements) spots are done for radio and TV.
o Coordinates with those responsible for website, banners, and signage.
o May facilitate promotion of your event at other events.
o Finds creative, out-of-the-box, low- or no- cost marketing tactics.
o Does all in their power to deliver the public to the event.

TIP   There may be special individuals in your community that you would like to be invested in your event. For example, you might invite someone on the local newspaper staff to the meetings.

Web Wizard
- o   Responsible for keeping website current.
- o   Works with graphics person and committee chair.
- o   Has the technical expertise to do the job.
- o   Has ability to listen to folks and hear what they are saying.
- o   Has enthusiasm, know-how, talent, follow-through, and the ability to meet deadlines.

7. It would be nice if we had...

Pinch Hitter

Event leaders would do well to find some good individuals who will do a quality, reliable job on their own. It is a blessing to be able to say to someone, "This is what we need to have done" and then leave them to it, secure in the knowledge that it is taken care of. You check in and they report back. These individuals are of great worth. They might be tapped to fill in when a committee member cannot finish his task.

Secretary

If you don't have someone to do this, invest in a little digital recorder to record the meetings. Always have a sign-in sheet for those attending. *Minutes are very important.* The secretary:
- o   Takes minutes or notes at meetings. (The Appendix includes a "Guide for Taking Minutes at Meetings" which is helpful for someone new at being a secretary.)
- o   Keeps binder of archival information, correspondence, press releases, handouts, posters, promotional items, etc.
- o   Distributes minutes to members in a timely manner.
- o   May prepare correspondence at the direction of the chair.

Archivist

It is an added bonus if you have someone who can devote their time at the event taking photos and videos. You want to have a large selection of shots from which to choose for your website and for promoting future events. You can also document the pre-event process and the event itself.

Database Keeper

o Responsible for databases of names solicited by drawings, contest entries, and "please send me information" forms from event, and queries on your website. A database only has worth if it is organized and used. Enters the information into the database, and makes a plan for using and following through on the plan.

o Works in conjunction with volunteer chair and promotion person.

Hired, Paid Workers

These are workers that the event has direct responsibility for hiring and paying. These are not on the committee level. They are under the authority of the administrative function that can hire and fire them, but they will probably take their direction from the logistical folks. Examples of these workers are physical labor for set-up and clean-up or off-duty police who provide security.

Resource Person / "Expert"

If your event is about a particular time period, or about a particular product, or body of knowledge, it might be prudent for you to have an expert volunteer for your committee. This person could save you a lot of leg work and keep you from going off on unhelpful tangents. For example, if you are having a school event and want to highlight some of the educational standards, it would make sense to have someone on board who knows the standards or how to access them readily. For a green event, someone who by avocation or vocation works with eco-friendly ideas, who has passion for the vision, and who has contacts, the education, and background is very valuable.

4. The Committee at Work

Structure

Do you need nonprofit status?

Consider the formal structure of your event committee early on in the process. I am assuming that the event you are planning is under the auspices of a larger group: a school, a church, a chamber of commerce, a tourism board, or some other entity. This parent group will dictate some of the procedures that you follow, especially if it already has a nonprofit status. There may be rules about posting agendas. There will certainly be rules about finances, budgets, and record keeping.

If you are not under a larger body, you may wish to have the event committee seek nonprofit corporation status. You will need to form your board and hold your meetings in accordance with those rules. The status is important, especially if you will be looking for sponsors and donations. If you don't have that 501(c) (3) status, your supporters may not be able to deduct their gift from their taxes. For guidance, consult a book on setting up a nonprofit corporation in your state. Be aware that there might be a three-to six-month delay after your paperwork is filed before you are granted a tax identification number. There are also considerable expenses involved.

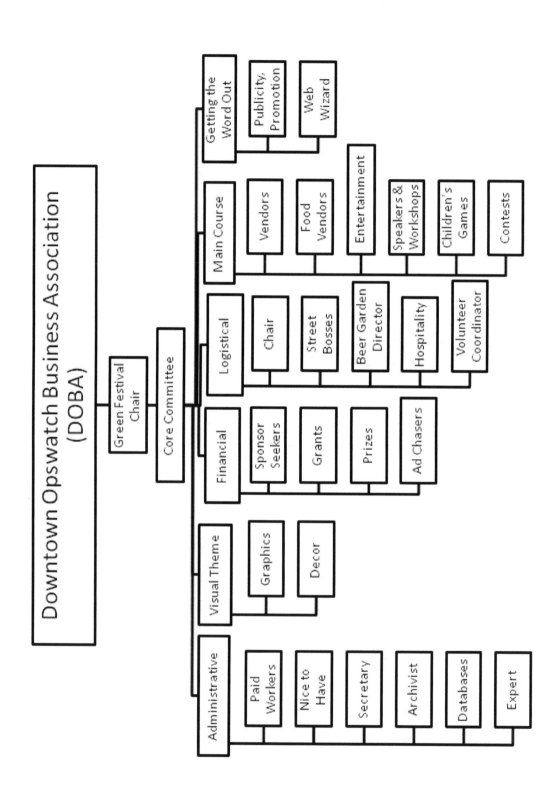

Basic Committee Structure

Let's look at the Opswatch Green Festival Committee to see how it is structured: see chart opposite. In reality, there is a lot of overlap on the chart. Some people wear more than one hat. The organization is informal and fluid.

The Green Festival is under the auspices of the parent group, the Downtown Opswatch Business Association Board of Directors. The chairperson reports directly to them.

The chairperson works very closely with the core committee, which is an informal, ad hoc group functioning basically as support and sounding board. It is similar to an executive board. It is a good group to work out tasks, such as the budget and the agendas for the larger committee meetings.

The work of the committee is divided into six functions: **visual theme, financial, logistical, main course, getting the word out, and administrative**. The seventh function, **"nice to have"**, mentioned in the committee make-up section, is shown in the chart under administrative.

The basic committee is made up of the subcommittee chairs from the working chunks. *A chunk is a smaller group of people or subcommittee working on a particular aspect of the whole.* You may have an entertainment chunk, a design-poster-program chunk, a costume-contest chunk, and so on. Some might have two or three people, some six or eight. Chunks are where most of the work gets done.

Who comes to the basic committee meetings? At least one person from each of the six functions is included. As the work of the committee moves along, other chunk chairs may attend when they have reports, questions, or just because they want to come. When the entire event is coordinated and last minute preparations are done, everyone should be present. Generally, the committee meetings are open to all interested.

Structure your work

A workable structure is to break things up in full committee meetings, chunk meetings, and work parties. You may choose to have five to nine full committee meetings during the course of the year, including the evaluation meeting. If your event is in its formative years, you will need more meetings than an event which is several years into its run. If your event is a one-time-only event, start your schedule early, and pencil in the number and type of meetings needed to bring the event to a successful conclusion.

The biggest challenge is to find a common meeting time for staff, busy volunteers, and those who work a typical work week. If you can't find a time when everyone can get together, try having two meetings with the same agenda, one at 8:00 a.m. and the other at 6:00 p.m. People could choose which to attend. It is more work for the leader, but it could pay off in greater participation. If enough of your core committee come to both meetings, things will be well coordinated. Notes and minutes are shared from both meetings.

Between full committee meetings, the work is done in chunk meetings. When needed, schedule work parties. These have specific goals, and are usually set to accomplish a physical task. You might come together to make banners and decorations, work on the program, coordinate all the schedules, and so on. Often there are specific details to discuss while your hands are busy cutting, folding, or gluing.

Start-up Meeting for a New Event

Because a shared vision is so crucial to the success of an event, the start-up meeting for a first-time event should include:

- Someone from the hotel and tourism base, if one of your goals is to attract more tourism to your area
- Key people who might be interested in working on the festival, who might give financial support, or whose opinion will help promote the festival
- Members of your parent board or group
- Those who are movers and shakers in your community or school
- Those who care enough about the concept to come and express their ideas
- Worker bees and potential committee members

Look at your goals and invite those who will be most affected by those same goals. They may become invested in the event and be your most positive promoters. Your efforts may begin an event that becomes a tradition and is passed on to the next generation in your community. Stress to your people that an event should not be judged on its first year. There is a learning curve. It takes a couple of years for things to fall into place, to iron out the wrinkles, and produce a popular and financially successful event. Concentrate on building a good foundation.

This meeting is the first opportunity to promote the event and get those who might have some influence in your community invested in your event. Promote this meeting well. Have a sign-in sheet with contact information for all who attend. This might begin your database of volunteers, potential sponsors, or even vendors.

Introduce yourself, distribute your agenda or speak briefly about it, and then have everyone introduce themselves. Ask them to share why they came, what their interests and hopes about the event are, and what group they may represent.

Be prepared. You may want to lay some ground work ahead of this meeting with your core group. Sketch out your goals, the vendor quotas, and the potential activities and entertainment. It is probably a good idea to talk to other major movers and shakers beyond the core group and get them on board before the meeting. It doesn't hurt to have vocal support that you have built beforehand.

If you are aware that there may be "nay-sayers", give some thought to answering their possible questions and dealing with their issues. A little forethought may help nip opposition in the bud. It may also turn skeptics into supporters.

At this meeting, plan to lay out your idea, your tentative goals, and what you think the event might look like. After the presentation, open up the meeting to discussion and brainstorming ideas. Ask for good suggestions for volunteers. Before closing the meeting, see if you can fill some of the spots on your committees. It may be wise not to assign chairpersons for chunks at this first, open meeting, especially if you are aware of underlying personality issues and troublesome track records.

 TIP   Photos, drawings, event programs, and websites of similar events may work wonders for your presentation. Bring what you can to inspire your people.

Agendas

It behooves the committee chair to set agendas for meetings and keep the conversation on track. Agendas mean less possibility that important topics will be forgotten or given short shrift in time. Let people be heard, allow time for ideas to germinate and for fresh ideas to be born, but don't let the meeting disintegrate into unproductive chatter or small groups talking among themselves. Don't waste your committee members' time. If minutes and agendas are emailed or distributed early enough, you won't have to waste meeting time reading them.

The core committee or the subcommittee chairs should help set the agenda. Consult your complete list of all of the activities and processes that are the puzzle pieces of your event. Also check your timeline. Consulting the list and the timeline means there is less chance of leaving something important out of the agenda. Reports or queries from your parent board should be added to the agenda.

Keep the agenda from the previous meeting to use as your template. The following agenda is an example.

Sample Agenda

Name and Date of Event
Agenda – Meeting date, time, location

1. Comments from the floor

    There are always latecomers. Use this time for reporting, not for action items. This might be a good chance to have the report from the internet seeker about what they have learned about other events.

2. Agenda changes, additions

    Agendas often need adjusting. Someone who is to report far down on the agenda may have to leave early, or something may have come up that must be added.

3. Introductions

    Each should give their name and what part of the festival they are working on. You might also report on those who have been excused and those who said they are coming, but have not yet arrived.

4. Old business from minutes

    When you set the agenda, note the items that were left hanging or tabled from the last meeting.

5. Budget

    Expenses

    Income

6. Chunk progress

    List all of the chunks. Items that you know will be reported on, or reports that the committee wants to hear should be bulleted under their chunk. Not all chunks will report, but if you list them, you won't forget them. It also provides an orderly way for folks to ask questions about a specific activity.

    A. Vision

    B. Entertainment
    - Staged
    - Walkabout

    C. Sponsors

    D. Prizes

    E. Vendors
    - Arts, crafts
    - Nonprofits
    - Food

    F. Website - updates needed, traffic reports

    G. Publicity, promotion

    H. T-shirts / totes

    I. Contests

J. Program
K. Volunteers
L. Beverage booth
M. Signage
N. Children's activities
O. Décor / ambience
P. Information booth
Q. Art contest
R. Logistics

7. Set next meeting date, time, and location.

Don't forget to thank everyone for coming. Their ideas, input, talents, loyalty, and perseverance are important.

Cell phones and other devices in meetings

Cell phones, lap top computers, and other electronic devices can be either disruptive or an asset in meetings.

- Use common courtesy and common sense to guide you.
- Devices should be turned off or put in a quiet mode to avoid rude interruptions.
- Use when information or answers are needed to keep business moving smoothly.
- Don't let the tools become distractions. Keep on track with your agenda and task.
- Be sensitive to those who are still hovering on the edges of the electronic age. If they don't get emails, make certain that they receive hard copies. If they do not subscribe to a social network used by many in your group to update folks, make certain that they have all of the information to function effectively. It is not productive to make good volunteers feel as though they are second class citizens, or to talk in a language that causes people to feel left out or alienated.
- For chunk meetings to accomplish tasks related to graphics, ads, or press releases, much of the work can be accomplished using laptops with everyone present. Sharing between computers with CDs and flash drives lets the work proceed and might reduce the need for some meetings.
- Occasionally, cell phones and emails may allow you to take care of business without a physical meeting. Sometimes the weather, people's schedules, or the fact that something has not yet fallen into place get in the way of meetings.

There is no substitute for face-to-face meetings. Some things will only be accomplished by interaction with other people dedicated to the same task. Reading people's facial expressions and body language and hearing the nuances in voices cannot be done through email. Seeing how new volunteers interact with people cannot be done by cell phone or computer. Rapport can be accomplished over a cup of coffee in a way that a conference call or electronic media cannot duplicate.

Supporting Committee Members

Treat them well, keep them informed, let them know that they are appreciated and of great importance to the event.

TIP   I was at an early planning meeting in the fall for an ongoing event to be held in late May. The committee chair handed to each activity leader a folder including the past history of that activity, information on where the event was held, how it was set up, how many participated, the people involved, and how it went. I was impressed. They didn't have to start from scratch. The set-up was there to build on.

It is much easier to get volunteers if there is a template or model for them to follow. From the experience above, I learned to develop guides for the subcommittee chairs and for each activity. (See the sample, "Guide for the Green Vendor Chair" in the Appendix.) Some call the activity leader's folders "continuity folders". Make sure that the archival binders in the office or other location keep the originals for backup.

The basics are available to build on. Chair people can still make changes and try new things. Communication back and forth is important.

Organization Is the key

If you plan well, divide up your responsibilities, pay attention to detail, and learn from your evaluation, your event will have a solid base. Once the template is in place for a well-run event, the next year is far easier and will take far less time. Distribute a committee list with contact information and responsibilities to all of your committee members. They will see how the responsibilities are divided and know whom to contact with their questions. They can also steer new volunteers to areas of interest.

A well-organized event committee means that no one person is overwhelmed. Volunteers are happy and willing to work again if they know what they have to do, if they get good direction, if they feel supported, and if they feel appreciated.

> **TIP**   After the event make certain that all of the folks in charge of different segments have submitted their reports, their databases, their templates for forms, their volunteer lists, and so on to the office or the chairperson. You need to have all that information together for the next year. If a subcommittee chair's spouse is transferred to a different part of the country and they move away, you do not want to have to re-create what they did. The new person in that position will want to hit the ground running with the history and data in hand. You may need to be diplomatic and persistent to get some of this material, but you will be glad to have it. Life is uncertain; change is inevitable.

Combining forces with other groups

It may seem like a good idea to share the labor and the income with another nonprofit group for a fundraiser. Usually this will result in benefits for both groups. There is a bigger pool of volunteers to share the work and a greater potential of reaching a wider audience. But on rare occasions this road may lead to quagmires, stressed friendships, grumbling, and bitter feelings.

The relationship has a better chance of remaining positive if the groundwork is laid ahead of time. Before you agree to combine efforts, find out how well the board or committee of the other group functions. Are you impressed with the planning and executions of their tasks? Do they handle their work in a businesslike manner? Think about it. Ask yourself if it would be a good idea to share responsibility with them for the whole event, or let the other group take the total responsibility for a certain segment of the event.

For everyone's protection, write up an agreement that spells out in detail which group is responsible for each tasks, who will pay for what, and how the proceeds will be split. Include a miscellaneous clause for unforeseen expenses and how they will be divided. Decide which organization will provide volunteers for certain tasks. Include members of both groups for tasks involving money handling and tickets. Don't just say that each group will use their "normal publicity channels" to promote the combined effort. Spell out the publicity tasks. The other group may not do a good job at publicity, leaving most of the task up to your group which has a clear vision in mind for press releases, flier and poster distribution, and emails to contacts. The other group may distribute 15 posters three weeks from the event and call it done! Work hard to make sure everyone is on board and that they all understand what is expected of them.

5. Choosing Dates / Location

Finding the Best Time for the Event

You will want to choose the date that has the best potential for delivering the biggest audience for your event. You also want to avoid dates that will take away your vendors, your volunteers and your potential entertainment. Of course, there will always be something else scheduled no matter what weekend you pick. Weather is unpredictable in any given month.

Here is a check list of items to consider before you set the date for your event:
- Holidays, school calendars, and vacations.
- Dates appropriate to your theme.
- If your event is based on a certain food like pears or asparagus, make sure you set the date when that food is being harvested.
- Other events locally or regionally.
- Potential weather problems.
- Similar competitive events in your wide region that might limit your choice of vendors, entertainers, and volunteers.
- Events that tie up your potential parking.
- Availability of your chosen venue.
- Other activities preventing a good turnout—local harvest seasons, school testing times, holidays, other events, local traditions, and so on.

Consider the thought process for choosing the Medieval Fantasy Festival dates:

- January and February are too close to Christmas; there isn't enough lead time to get ready for a major festival.
- March has St. Patrick's Day, meaning many of our Celtic entertainers are already booked. Weather is pretty iffy in California in March.
- We looked at the date Easter falls on and when the local schools have their spring break.
- May is really busy in our area with several long-standing festivals as well as Mother's Day. Schools are winding down with testing and finals.
- June has graduations, Father's Day, and people going on vacations.
- June, July, and August get pretty hot. If you want folks to be in costume, you don't want to schedule your event in 100-degree-plus heat!
- September and October are hectic with schools beginning and other events. The Northern California Renaissance Faire runs from mid-September to mid-October involving lots of our vendors and volunteers. Later October could be a possibility, but could be hot or rainy.
- In November rain is likely, and folks are gearing up for the holidays.
- There was no way that we would choose December.

So we chose April. Nothing else was happening except for the income tax deadline. If we stayed away from Easter and the last full weekend of April, which has two popular regional festivals, we would do pretty well. We deliberately picked the closest weekend to Earth Day (April 22) because we wanted to connect to the green, eco-friendly folks.

TIP Sometimes it is beneficial to look at obscure holidays when you are seeking a theme or date for your event. Even if the holiday will not be your major theme, it might suggest a fun, unusual activity for you. If you find your date coincides with the anniversary of Johnny Appleseed's birth, bring in apple-related activities. Perhaps your date is on the anniversary of the Sack of Rome, or during Mold Awareness Month. Check out a volume of "what happened and who was born on this day" such as *Chase's Calendar of Events* from your local library. Have fun perusing this compilation of facts and put your creativity to work.

Location Considerations

Check out the choices of location (venue) in person. Picture your event in each location. Think of your intended activities and your target audience. What do you like? What don't you like? What is lacking?

 You may wish to have your parent group or an attorney look at the venue contract before it is signed. Who from your committee is authorized to sign? Can you meet the deadlines reasonably? What are the costs — deposits, etc? What are the services offered, liability for damages, cancellation risks?

Consider these questions:

- Is the facility (structure) or site (outdoor location) available on the dates you want it? (Some are booked a year or more in advance.)
- What are the rental costs? What do they require as a deposit?
- Will the location fit the size and theme of your event?
- Is the venue handicapped accessible? Are parking and restrooms suitable?
- Will the public have trouble finding the location?
- Is it easy for the public to get to? Are there traffic bottlenecks or one-lane, winding roads to navigate? Is there public transportation?
- Will you have to share the venue with another event? If so, will the other event be compatible with your intended audience, or will it clash? If there are other events nearby, will they affect yours (and vice versa) with noise, parking problems, traffic, confusion and attitudes?
- Will your event be sandwiched between other events on the same day? If another group runs over their time or they arrive early at a celebration, what does that do to your event?
- How about access before the event in plenty of time to take care of set up and décor? Do you pay extra for this access? After the event, how much time do you have to get everything cleared out?
- Are there restrictions on the type of signage the venue owners will allow?
- How easy will it be to do crowd control and keep the area secure? Will you have to foot the bill for fencing an outdoor site?
- Will there be enough parking for vendors, for volunteers, and for the public?
- What are the insurance requirements?

- Will the venue allow liquor to be served?
- Will you have to deal with a tobacco smoke smell? How about other odors—musty, damp, unused stale odors or glue from new carpets? How about upkeep and cleanliness of the venue in general?

> **TIP**   Consider this when renting a city venue: You may be able to ask for a waiver of all or part of the fees if the event is seen as bene-fitting the community or if you are nonprofit. If an event adds to the city employees' work load, your request may not be looked upon as kindly. It doesn't hurt to ask if you can negotiate some costs.

- Note the direction of the wind for outdoor sites. Ask about the prevailing wind patterns. This may affect your set up of vendors, stages, and so on.
- How much of a hassle will it be for vendors to offload and set up?
- Does the venue provide electricity in the amps that your equipment requires? How about your entertainment or vendor equipment?
- Will your evening's entertainment have appropriate lighting?
- Is it in an area where people feel safe?
- Will they be able to move easily between your different activity locations?
- Can you live with the rules and restrictions the venue has?
- Will you have to close off streets? Will that create a traffic problem and animosity?
- If your event has loud music, will that be a problem for neighbors or neighboring businesses?
- Does the location provide a "Plan B" in case of inclement weather?
- Does the venue have requirements about booth and décor materials? Do they have to be made out of a fire-retardant material?
- Do the kitchen/dining facilities and toilet facilities allow you to accommodate the number of folks you want to attend?
- Are you able to talk to other groups who have used the venue to evaluate it for your event?
- Is the venue in financial jeopardy? Who might know? The last thing you need is to pay your deposit, plan and publicize your event only to have the venue declare bankruptcy and cancel their schedule. Getting a refund of your deposit (if it is even possible) may force you to join other creditors in line and take months.

Develop a venue possibility form for each activity in your event that needs a special location. A sample has been included here.

Indoor Venue Possibility

Activity _____

Location _____

Date _____ Availability _____

Cost _____

By hour? _____ Set-up, tear-down time extra? _____

When can you get in? _____ Hours _____

Security deposit _____

Contact person _____Phone _____

Email _____

Number of people capacity _____

Bar? _____ They run _____ We run _____

Catering? _____ Hours _____ Cost _____

Sound? _____ Restrictions _____

Décor possibilities _____

Stage _____ Lighting _____Dance floor _____ Chairs _____ Tables _____

Security needs _____

List the amenities, services, products the venue provides.

List the what the event would have to provide.

Notes:

_____

Whatever location you choose, map it out and place each activity on it. Get all of the location-related deadlines into your timeline—for choosing menu items, letting the venue know the final headcount of attendance, and so on.

Some locations are chosen by default. If your goal is to raise funds for a particular school or church, it might make the most sense to have the event there. You had better have a pretty good reason to choose a different venue than the one you are raising funds for, especially if you have to pay rent for the other location. The Medieval Fantasy Festival was in the historic downtown on the streets. Since one of our goals was to bring business and visibility to the downtown, it was the obvious choice even though there was a park close by.

Using a park may add prohibitive rental costs and many more city hoops to jump through. For some city parks, for a two-day event, you could easily run up a bill of several thousand of dollars for police, fencing, a stage, park rental, sprinkler covers, and so on. Your profit would be non-existent, you could be in the red, and your event could be looking at its demise.

TIP   When you scout a location, take notice of everything and allow enough time to think about the ramifications of holding your event there. One event group planned to use a closed-off parking lot for all of their booth spaces and activities. They had noted the garbage dumpsters in the parking lot behind some restaurants. The booth spaces near them were the last ones to be used. The planners had not, however, counted on the event day being a breezy, 105 degrees. The dumpster stench was deadly, surpassed only by the rank odor emanating from the parking lot storm drains—a nasty surprise!

Moving People Through the Event Location

How do you see the public moving through your event? Do they move up and back; do they move in a circuit? Could they miss event activities because their locations aren't obviously visible to someone who doesn't know the area? A list of "people movers" follows:

- Comfort and physical needs (shade, bathrooms, and food)
- Certain performers and music
- Announcements over the public address system
- Visual activity

- Signage and program maps
- Contests or scavenger hunts

If your event is in a downtown area, there will be certain businesses that want the foot traffic from the event. What is the best way of accomplishing that?

If your event is in a school and will use classrooms and multi-purpose rooms, how will you draw them from one activity to another?

Even if you don't have a formal program, a hand-out with a schedule and a map are excellent ideas. This is especially true if your event is too large to have it all visible at one time. Provide the public with easy access to *What, When,* and *Where* things are happening. Actively distribute the handout; don't make folks look for it. Announcements are good but should only augment or remind about something written; it is too easy to miss part of what comes over a loudspeaker. Too many things are competing for attention. You have worked to pull all the pieces of an event together. Don't let the lack of a schedule and map get in the way of the public's enjoyment of your hard work.

What's with the tracks? Read on!

The Medieval Fantasy Festival grew in its first years from one block only to a triangle of streets with a continuous flow of foot traffic. In the beginning, we struggled with the foot traffic flow. We didn't have any activities or vendors on the far side of our triangle of streets, but we still had a retail merchant there who wanted the foot traffic.

We got the idea of printing dragon tracks on the sidewalks and streets for the public to follow. We designed a huge dragon footprint, cut the print pieces out of thick sponges, and glued them to a piece of plywood. Then we put handles on the other side of the wood so we could put firm, even pressure to our "stamp". We mixed up poster paint in a paint tray and applied it to our stamp with a roller.

Always test things first. We knew that.

We experimented with green poster paint and found that it washed off easily. But the green paint didn't show up well against the street or sidewalk. So we added white and blue, loved the effect, and proceeded to stamp dragon tracks all around the downtown triangle of streets. The tracks went up to the doors of all businesses who had advertised event specials. At the door the dragon left a double track.

Grandparents and kids loved the tracks. They followed the tracks; kids jumped on them and talked about the creature that must have left them. It was very successful.

When the festival was over, we discovered that while green paint comes off with water, white and blue don't. With a steel brush, lots of elbow grease, and some pretty caustic soap, we eradicated the tracks in 'sensitive' areas to avoid complaints by the city. The ones on the actual street eventually were worn away by traffic. The rest are there, years later. Visitors to our downtown ask, "What's up with the big bird tracks?" Kids still run and jump on them. The tracks are fading at last, but we definitely left our mark on the city!

6. Budget / Finances / Regulations

So far we have talked about *What* you want to do, *Why* you want to do it, *Who* is it for, and *When* and *Where* it will be. Before you nail down the particulars, you must address ***How are you going to pay for it?*** Later we work on *How* you will find *people* to pull it off.

While working on the finances, you will wish to refer to the sample budget for the Green Festival which follows the sections on Sources of Budget Income and Types of Budget Expenses here.

Sources of Budget Income

There are several possibilities available to pay for your event:
1. You or your group could foot the bill. Depending on the size of the event and its purpose, this could be appropriate.
2. Charge admission. Think through the pros and cons with your core committee:
   o Some of the public won't come if you charge them to get in.
   o Some have the theory that if people come with $40 to spend and it costs them $6 to get in, that is only $34 left to spend on food and on items from vendors.

- o You may have to deal with the public attitude, "Why should I pay to get in and buy stuff?"
- o There is a theory that people won't value what they get for free. If it costs them money, it must have more worth.
- o If you charge, be prepared to deliver that worth, and set the price accordingly.
- o For some fundraisers, the ticket price is set high and becomes the major source of income for the event.
- o If you want the public to experience the event—to learn about and have their minds enlightened about a certain subject—you might not want to charge.
- o If your goal is to help a food bank, make the price of admission some nonperishable food items.

3. Ask for donations or a free-will offering.
4. Find sponsors or grant money. (Start early!)
5. Vendor booth fees.
6. Selling merchandise, beverages, T-shirts, tote bags, and so on.
7. Selling ads in the event program. (See Chapter 17 under Programs.)
8. Selling ads to include on your website. (While it may bring in income, the feel of your design may be compromised by ads which bring clutter and distraction.)
9. Charging for a particular activity. Some activities are very entertaining just to watch. You may be able to charge the participants for some activities.
10. Raffle prize tickets.
11. Combination of several of the above.

The Medieval Fantasy Festival created a popular activity called the Ratapult. This idea caught on and became a good fundraiser. Read more about the Ratapult in Chapter 17.

Types of Budget Expenses

There will be expenses related to your event. Some will be dictated to you and some you will incur because you want the event to include that luxury or activity.

Many of these have been listed previously as responsibilities of committee chairs. This list has items that will be in your budget.

1. **Leader education and preparation**

    Some of this will be borne by individuals. This may be in-kind support (donation of service or goods, not cash). If so, it should be acknowledged as such. If reimbursement is needed, it should be authorized beforehand. The person should provide receipts, and careful records should be kept. Some of these expenses may be:

    o   Sending someone on your committee to a "how to" conference or workshop.

    o   Purchasing how-to books (like this planning guide!).

    o   Subscriptions to pertinent, valuable magazines such as craft show guide magazines.

    o   A planning retreat for core group on vision. This may be as simple as providing coffee and donuts or pizza in a large room. It may be as elaborate as taking the core group to the location of the event for in-depth planning, out of the range of other distractions.

    o   Visiting other similar events, mileage, parking, meals, tickets, and so on.. The purpose of these visits may be to find vendors and entertainment.

    o   Nonprofit incorporation expenses—if there is no parent group to whom this expense properly belongs.

2. **Logistics and amenities**

    o   Chairs, tables, porta potties, garbage and recycle toters

    o   Water and ice

    o   Pop-ups, tents, weather cover

    o   Phone, postage, copies, paper, printer ink

    o   Insurance, business license, permits, health department fee

    o   Venue rental

    o   Catering, refreshments, meals, beverages

    o   Security

    o   Hospitality for volunteers

    o   Lighting, sound

    o   Signage, décor

    o   Paid staff

    o   Space, electricity for event administration

    o   Accommodations and hospitality for entertainers and speakers

3. **Promotional**

    o   Posters, fliers, tickets, newspaper and other media advertising

    o   Promotional merchandise, T-shirts, name-dropped items

    o   Programs, other written material

    o   Prizes for contestants, raffles

4. The main course of your event

- o Entertainment
- o Speakers, workshop leaders
- o Games and activity expenses

 TIP   Always include a budget with your anticipated income and expenses in your proposal to your parent group or organization.

Green Festival Budget - April 18, 2015

INCOME			
Activity	Total 2014	Budget 2015	Notes
Sponsors	1000	1200	
Merchandise Vendors	4800	6000	
Food Vendors	700	700	
Program Ads	450	600	
T-shirts	900	1100	
Tote Bags	0	200	No tote bags done in 2014
Beverages	940	1000	
Total Income	8790	10800	

EXPENSES			
Activity	**Total 2014**	**Budget 2015**	**Notes**
Logistics			
Chairs, Tables	381	400	
Porta potties, Greywater Tank	448	500	
Phone	25	25	
Insurance	650	650	
Ice, Misc.	85	100	
Signage on Site	24	25	
City Business License	250	250	
Postage	44	50	
Garbage / Recycle Toters	0	0	In-kind Sponsor
Health Dept. Fee	300	330	
Advertising / Promotional			
Posters	181	200	
Fliers		50	In-kind Sponsor 2014
Newspapers	250	350	
Schools	68	75	
Other Publications	50	150	
Freeway Sign	100	100	Free to nonprofit, cost is graphics
Program	135	150	
Other		100	
Entertainment	250	400	
Speakers, Presenters	600	800	
Accommodations	179	200	
Meals	58	75	
T-shirts	781	800	
Tote Bags	0	140	
Activity, Contest Supplies	248	200	
Total Expenses 2014	5107		
Total Expenses 2015		6120	
Total Profit 2014	3683		
Total Profit 2015		4680	

Handling Money and Tickets

Do your homework. Besides doing the proposal and tentative budget, spend some time becoming familiar with your own organization's policies and procedures on budgets, handling money, and finances. Start from there and follow the rules religiously. Keep good records, do things decently and in good order: keep your financial dealings transparent. Put people you trust in positions of money handling, but back that up with good accounting practices and oversight. Keep it simple, keep it clear, and keep it clean.

 TIP   Don't even think of running event money through your own personal bank account. If your parent group cannot handle the banking for you or there is no parent group, set up a new bank account strictly for the event. The account should have at least two people named from your committee. Keep the records and accounting for this account meticulously. If a check is written to any person named on this account, have another named individual sign it.

Second, set your own event procedures on handling money:

- Who will be authorized to make purchases on behalf of the committee? What procedures must be followed if someone is to be reimbursed for a purchase they made with their own money? Is there an amount they can't exceed without board or committee approval?
- Keep the duplicate receipt book handy. When someone gives you a cash donation, pays cash for a T-shirt, or gives you three cases of water, give them a receipt. Make sure the receipt book itself, with the carbon copies, is kept in a safe place and that the information gets recorded properly.
- For petty cash drawers, keep a record of the starting amount and what is spent. Either the money should be there, or corresponding receipts should be in its place—from those who made purchases, of what items, for what subcommittee, and how much spent.
- How many people will count the gate receipts or the money received from the beverage concessions? Where and when will they do the counting? How will the money be labeled? How will you get it to the bank safely? Where will it be kept until you take it to the bank? Who will be assigned to handle it? Think through all of the steps from the customer handing you the money to the actual bank deposit.
- For a multi-day event, how will you keep track of each day's money?

- How much of a start-up cash drawer do you need for any activity that is handling money?
- If you take checks, what kind of ID is required and what information is required on the check? Do you plan to take charge or debit cards? How will funds be verified? Be aware of state and federal regulations regarding the kind of information you can ask for.
- Insist on a complete paper trail for all financial transactions.

If a person deals with money, merchandise, or tickets, they should be organized in such a way that tracks all that they have done. Think about how tickets will be handled before and during the event. Where will they be sold? Who will sell them for you? How will the money be handled? What kind of records need to be kept? What kind of information do you want from the purchaser? Is seating assigned? How will you know if someone has paid admission if they leave and want to come back?

Tickets should be numbered in order to track them. Those selling tickets need to sign off for a certain number of tickets at the beginning. If they began with tickets numbered 1–20, they should have either the tickets or the money for sold tickets when it comes to signing off at the end. If you are charging admission to get into the event or to get in to a particular performance, think through the procedure.

TIP   Decide early on about who gets complimentary tickets and perks among the committee leadership. If there is a policy set up at the beginning and the guidelines followed, there will be less chance of folks getting bent out of shape over who got tickets and who did not. Will the chair of the costume ball committee be expected to buy his or her own ticket? How about the costume ball decoration committee helpers? Who gets a festival T-shirt at no charge? Does anyone get free beverages?

Be careful of how much profit you are giving away. Balance this with care and consideration of your volunteers.

Make it clear ahead of time exactly which people are authorized to spend or to promise money on behalf of the event. Who is responsible for each budget chunk? What is the procedure if it is necessary to spend more than the budgeted amount? A clear chain of command, for both budget responsibilities and reimbursement policies, should be in place.

A budget is just a plan, not a blank check. Just because a certain amount is budgeted for an activity doesn't mean that it all has to be spent. If the event's goal is raising funds for a particular cause, any "extra" will help the bottom line. Do the best you can, spending as little money as possible without stinting on the integrity of your activity.

Don't expect that a first-year event will make a lot of money. You will be fortunate to break even. You are getting your feet wet, trying new things. It is impossible to know what to expect. If you put on a good show, however, future years will see improvement in the number and quality of vendors, the attendance, and the strength of the event. Consider the first year or so as building blocks for a strong, successful venture. In your proposal to your parent group, emphasize this.

Tax Reporting, Money, and Regulations

The treasurer or accountant from your parent group or your own nonprofit group will be interested in helping you provide the information they need to file reports and tax returns correctly. You will want to check on the current tax rules that apply to your group. Be aware of federal, state, and sales tax laws. Make sure that you keep up on the rules for what you must report and what you can and cannot do. Be aware of the forms that must be completed and the information they ask you to complete. Note any deadlines for reporting on your timeline.

Make sure that you handle the sponsors and donors properly, giving them the paperwork to verify their financial gifts for tax purposes. Make sure that your donors receive acknowledgement and thank you letters. Be sure to know the federal and state tax regulations about who can receive goodies as incentives for their gift and who cannot—like tickets and T-shirts.

Any vendor needs a resale permit in most states. If your event committee is also a vendor because you are selling T-shirts or beverages to raise money, you will need to collect and pay sales tax to your state agency. If you are selling raffle tickets or event tickets, you may have to pay sales tax on them as well. Make a point of finding out the rules for your state.

Your insurance company, your city's insurance company, or your venue contract may have some regulations that you must follow. One of these might be a "volunteer hold harmless agreement". A sample of this is found in the Green Festival Documents in the Appendix. Frankly, the language is off-putting, but it may be necessary to satisfy the agency in charge. Please note: this is only a sample form. Each state has its unique waiver language. Therefore, don't just copy this or one you find online. Get the advice of your attorney for drafting this document for your event or use a recommended waiver form from your city.

Treat city, county, state, and federal regulations as a mine field that you must cross with care. As the organizational person, you should take the trouble to find out how they affect what you want to do and how you want to do it. Ignorance is not an excuse.

You, your parent group, or someone on your committee must be responsible to learn about and comply with regulations and policies of any ruling body that may have jurisdiction over your event and activities. I*t is beyond the purview of this book to give definitive tax advice or reporting advice on other bureaucratic policies.* The checklist below notes some of the possible areas with regulations you may have to deal with.

Checklist for rules, permits, licenses, and regulations

A few examples of possible regulations are given for each jurisdiction below. Don't assume that if something is not included on this list that you don't have to find out about it. Every location will have different policies and practices. A city might have jurisdiction over something that a county will regulate in another location. Some items like alcoholic beverage sales may necessitate cooperation with more than one agency, such as the local police department and the state.

Police and Fire
- ☐ Background checks, security requirements
- ☐ Use of weapons, black powder, pyrotechnics
- ☐ Building occupancy limits
- ☐ Fire-retardant materials for tents, decorations, fire extinguishers

City
- ☐ Special event application, parking, street closures
- ☐ Business license, signage regulations, volunteer hold harmless agreements
- ☐ Curfews, noise limits
- ☐ Use of parks, public property rules
- ☐ Animals at events

County
- ☐ Health department regulations
- ☐ Food vendor regulations

State
- ☐ Raffles
- ☐ Sales of alcoholic beverages
- ☐ Sales tax
- ☐ State registration of your group and its fundraising activities

Federal
- ☐ IRS reporting, documentation for sponsors, donors
- ☐ 1099 workers (those who receive $600 or more in payment)
- ☐ ADA (Americans with Disability Act) requirements for accessibility

Event Venue / School Districts
- ☐ Security requirements
- ☐ Activities—are there restrictions?
- ☐ Background checks for volunteers
- ☐ Compliance with district policies about what activities can and can't happen

Your parent group
- ☐ Money-handling restrictions, reporting, documentation policies
- ☐ Restrictions because of your insurance policy

Medical emergencies, first aid
- ☐ What jurisdiction is in charge?
- ☐ What can you do, what can't you do legally?

Environmental impact
- ☐ What jurisdiction is in charge?
- ☐ Policies about recycling, garbage disposal

7. Developing Timelines

Doing things decently and in good order requires planning for what happens when and who is responsible to see it done and report back. Sit down with your core committee or someone in your area who has done events before and think it through.

The following timeline is only a template. It is not complete and will need to be tailored for your particular event and your particular organization and city. Put the tasks in the order on the timeline where they make sense to you. Starting times and deadlines for tasks should be included, allowing your workers time enough to complete the work without hitting the panic button.

There is a lot of wiggle room in the following timeline. When doing a start-up event, you will need more time to lay the foundation. If you are using volunteers who are new at the game, you will need to build in time for a learning curve. It takes time to develop databases of craft vendors, a good working committee, and enough dependable volunteers and leaders that can nurture an event to a successful conclusion. Those with a lot of event experience under their belts can accomplish their tasks in a much shorter period of time.

Be aware of the regulations that your state, county, city, school, church, or your parent organization might have that might have to be included on your timeline. If your event is part of a larger organization of events, for example, a sanctioned chili cook-off or a race sponsored by a larger sporting association, their governing body will have procedures and deadlines of their own. You will have to discover these and plug them into your general timeline.

Throughout the process you might want to document the steps and progress with photos. Throughout, you need to keep your website current and interesting. Keep your parent group in the loop—especially with exciting developments.

Organize the tasks that must be done on a list or chart that will list the specific tasks: who will be responsible for them, when they were assigned, what the deadlines are for completion, and who reports back.

I have organized the items plugged into this timeline in the same categories that the committee make-up has in Chapter 3. This organization is loose and subjective because the tasks don't fit neatly into compartments. The administrative category ended up with the lion's share of these items without an obvious home. You don't have to use the categories suggested here. Draw up categories that make sense for you and your event, making sure that all of the tasks are covered.

These are the task categories:
1. *Administrative*—the theme, planning, organizing, vision, and budget
2. *Financial*—the actual fundraising, getting sponsors, selling ads, handling money, and so on
3. *Visual Theme*—graphics and décor
4. *Logistical*—what you need to make it run smoothly behind and in front of the scenes
5. *Main course*—what the public will come to see and do
6. *Getting the word out*—your publicity and promotion people

Go through the timeline with each of the above categories in mind. What should they be doing?

18 months out

Administrative
- [ ] Draft budget.
- [ ] Pitch proposal to your parent group.
- [ ] Research for event ideas.
- [ ] Work on vision, theme, goals, and new ideas for event.

Financial
- [ ] Apply for grant funding.

- ☐ Identify and lay the groundwork with major sponsors.
- ☐ Research for grant possibilities for following year.

Logistical
- ☐ Research venues.

Main Course
- ☐ List possible entertainers, speakers.

12 months out or earlier

Administrative (The first two are crucial.)
- ☐ **Reserve main venues. Get any facility rental waiver in writing.**
- ☐ **Set date for event. Search out all other events that might conflict, taking your audience and your participants.**
- ☐ Contact your chosen folks and get commitments for major positions on committee—for example, website person.
- ☐ Continue work on vision, goals, and new ideas for event.
- ☐ Gather together volunteers for your committee.
- ☐ Finalize contract details, if you are contracting with an outside organization to handle the vendors.
- ☐ Plug meetings of your parent group into this outline. Plan to make brief reports.
- ☐ Prepare calendar of other upcoming events that you may attend for ideas, vendors, and insight into planning.
- ☐ Put together database of resources in your community, groups and organizations that might be of help.
- ☐ Research the internet for ideas.

Visual Theme
- ☐ Begin plans for coordinated theme ideas for design, logo, T-shirt, signage, décor.
- ☐ Begin a folder of ideas collected from other events and resources.

Financial
- ☐ Begin contacting the corporate sponsors whose decision-making wheels may turn very slowly.
- ☐ List potential sponsors and supporters.

Logistical
- ☐ Find out about any city or other organizational hoops that you need to jump through and when these must happen. For example, do you need a city business license? Does the city require event leaders to meet with city police, ADA folks, fire department, and so on? Do you need to plan for street closures?

☐ If you plan to serve alcohol at your event, find out about obtaining a liquor license and getting your servers properly trained. Integrate this information into the timeline.

Main Course

☐ Refine speaker options to a short list, prioritize, and begin contacting.

☐ Seek entertainers; research possibilities.

☐ Seek vendors; collect possibilities.

Getting the Word Out

☐ Create a website if you don't already have one. Update it if you do. Coordinate it with graphics people.

☐ Prepare publicity and promotion plan outline. Plug any deadlines for publications into this outline.

☐ Submit publicity to magazines and other media with long lead times. Get included on their calendars.

☐ Update your list of media outlets and contact persons.

11 months out

Administrative

☐ Chunk groups should meet to make basic plans.

☐ Meet with décor subcommittee; make plans for overall décor and signage.

☐ Plan your year's committee meeting schedule as best you can and plug it into this timeline.

☐ Update or put together guides for the leaders of each chunk.

Visual Theme

☐ Complete logo, get authorization from committee, and begin using it.

Getting the Word Out

☐ Advertise date on your website as soon as known.

☐ Get on city/school/community calendar

10 months out

Administrative

☐ Brainstorm for new ideas, ways of keeping event fresh.

☐ Review last year's budget—income and expense.

☐ Set a more complete budget for coming event.

Financial

☐ Compose sponsor packets; set sponsor menus.

☐ Seek donations and prizes from corporations and big businesses.

Logistical

- ☐ Book important and crucial amenities—security, porta potties, venues, tents.

Main Course

- ☐ Compose entertainer and vendor applications.
- ☐ Determine vendor application deadlines; plug them into this outline.
- ☐ Contact members of your own organization if they get first crack at vendor spots,
- ☐ Set up criteria for choosing vendors and vendor wish lists.
- ☐ Set vendor fees, ticket prices.

Getting the Word Out

- ☐ Get applications onto website.
- ☐ Update website as needed.

9 months out

Administrative

- ☐ Begin collecting bids for posters, shirts, programs and other promotional materials.
- ☐ Contact county health department for health regulations.

Main Course

- ☐ Make sure all of your most wanted vendors and entertainers have been contacted.
- ☐ Work on new activities; flesh them out. Find volunteers to run them.

8 months out

Administrative

- ☐ Core committee sets up or reviews money handling procedures with treasurer and budget folks.

Financial

- ☐ Continue contacting potential sponsors.

Main Course

- ☐ Begin accepting vendor and entertainer applications—the jury process should be ongoing from this point. (The jury process is explained in Chapter 12.)
- ☐ Book most crucial bands, entertainment, speakers, vendors.

Getting the Word Out

- ☐ Send out "Date set for…" press releases. Include looking for volunteers, vendors, entertainers, art show entries, and so on. Include all elements of the event that need a long lead time.

6 months out

Visual Theme
- ☐ Begin plans and work on creating décor.
- ☐ T-shirt design should be well along.

Logistical
- ☐ Contact remaining amenities including garbage/recycle toters.
- ☐ Obtain city special event application form.

Main Course
- ☐ Send out enticing invitations to vendors you really want.

Getting the Word Out
- ☐ Begin promoting event within your base. Highlight any activities or contests they might participate in.

5 months out

Vision Theme
- ☐ Make a list of signage needed. Assign the completion of signs to individuals or work parties.

Financial
- ☐ Contact local, smaller businesses and mom-and-pop businesses for prizes and donations.

4 months out

Visual Theme
- ☐ Begin layout for program. Develop ad sell sheet.
- ☐ Determine how many vinyl promotional banners are needed and where they will be located. Get bids and order.
- ☐ Finalize T-shirt and promotional materials designs. Order in a timely manner.

Financial
- ☐ Continue contacting potential sponsors and supporters.
- ☐ Solicit ads for program.

Main Course
- ☐ Be in touch with your county's health department. Find out about their regulations for having food vendors at an event. Request an application from them.

Getting the Word Out
- ☐ Send out a second round of press releases. Feature the theme of event and any major attraction booked.

3 months out

Main Course
- ☐ Contact vendors again. Send out a bigger net for vendors beyond the first choices you have already contacted.
- ☐ Finalize any menus and other arrangements with caterer.
- ☐ Evaluate your food vendor applications to date. Look at the menu choices you have for the event. Contact folks to "fill the holes".

Logistical
- ☐ Take care of any travel arrangements that must be done for speakers and entertainers.

Getting the Word Out
- ☐ Send out another round of press releases. Highlight new attractions.

2 months out

Administrative
- ☐ Finalize schedule. Get program wording finalized.
- ☐ Complete orders of any merchandise needing logo and design.

Visual Theme
- ☐ Work parties meet to make décor and prepare for games and activities.

Financial
- ☐ Begin pre-selling shirts.
- ☐ Get ads for program proofread.
- ☐ Plan for soliciting prizes. Continue to seek prizes and donations.
- ☐ Make arrangements to pick up.

Logistical
- ☐ Go through items in storage. Will any of them need to be repaired, refreshed, or replaced? Update your shopping list. Plan work parties if needed.
- ☐ Prepare site map with location of amenities.
- ☐ Submit your application for the permit to serve alcohol.

Main Course
- ☐ Finalize speaker and entertainer accommodations—travel, hotels and anything else needed.
- ☐ Send in application to health department for the event food vendor permit so the department has it within the number of days required prior to event.
- ☐ Get contracts from major entertainers.

☐ Place vendors on street maps. Send out confirmation and space assignment emails.

Getting the Word Out

☐ Send out another round of press releases.

☐ Prepare schedule and short blurbs about people and activities for website.

☐ Do draft of newspaper and other media ads.

☐ Have poster ready this month. Follow up on plans to distribute so they will be in place one month from event.

☐ Obtain permission to distribute fliers to schools.

☐ Pass out fliers, bag stuffers, other promotional materials to stores and businesses.

1 month out

Administrative

☐ Hold one-on-one coordinating meetings with key players like the stage manager and street bosses.

☐ Find volunteers to fill holes on committee and activities.

☐ Create a master file of contest entries and other needed forms.

☐ Make enough copies of all forms needed at event.

Financial

☐ Review the sponsor goodies that have been promised. Make arrangements for them to be picked up.

☐ Make a list of all contest prizes needed and make a plan to have them in the right place when they are needed.

☐ Pre-sell T-shirts.

Visual Theme

☐ Complete all signage needed.

Logistical

☐ Address vendor requests for water, electricity, and other needs.

☐ Notify local merchants of festival hours and street closures. Keep them in the loop.

☐ Hang large vinyl banners. Obtain permission first. You don't want folks ripping down and throwing away your expensive banners.

☐ Begin preparing "chunk boxes" with supplies for each area. Note anything that needs to be purchased.

☐ Plan what will need to be moved and set up on the day of the event.

☐ Secure volunteers responsible for clean-up and set-up.

☐ Double check on crucial amenities and logistics.

☐ Double check on permit for serving alcohol.

Main Course

☐ Send out any remaining space assignment letters to vendors.

☐ Secure any outstanding credentials from vendors, entertainers.

Getting the Word Out

☐ Deliver promotional fliers to schools in accordance with their rules.

☐ Reserve ad space in local newspaper.

During the second week out

Administrative

☐ Draft evaluation questions for committee to think about.

☐ Draft vendor evaluation form to hand out at the end of the event.

Financial:

☐ Pick up donated prizes.

☐ Make list of anyone who will get paid by check during event.

Main Course

☐ Double check on speakers and entertainment accommodations.

During the last week

Administrative

☐ Hold last-minute coordinating meeting.

☐ Fix binder with needed reference information.

☐ Prepare cell phone list or walkie-talkies for staff.

Financial

☐ Buy last minute supplies—water, duct tape, first aid kit supplies, and other items.

☐ Get cash for drawers for drinks, tickets, or T-shirt booths.

☐ Cut checks for entertainers and others to give out during event.

Logistical

☐ Put out "streets will be closed on this date" signs.

☐ Double check all equipment.

☐ Put up décor as appropriate.

☐ Fix "tool kit" for possible repairs during event.

☐ Finish chunk boxes, supplies needed list.

☐ Reserve parking for entertainers, VIPs.

EVENT

During the week after

Sleep

Administrative

- [ ] Finalize the evaluation questions and distribute evaluation forms to committee members.
- [ ] Schedule and hold evaluation meeting.
- [ ] Prepare list of supporters and volunteers to thank.
- [ ] Make sure all paperwork is put away properly in the appropriate binders.
- [ ] Save a hard copy and a computer copy of all application forms, fliers and handouts to use as templates for the next event.
- [ ] Note any items that need repair or replacement.
- [ ] Figure budget to date.

Financial

- [ ] Count and bank monies according to your organization's policies.
- [ ] Collect all invoices and financial information.
- [ ] Return food vendor cleaning deposits.

Logistical

- [ ] Return all borrowed items.
- [ ] Put away equipment, supplies, décor, and so on. Organize items by activity or list contents on boxes for easy finding when next needed.

Getting the Word Out

- [ ] Print out a hard copy of all your website pages. Put copies into your archive binder.
- [ ] Update website with photos of event. Add a thank-you page listing those who made it all possible. Thank those who attended. If date for next year is known, highlight that as well.

2 weeks after

Administrative

- [ ] Evaluate festival; prepare report for overseeing body.
- [ ] Organize and tabulate responses from evaluations.
- [ ] Look at expenses, income, and think about next year's budget.
- [ ] Put prospective volunteers and contacts gathered during event into the appropriate databases.
- [ ] Revise this timeline for next year with wisdom gained from your evaluation.
- [ ] Make sure that everyone has been thanked formally.

☐ Schedule and hold social event for volunteers; enjoy their company without the stress and the clock ticking toward deadlines.

Financial

☐ Submit report to foundations from which you received grants.

☐ Send out thank you notes to sponsors and supporters on letter-heads. Include your tax ID number and donation amounts.

For a model on event planning, do an internet search for "Strawberry Days Planning Guide". You should find a PDF file for the Strawberry Days Festival in Strawberry Point, Iowa. It includes their timeline. While specific to that event, it is a good model for someone else's festival. It is well-planned and is the kind of document you might generate to help your event from year to year.

8. Décor for Your Event

No matter the size or type of event you are planning, you want the ambience and the look to be pleasing to the public. You want the décor to add to the festivity.

Crank up your imagination. As you walk through craft, hardware, teacher supply, thrift, and fabric stores, look at what is available and ask yourself, "What could this material or item be used for?"

Before you design your décor, find out if your venue has restrictions. Masonic lodges or churches, for example, may have certain memorabilia or artifacts that must not be moved or covered up even though they clash with your décor or theme. Here are some questions to ask about your venue:

- Are there any restrictions or requirements on what we can or cannot do for décor?
- Can we use ceiling clips to hang items from acoustic tile ceiling grids?
- Are there any rules about attaching items to walls?
- Do you have ladders available and are we allowed to use them?
- Is there anything that cannot be moved or covered?
- Are decorations required to be made of fireproof material?

Event Theme Determines Your Décor Style

For the maximum effect, your décor should be coordinated with your program, your website and advertising, your signage, and definitely your theme. Share the décor ideas with the whole committee so the planning will be coordinated by all involved. Don't let your workers become invested in marvelous ideas only to have the ideas shot down because they clash with the theme.

You will want to choose appropriate materials for your theme. If you are planning a green, eco-friendly event, you will want to stay away from polyester film balloons and plastic one-time-use items. If you are planning a Mardi Gras event, purple, gold, and green balloons, plastic beads, and glitzy gaudy items fit well.

Think of ways that you can carry out your theme in large settings like stages and outdoor spaces. Find ways of using your theme indoors with your welcome or registration table and your dining area. Think of smaller-detailed décor for your tables where guests will dine and for the buffet and food service tables. Use posters of the musicians and related artifacts at a table where artists' CDs are sold.

Whatever décor you choose, it should complement the activity rather than conflict with it. Keep the décor in contest-entry displays in neutral colors and in the background. The focus should be on the entries.

Get the Maximum Impact for Your Dollar

Since you are probably on a limited budget, whatever you do should give the biggest bang for your buck. You can plan for what you eventually want the event to look like in the future, but it doesn't all have to be done the first year. You can build year after year, adding as your budget allows.

Think about where the public attention will be focused. If it is a stage for music or other entertainment, put a significant part of your resources there. After that, you can spread out and deal with the smaller activity areas.

If you plan ahead, you can collect materials during the year that will be useful with your theme. Take advantage of sales. If some on your committee enjoy visiting thrift shops, rummage sales, and garage sales, brainstorm with them about what could be useful to you. You may find real treasures for your theme for pennies on the dollar.

Keep your eyes open for displays at local businesses, theaters, or in the big box stores. If you see something that would be a super addition to your theme, ask the manager if it is possible to donate it to your event when they are through with it. For many businesses, when the promotion is over, they have no use for the items. A pizza chain may have cutout cardboard knights that may be perfect for your medieval banquet. A set of huge snowflakes hanging in a department store may be just what you need for your Winter Wonderland event next year. Don't forget to give credit where credit is due. Acknowledge the donations by announcement during the event, by program notes, or by a thank-you page on your website.

Your parent-group membership may be the source of materials as well. Artificial flowers, baskets, ribbons, and fabric are items that they may be ready to discard. Ask at a meeting. Put a request in the group's newsletter for certain items to help with décor, prizes, and costumes.

Getting Others to Create Décor for You

Take advantage of what is already in place. If you are in a park setting, use the features and plants that are already there as a backdrop for your activities.

Use an activity as décor. All the activity at a kite festival is the décor. Folks watching fantastic kites overhead in the breeze need no more décor other than a backdrop of the ocean or a grassy field with no kite-eating trees. You can add appropriate table decoration at your information booth and signage in kite shapes or on kite fabric, but this just augments the activity itself.

The art contest itself becomes décor. Children doing chalk art are doing décor. The high school art class using a better type of chalk makes a more impressive display with folks watching as the creations take shape. In a car show, the entries are the focus. In the children's activity area, the games and their components become the décor. If one of your vendors is supplying bounce houses or children's rides, choose those that correspond with your theme.

If your event in the fall has a scarecrow contest, the entries become part of your décor. Add some borrowed straw bales and bundles of corn stalks and you make a very good impact. In all these, contestants have provided the work and the investment. You have only added some props, drapes, and perhaps signs.

The costumed rats in a window display and also the people who entered the people-costume contest were all part of the décor in the Medieval Fantasy Festival. The costumed rats paraded with their "handlers" in a special parade before the Ratapult event. The winners of the people-costume contest also had a parade through the festival site.

For a downtown event or an event at a shopping center, get the businesses involved with window displays. That brings more décor and more promotion for your event, and somebody else is paying for it! If you want greater participation, have prizes for the best. If you can get the prizes donated, that is even better. Try to give the winners good publicity. List them in your media press releases. Note them in your program as sights the public must see. Take pictures of them for your website. Announce the best on your stages between entertainers. Thank the businesses for participating.

Ask your art and craft vendors to decorate their booths as appropriately to your theme as they can. Tell them about the ambience you are trying to create and the look and colors you prefer. Some vendors will do amazingly well. Prize winners who get good recognition will inspire greater creativity at the next event. A free booth space or a coupon for $100 off next year's booth is a prize they will love and one that you won't have to cough up any cash for. Your only cost is the missed revenue on their booth space next year.

Have a tableau contest. Invite contestants to come up with their favorite painting from the masters. Use live, costumed characters and props and backdrops from the paintings. Have them create and hold their poses for a certain length of time. Create an historical or literary scene. The major expense here will be the costumes and props, and they are provided by the contestants!   Tableaus provide excellent photo-ops for festival goers and also for professional photographers.

Make Functional Décor

Barricades

You can turn some barricades into décor. Make cloth covers for A-frame barricades with a pocket for the front feet and ties for the rear feet. You don't need to worry about the sides. On the side facing the event you can put your logo or appropriate, colorful graphics. On the other side you can put signs, "Street Closed", or other directions.

We made barricade covers for the Medieval Fantasy Festival. One of our committee sewed them from donated, inexpensive black cloth. Heraldic designs were cut out of felt and attached with a glue gun to the fabric. These barricade covers were large and colorful enough to make an impact and could be used again and again. They stored easily.

Signage

Coordinate your signage into the décor. You have to have the signs anyway. You may as well make them decorative. If you are required to have signs saying, "No pets within 20 feet of food booths", make those signs worth looking at. At a fiber arts fair (textiles, spinning, weaving) use sheep-shaped signs to highlight different areas. At a daffodil fair, coordinate the signage by using the same daffodil graphic on each sign.

Pop-Ups and Shade Structures

If you want some uniformity and a festive look on your shade structures, try decorative borders sewn simply in scallops, triangular teeth, or squares, like a fringe. Figure out how to attach it so it looks good and is easily removed without damaging the pop up.

TIP   Some outdoor period fairs have implemented a good idea that is functional as well as decorative. They set tall wooden poles in the ground and attached a "shade cloth" made from long lengths of burlap in muted colors sewn together. This was done at entertainment areas over audience seating and in other areas as well.

Other clever and functional bits of décor were found in meeting areas where fairgoers could relax and mingle with other folks. Straw bales were used for seating. One area featured a Celtic cross with potted flowers and flower garlands. Another area was a water well where the village washerwomen hung out and interacted with passers-by.

Roping Off Areas for Serving Alcohol

If your beverage area or beer garden needs to be sectioned off, is it possible to make the division part of the décor? Will garlands of fake flowers do the trick rather than a boring rope or chain? They may weigh more than the rope, so plan on having more supports along the way. A heavy cord or lightweight rope threaded through the garland may give it more strength and cause less trouble for you than the garland alone.

Display Panels

If your event has an art show included as one of the activities, you will need sufficient wall space or panels to display the art. Panels may be pegboard, framed wire grids, or of other material, connected with hinges and arranged into a Z or W shape. You get more space for your art if you can hang it on both sides of the panels.

Since you will want the art hung at or near eye level, the number of your entries may be limited by the space you have available.

You will want to construct the panels in such a way that they are attractive and as lightweight as possible. They should be sturdy enough to securely hold several heavily-framed art pieces. They should be braced or have a base that makes them impossible to tip over, resulting in damaged art and broken glass. Even though children are warned not to run, there are always some whose behavior is less than ideal. Sturdy and stable construction is the best way of preventing accidents. Panels should be constructed so that the base is not a tripping hazard. People will be looking at the art, not where their feet are going.

You might be able to borrow panels if you are lucky. Otherwise, look into costs of renting or constructing your own. Remember that you will need to store them as well. Which solution fits with your budget, your possible future use for the panels, and your volunteers with construction skills?

Using the Five Senses

Vision

This is the sense that we probably think of first with décor, but depending on the occasion, other senses can be brought into play as well.

Color and light deserve careful planning. Movement also catches the eye. Flags, banners, and ribbons move in the breeze. Fountains splash. Whirligigs and pinwheels go around. Mirrors and holographic material reflect and change.

Hearing

When the public enters your event space, what do they hear? Is it the bands you have hired? Is it the sound of water moving over rocks or waves breaking? If you have created a rainforest effect, is there a CD playing bird sounds? If you are in a large room and people are mingling and talking, is there a harpist playing music chosen to fit your theme?

Think about what you do want the guests to hear. Music can set an emotional tone. It can draw a crowd to a location, bring back memories, touch the soul, stir the body into dancing, calm tempers, incite action, put people to sleep, or just drive people away! While the music may not be the responsibility of the décor committee, it is part of the whole picture.

Taste

What? We don't want the public to be licking the decorations!

Yet for some events taste plays a major part—those featuring a food crop certainly do. Chocolate, wine, and strawberries can each be featured in events in their own right. Holiday events are tasteful (pun intended) as well. Think of décor for a banquet table at Easter with jelly beans, dyed Easter eggs, and chocolate bunnies. Think of Valentine's Day with red cinnamon hearts and candy hearts with sayings. Think of adding candy corn to the fall décor. (You may have to have these goodies in tiny paper cups rather than scattered on the table or have the candy wrapped. Know the rules.) If you have a pirate theme, you can use gold-wrapped chocolate coins.

If it is appropriate for your event, a chocolate fountain uses the sense of taste in a very elegant way. It is even better if someone sponsors the cost and monitors the area to maintain safety, cleanliness, and proper usage.

Smell

Anyone who has visited an event with kettle corn knows how tantalizing and festive that smell is! People who decorate for Christmas know that the wonderful smell of pine makes it just right. There is no reason that fresh greens, including pine, can't be used for other occasions as well.

Scented candles on the tables may work for your event. Know the rules about open flames.

Rosemary, peppermint, spearmint, or citrus can be added to the floral arrangements, or laid down the center of a banquet table with other herbs. Rosemary is not going to wilt and turn ugly, which makes it even more useful. Herby, spicy smells, cinnamon, peppermint or spearmint, and citrusy smells are generally well-tolerated. Don't go heavy with strong floral scents. While some people love gardenias and jasmine, others want to leave the area as soon as they get a whiff.

Be careful about strong scents near where singers will be performing. Any choir member can tell you horror stories about other singers with strong perfumes or the difficulty of trying to get a good breath for sustained notes near a bank of Easter lilies.

TIP   Before you use greenery on your tables or the food service area, wash it first. Inspect it for critters. You don't need six- or eight-legged beasties frightening, offending, or amusing the public at your expense.

Touch

This is maybe the hardest, but in some décor it might be important. Sculptures of polished wood or bronze invite touch.   Velvety, furry, or silky materials invite touch. Canvas pads on your prickly straw bales used for seating provide a more comfortable touch!

The Whole Picture

You work to have your event pleasing to the eye and inviting to the public through all of the senses in a positive way. Think about the memories that the senses might evoke.   Some memories associated with smell, hearing, and taste can be very powerful.

Don't forget to limit the negative side of the five senses. Walk through your site, through all of its parts. Go through all of the places the public will go, including the rest rooms. Imagine you are a guest at the event. What do you notice?

While you were busy thinking about décor, have you overlooked something unsightly? Will your senses find anything negative that threatens to overwhelm all of your positive work? Is there rubble, clutter, or some other eyesore in your downtown? Is there a vacant lot full of weeds, tall grasses, and trash? Do any of the venue rooms have a stale smoke smell or musty odor? Is there a sickly plant in a container in the entryway? Are any of your vendors assigned to spaces too near storm drains that may become noxious in the summer heat? Are those privet trees lining the street going to be in full bloom? Very pretty, but accompanied by an unpleasant smell.

Some of these situations you will have the ability to change; some, unfortunately, you will not. If you are forewarned, you may be able to rearrange tables, activities, or booths to minimize the negative. Some things you will be able to hide with a screen or draped fabric. Some things you will be able to clean up or move. Consult with the city which may have the authority to get that lot mowed. Some odors you will be able to mask. Some negatives you might have to live with as being beyond your control. Accept them, don't lose sleep over them, accentuate the positive, and move on. Make notes for your evaluation and plan next year's event with your new wisdom in mind.

Décor Materials and Ideas

Color

Choose your colors with deliberation. Color makes a statement and evokes moods. It can create energy, healing, excitement, power, tranquility, patriotism, anger, and celebration. Wearing school colors shows loyalty and community. If you have chosen certain colors for your theme, or if you have school or logo colors, use them consistently. Your color choices carried through in all of your design areas will give greater impact than colors chosen willy-nilly for each sign and activity.

Certain colors may mean one thing in our culture and another elsewhere. Also, in our lifetimes we have seen color associations come and go. Yellow ribbons mean bring home the troops; pink ribbons mean you support the fight against breast cancer. In this book we talk about 'greening' an event, meaning we are planning with regard to the health of our environment. For the next generations, these colors may not mean the same thing.

Fabric

Fabric is very versatile, comes in many price ranges, can be used again and again, and stores easily. You can drape it, swag it, hide supplies with it, cover tables and other surfaces, use it as a curtain, or as a backdrop. It works indoors and out.

If your event includes dining, tablecloths can make a huge statement for you. They can be anything from casual, red-and-white-checked picnic to pristine white with over-drapes, runners, and napkins in your chosen colors.

Use durable, washable, cloth table coverings and skirts if possible. They hold up better, look nicer, and can be reused. If they are not available to your event through your parent organization, consider investing in them—at least little by little. Avoid one-use plastic coverings which are tossed out and live for years in a landfill or floating in the ocean. If you do use plastic, save the good ones and use them again.

For ethnic or national celebrations, use fabric from the cultures: tartan at a Scottish festival, denim and bandanas for themes set in the Old West, and tie-dyed bright colors for a celebration of the sixties. For a patriotic celebration or a Fourth of July parade viewing stand, use red, white, and blue fabric draped as bunting.

TIP   If you have a panel discussion in front of an audience, cover the panel's table with a plain cloth and add a skirt that goes to the floor. Keep the focus on the panel, not metal table parts, purses and briefcases, and various skirt lengths and legs.

Murals or Collages

There are several ways of creating a mural. It can be done with chalk on the street. Rolls of white butcher paper can be used for wall murals. Murals can be painted, colored, or done with markers. You can create large "rubber" stamps out of sponges and stamp a mural. Get the art classes from your schools involved. You can keep control over the mural and have it done ahead of time, or it could be done as an activity during the event.

For a patriotic event or celebration of a part of history, photos blown up to poster size may be included in your décor. Print them in sepia tones to capitalize on the historical look.

Especially for a group or community celebration, collages of the event from previous years might be made. People enjoy discovering pictures of themselves, their friends, and family from years before. At a family celebration for a fiftieth wedding anniversary, a collection of photos from the past years is very effective.

Your collage doesn't necessarily have to be a static creation on a wall. It could be multimedia, either with a slide show and music or created as a computer PowerPoint display. It could be scheduled at certain times or done continuously on a loop.

Other Paper Creations

Besides the mural and collage use of paper, you can cut out paper "chains" created with accordion-pleated paper and scissors. These can be swagged from booths, on walls, or on table skirts.

Use cut out silhouettes—unlimited ideas, adaptable for all themes.

Tension Fabric Décor

The event industry uses tension fabric décor to create dramatic effects. Basically it is stretchy fabric stretched over a frame. Whatever the industry uses as a frame allows them to make large-scale three-dimensional shapes. They can be big enough to walk under, rise high enough to cover tent poles, or stretch over head in star-spangled free-form pieces. They can be very dramatic when combined with the right lighting. (To get an idea of the scope of tension fabric décor, do an internet search and click on images.)

Though spandex fabric is often used, other less expensive fabrics will work as well. Crushed panné velvet material is relatively inexpensive and seems to have the needed stretch. It does not ravel. The raw edges curl in on themselves, but that could be an advantage.

One construction idea uses nylon filament fish line tied on each corner of the fabric. The fish lines are then attached to trees, poles, or structural elements. Visit a fabric store to do a reality check and reconnoiter. Pull gently on different types of fabric to see how they stretch. If you have access to a kite store that sells components used in the creation of kites, visit it and ask questions. Maybe they will have fiberglass or carbon tubes and rods, and fittings and connectors you will find useful. Tell them what you are trying to do and ask for their suggestions.

Windsocks, wind spinners, and fabric whirligigs also fall under tension fabric décor and they are much simpler to come by. They are available in every holiday theme and every color as well.

Felt, Scissors, Fabric and Glue Guns

The possibilities with these materials are endless for any décor, for any budget, and for any skill level. Banners and soft sculpture can be created. Your signage may be made using felt with cut-out felt letters. Use paper to make patterns and to plan your creation before you cut into the felt. Save the felt scraps to use where smaller shapes are needed.

If you are using glue guns with younger children, choose the kind that works with a cooler temperature of glue. Tell workers of the dangers, ask them to think about what they are doing, and provide supervision.

Natural Artifacts and Dried Flowers

Bare tree branches can be used for hanging decorations or making a paper money tree. Think about the uses for these:
- Corn stalks, wheat sheaves, fall leaves
- Pine boughs, holly branches, mistletoe
- Tumbleweeds, teasels, cattails (Spray with polyurethane to keep cotton from getting all over the place.)
- Eucalyptus branches, artichoke flowers, palm fronds, bamboo
- Wreaths, sprays, bouquets
- Pussy willows, statice flowers, lavender, hydrangeas

How do you make fall leaves stay nice? For individual leaves or small branches, immerse them completely in a solution of one part glycerin to two parts water for two to six days. They should be pliable when they are done, not dry. For larger branches of leaves put them in a vase of the same solution. Slice the stems at an angle so they absorb the liquid better. Eventually the liquid will be drawn up into the plant, and beads of the solution will form on the leaves. Wipe them carefully and take the stems out of the solution. Do an internet search for more ideas on preserving branches of fall leaves with glycerin. Glycerin should be available from your pharmacist.

For a small eye-catching display on a registration table, rocks and shells may be used. In the fall, pumpkins, gourds, and Indian corn are attractive and readily available.

Every year in a Sacramento park, the groundskeepers prune and groom the palm trees. A nearby church has made arrangements with the park to use the palm fronds in their liturgical procession on Palm Sunday. It is a win-win situation.

Real Flowers

If you look at other special-event books or wedding planners, you know that you can easily rack up thousands of dollars in costs if you rely on floral designers. Here are some ideas that may help if you want to use real flowers:

- Use flowers from your members' gardens if available. Ask your committee to prune appropriate plants at the right time and use their cuttings. Use a garden trellis with flowers.
- Borrow the "flowering the cross" idea that many churches use at Easter. Put together an appropriate shape that fits with your theme using chicken wire and add flowers. For an event that doesn't last too long, real flowers can be used. If you want it over several days, use fake flowers.
- Floating candles and flowers on water. If your venue has a fountain, dress it up with floating flowers.
- If there is a garden club in your area, they might be willing to "strut their stuff" and do some flower arranging for you. It might be good publicity for their club and would help you out.
- Sometimes home improvement stores can lend live plants for your event.

TIP   For greening your event, take advantage of local plants for décor. Use potted plants that can double as raffle prizes. If your committee members are planning on adding to their landscape, have them time it right to use their purchases as your décor first. Don't fly in flowers and especially don't choose out-of-season flowers. You will save money and your carbon footprint will be less.

Flowers Created by You

Flowers can be made with tissue, paper, crepe paper, and ribbon. There are challenging techniques and even simple techniques for children. Cut-out, two-dimensional flowers can be scattered on a table top or hung from branches.

Facial tissue can be made into flowers. Many a parade float has been decorated with this type of flower attached to chicken wire.

Marvelous flower creations can be made from crepe paper. Crepe paper is inexpensive and versatile, but is not as readily available as it once was. It comes in many colors—both in folded flat sheets and pre-cut streamers. Check with your local craft stores and party stores. Look for it on line. Look in your library or on line for books giving directions for using crepe paper for making flowers, costumes, and so on. Most people, old and young, can create effective décor using this material.

Fake Flowers, Fruit, and Garlands

These items can be used again and again, adding color to different contexts. Craft stores often have good selections of silk and plastic flowers, fruit, and garlands. Often craft store chains will have deeply-discounted sale items and coupons in the local Sunday papers. As each season draws to a close, discounts get even bigger. This is a good time to plan far ahead and get what you need.

While you are collecting flowers that may be useful, think of collecting baskets and other containers as well.

Banners

Banners can be easily stored if they roll or fold. Displaying them may take hardware and poles. Figure out how and where to display them before you commit to them. Otherwise you will have wonderful banners folded in a box during the event! What size banner will you need to get the visual effect you want? They can be made with cloth material and felt. Some of the graphics may be attached with a glue gun; some may need to be appliquéd. What kind of weather, wind and rain, will they be subjected to? Do you want a uniform size and look with the banners, or a kaleidoscope of offerings?

Banners in procession—if the event is made up of different entities or groups have each make their own banner. It is probably a good idea to standardize the size somewhat. If you are having a school extravaganza to which clubs or visiting teams have been invited, ask them to bring a banner they have created to represent them. Even if you don't carry the banners in procession, they will look good on your stage or walls. Give the creators guidelines as to size.

Flags

For patriotic events and for ethnic or national heritage events, flags may be chosen as part of the décor. Probably your theme colors will be those in the flag. Treat the flags with respect.

Balloons

They can be combined to make a significant impact, especially in a large room. Balloons can be made into arches, pillars, or gigantic bouquets. They can be released in huge quantities outdoors. There are pros and cons about using balloons. There are also guidelines for safety. Pay attention to this information on balloons if yours is an eco-friendly event.

Balloons are made out of one of two materials. The first is latex—these are the stretchy balloons. Latex balloons are biodegradable, like leaves from a tree, as they are made from the sap of rubber trees. This is sustainable agriculture much like the maple syrup industry. In this way, you are saving the rain forest. In the third world, harvesting latex can be more profitable than wiping out the forest and raising cattle. The forests, besides producing latex, protect the ozone layer.

When latex balloons filled with helium get away from you and rise into the sky (either intentionally or not), most of them rise to about five miles. There in the freezing cold they shatter and send little pieces of biodegradable material back down to earth.

The other balloon material is polyester film:
- These balloons are made of sandwiching layers of polyester together.
- Some have a layer of aluminum added and become foil balloons.
- Polyester film balloons are not biodegradable and should never be released into the atmosphere.
- When you use polyester film balloons with helium, make sure that the strings are weighted, and do not tie them together. Foil balloons, especially in a cluster, can get tangled in power lines and cause power outages.

 Some claim that polyester film balloons are "dirty" both in production and in disposal. If you are going green, this choice is not what you want.

What is used for strings, ties, and weights is perhaps as important as what balloons are made of. In your effort to use fewer manufactured resources, avoid tying anything to a helium-filled balloon that is metallic or shiny—a pretty good indicator that it will not decompose. If you must have a string, use one that is biodegradable. Metallic strings on latex balloons could still wreak havoc with power lines. When professionals do mass balloon releases, they use self-tied, latex balloons with no strings.

Whatever kind of balloon you choose to use, make sure that they are disposed of properly after the event. If you see balloon fragments on the ground, pick them up and put them in the trash.

What about using helium?

This lighter-than-air gas is non-toxic, will not burn or explode, and will not harm the earth. It is a natural by-product of decaying rock within the earth. It is found with natural gas and is separated from it in production. It is common on earth but is a finite resource. It has many uses, including the manufacture of LCD screens.

Do not inhale helium. It is not poisonous, but it can displace oxygen that you need to sustain life. Too much helium can give you a headache, make you dizzy, and may cause you to pass out.

You may also have heard that birds, land animals, and marine animals ingest balloons and suffer health problems or die. They might get tangled in balloon ribbons as well. The research that I did indicated that these reports may not be validated. Even so, why not err on the side of caution. If you use balloons, use them responsibly.

> **TIP**   A safety note about using balloons with children—no child under eight should play with a balloon unsupervised. Just as plastic bags are a suffocating hazard, balloons and balloon fragments can be a choking hazard. When a balloon breaks, dispose of all the pieces in the trash immediately. Don't allow children to play with un-inflated balloons or balloon fragments. Entertainers who make balloon animals for children should be aware of this. Perhaps they can work a note of caution to the parents into their talk as they create these critters.

Lighting

Dramatic effect can be found with clever lighting. Some venues come with built-in spots, mirror balls and so on. Light covers with cutouts (gobos) can be made to project shapes appropriate to your theme. Light can be projected with revolving, constantly changing patterns. Ask your local theater or high school drama teacher for help.

Another way of getting decorative lighting is by using Christmas lights or other holiday lights. For your southwestern theme, use chili pepper lights. Use rope lights to get certain effects or outline an area. Hang star or icicle holiday lights. Use Chinese lanterns.

Luminarias

Luminarias are paper bags with decorative cut outs, letting the light from a candle or other source inside shine through to light a pathway. The whole luminaria glows. These are for outdoor use and should be used only when there is no danger of starting a fire. Weight the bag with a little sand. Set a small votive candle inside. Use these to light a path. Use appropriate safety measures and cautions when real flames are used. If you are using many luminarias, remember that it takes a while to light them all. An electronic match will come in handy.

Dry Ice

The creeping, flowing fog can be very atmospheric—spooky, mysterious, and haunting. Follow the rules for the safe handling and use of dry ice in special effects. It can be dangerous if you don't know what you are doing.

Pennants

Make pennants using V-shaped fabric, plastic, or paper pieces on a piece of twine or thin rope. You want the public to see them and think "Celebration!" and "Festive!" Use your theme colors. Pennants are effective unless the public in your area has strong associations with their use in another context. You don't want them to think they are entering a used car lot.

For an old-fashioned, frugal way of making pennants to cordon off a certain area, use twine with strips of fabric tied every twelve to eighteen inches. Fabric can be donated; work parties can tear it into strips. Store this "rope" by wrapping it around wood or stiff cardboard to avoid a tangled mess when it is used again.

Ribbons

Ribbons are another versatile yet inexpensive material to use. Wired ribbon is a wonderful resource that comes in wide widths for good impact. Besides making spectacular bows, it can be swagged or arranged in your greenery, on poles and other architectural components. Wired ribbon bows can be stored easily, for if they flatten, they are easily fixed.

Ribbon wheels These can be done by a work party for your event. Your local bicycle shop may be able to donate damaged bicycle wheels with their spokes popped out. Old hula hoops also work. When I made ribbon wheels, I used rolls of polypropylene three-quarter inch ribbon. (These rolls are readily available through the bag and packaging vendors that retailers use.) Cut the ribbon in 6-foot lengths. Using tape to attach a length of ribbon to the wheel, wrap each piece around two or three times and then glue it to itself. Leave the long end to flutter. Continue on until the entire rim is covered with long, hanging ribbons. Choose theme colors for some and rainbow colors for others. Using clothesline rope, hang the wheels from trees in the event area high enough to walk under. The ribbon wheels make a big splash of color and look really pretty in the breeze. Each can be stored in its own large garbage bag between festivals.

Tie ribbons around poles and trees, leaving enough to flutter nicely in the breeze. Tie donated silk flowers in with the ribbon.

TIP   Take care that whatever is used to secure the ribbon doesn't damage paint or mar the surface. I don't recommend winding ribbon around poles, making them into barber poles, or weaving ribbon in and out on park benches. It adds a lot more work and time to the clean-up process. If you have the same folks do the cleanup that did the decorating, they learn quickly what works best and what is a pain to undo.

Papier-Mâché

You can create large or small sculptures using this medium. Be creative; use discarded recyclables, torn up newspaper, wallpaper paste or another glue mixture, and tempera or acrylic paints. It takes time as each layer must dry before another is added. Hollow shapes can be constructed by forming your papier-mâché on a blown-up balloon. Consult one of the books in the Appendix, or Wikipedia, or do an internet search for interesting information on papier-mâché.

Other Sculpture

Garden statuary or large teddy bears or soft sculpture may work where you need a large focus. Someone in your group may surprise you with a talent for this. Ice sculpture is also a possibility, making a very unique centerpiece for your buffet table.

Collectibles

For smaller events with more of a sense of security like an afternoon tea, people may be willing to lend some collected items like teapots and china cups that fit in with the theme. At a western theme event, Breyer® horses may be used to advantage. Common sense prevails here also. Be careful with borrowed items, display them where they are secure, return them promptly when the event is over, and thank the lenders for their generosity.

Wood or Cardboard Cutouts

These can be added to year after year. One good idea to define an area for children to talk to Santa is to make wooden cutouts of large elves, gingerbread cookies, or snowmen and paint them appropriately. Construct stands for them as well. You might enlist the services of your local high school art class or shop class.

Another good idea is to have a large mural with life-sized figures that fit with the event theme. Mount these on foam core board or wood. Leave oval holes where the faces should be, and let folks have fun taking pictures of their family and friends looking through the figures.

9. Working with Volunteers

You can't have too many volunteers. Your committee will probably brainstorm and dream up more activities than time, budget, energy, and volunteers permit. Volunteering provides a way for those who don't have much money to give their time, talent and energy to a cause. This is one of the beautiful things about volunteering —it is a way of including more of the community.

One of the biggest challenges is matching volunteer with task. In anticipation of this, prepare a ready-made task list in some detail of jobs that need volunteers. Be prepared to set aside time to train your volunteers and guide them in the way you want them to go. You want them to succeed, not be thrown to the wolves.

Volunteers will work the hardest and reach the most success if they are working in areas that they enjoy or have a passion for. A good leader will recognize people's gifts and encourage them to work in that area. Good leaders have people skills and can be diplomatic, can inspire and encourage folks. Enthusiasm can be contagious.

Recruiting Volunteers

Go back to the sources for committee members mentioned in Chapter 3. Those who may not have wanted to commit to a long-term committee project may be willing to volunteer for specific tasks or work during the actual event.

Look again at:

- Your parent organization
- Your surrounding community
- Your friends, co-workers, and church members

Then cast your net wider and consider:

- **New people in the community.**
  A good way of getting acquainted and making friends in a new community is to become a volunteer. New folks come with experience, skills, new ideas, and enthusiasm. It is an excellent way of becoming part of the community—a win-win situation.

- **Use your event to find volunteers for following years.**
  This is one of the best sources for volunteers. There is an instant match of volunteer and interest. Set up some kind of system to get the names and contact information at your event. This could be at an information booth. You could also encourage each activity chair be part of the system and give them the volunteer-interest forms.

 You might also use the names you gather at your event for promoting your event the following year. Sending postcards might be cost prohibitive, but emails are a good way of reminding folks. At your information table ask them to fill out a form or put their names on a sign-up sheet if they are interested in hearing about future events. To lessen "email reluctance" you can stress that emails will not be sold, but will be used only for event purposes. Sign-ups might be increased by combining them with a raffle prize. Dropping a business card into a basket is a quick, painless way of entering (and often more legible) than filling out a form.

- **Business Sponsors**
  These might also be a good source of volunteers. A business can sponsor an activity by supplying the volunteers to staff it. Perhaps the beer garden, one of the contests, or the children's game area could be staffed by business employees. If they aren't able to do the whole activity, perhaps they could be worked into shifts. Of course, these folks need

training and guidance to keep the activity to your standards. Make it fun for them and provide oversight by your committee.

- **Folks currently "between jobs"**
  Volunteering is an excellent way to keep up one's skills and gain new ones. If people are new to the area, they might wish to become known and make contacts that they can use later as references in the job market.

- **Don't overlook teens and children as volunteers.**
  Working with younger folks can be a real serendipity. Serendipity is defined as the unexpected discovery of something good, pleasing, or useful. The younger generation may bring enthusiasm, fresh ideas, and energy to your event. You may find some volunteers in youth booster and service clubs (for example a Key Club, a Kiwanis high school organization) who are looking for ways to perform community service.

  Some may be brought into your event because their parents are volunteers. Encourage them to bring their friends as well. Work parties, making decorations, sewing, building sets and props, putting up decorations, working in the children's game area, handing out programs, clean-up, set-up, being runners (go-fors)—these are all good ways of involving young volunteers. Some will have the maturity to hold their own on your committee. Absolutely involve them, especially if the event is held as a benefit to their organizations! It is good training for young people to be involved in the planning and execution of events. The interaction of all ages involved in the event builds a stronger community.

Putting on an event is a

team sport.

You can't do it by yourself.

- **Use other events to promote yours and to expand your volunteer pool.** You might promote your event by setting up a booth at another event, perhaps in your same community, or in a wider region. You might have to pay a booth fee, perhaps the going nonprofit rate. You might negotiate a reciprocal agreement to let the other event do the same at yours. Use the opportunity not only to interest the public in your event, but to watch and listen for potential volunteers. Hand out fliers and include contact information and your website. Prepare a special flier for interested volunteers.

- **Your committee or group can support other events in your community.** Your help will be appreciated. You will make many new contacts and possibly gain some new volunteers. It won't hurt your event to be recognized as helping with other worthwhile events.

- **Send out a press release about the need for volunteers.**

  Use other media as well, not just public media. If it is appropriate, ask churches to put an announcement in their bulletins. Ask other organizations to put it in their newsletters. Put the volunteer information on your website.

- **Use social networking on the internet.**

  Especially among the younger, computer-savvy age, Facebook, etc., may provide a way of spreading the word about the need for volunteers.

- **Do an internet search.**

  Use the words "Volunteer Network" and name your city in the search. You may find an appropriate site to list your volunteer positions.

Screening Volunteers

It makes sense to get to know volunteers. You want to know what their interests are, whom they might enjoy working with, and how they carry out their tasks. In that sense, you will screen all your volunteers. For some prospective workers, it is helpful to invite them to a committee meeting and introduce them as volunteers. At the end of the meeting, ask them where they would like to focus their time. By that point, they will have a good idea of the scope of the event and be excited about working on some aspect of the tasks ahead.

But there is a more serious reason for screening. If you are accepting volunteers who are complete unknowns, be careful. Be especially cautions about folks who want to work with children or other vulnerable populations. If you are doing a school event, there is probably protocol with background checks to follow. Some cities and city events also require background checks for volunteers.

If you don't have any procedure to follow, think of setting up some guidelines. Many organizations have developed a volunteer application form to help them in their screening procedures. If you do an internet search using "volunteer application form" you will find a wide variety of samples from which to draft one specifically tailored for your needs. If it is appropriate for your event, you can include your volunteer application form on your website.

Your form might have several parts. The first part is contact information—what you need to know to get in touch with them. You could also ask for information about their employment, and someone to notify in case of emergency.

The next part is finding out about the time they have available to volunteer and what their interests, hobbies, and skills are. Find out about their education, special training, and any special certifications. In what computer programs are they proficient? Ask if they speak another language. Would they consider their proficiency basic or fluent? Have them tell about their previous volunteer experience. What other organizations are they involved in? What skills would they like to learn?

Include a list of what committees or activities your event has and have them indicate interest. This application process may even turn up surprising information for folks you thought you knew well. If you ask volunteers how they heard about your event or group, the information could be helpful in finding other new volunteers.

You can ask for references—those who have worked them on other volunteer jobs or who know them personally. Go ahead and check the references. You can ask simple questions, "How do you know this person? Have you worked with them on volunteer projects? What were their responsibilities?" You can also have the application ask if they have ever been convicted of a felony and for details about that conviction.

The application may have a section that satisfies a city's legal concerns by including a hold-harmless agreement for the volunteer to sign. There is a sample of this in the Green Festival Documents in the Appendix. Finally, a place can be provided for their signature and the date. If the prospective volunteer is underage, provide a space for their parent or guardian to sign, giving their permission.

Even if you don't have your volunteers complete a form, you can have folks sign up to volunteer, get their name, contact information, and their driver's license number. Depending on custom in your area, you may have to ask the police department to run the driver's license numbers of your volunteers. Whatever you do, be consistent, be fair, and make all volunteers jump through the same hoops. Be up front about your reasons—we want to keep our children safe, and we want to make sure our event is as successful as we can make it.

You may wish to do an internet search of the Megan's Law site. Other sites may also prove helpful in your screening. If you have a bad feeling, or if you see red flags about a person's interest in being a volunteer, *pay attention*. Certainly you will diligently check up on the information you have. You can decline their help in a diplomatic way: "I don't have any tasks left that match your skills" or "The area in which you want to work is under control presently."

You can do a lot to ward off potential problems by where you choose to assign volunteers to work. If you don't know them well, put them into groups in less critical areas where they will become known. Have them come to work parties, committee meetings, to task groups where the job is folding fliers or other necessary busy work. See how they interact with people, with different ages and groups of people, how their work is done, and see if they follow through on tasks. Get to know them. You wouldn't assign the poster design to someone whose graphic ability or habit in meeting deadlines is unknown. You wouldn't assign someone to contact potential sponsors unless you trusted them to be diplomatic. Let new volunteers work up to the jobs that are critical, sensitive, or that take initiative.

Retaining Volunteers

People will stay and work when they feel appreciated and when they can use their gifts in a way that brings satisfaction personally and to the group. Telling them thank you, going out of your way to thank them, saying what a great job they did in the presence of others to hear—all go a long way to keeping volunteers.

I can't stress the importance of appreciation enough. Don't kid yourself, even if you know that you are doing an important service, giving the community the gift of an event, and raising funds for a cause you hold dear, you and all your workers still need to feel appreciated. Thanks and appreciation might make the difference between a volunteer putting in even more effort or pulling back, letting someone else do the work, complaining about "casting their pearls before swine" and being a divisive person on the committee. Thanks and appreciation for work done may pay off in keeping the leadership for another year.

If your community has an annual event to thank volunteers, request that your event and workers be included in that event. Such volunteer recognition events may be hosted by seniors, the city government, the chamber, or your local media. If there is no vehicle for thanking your community volunteers, you have a ready-made need for an event to do so!

Ideas for keeping volunteers happy and working hard for your event:
- Keep folks in the loop so that they aren't caught in an uncomfortable place handing out misinformation. No one wants egg on their face.
- Post agendas, email about coming meetings, use meeting time wisely.
- Take the time to come to consensus in a meeting. Listening to individuals, clarifying issues, and working out differences—these are all ways of keeping the respect of your group.
- Treat everyone as you wish to be treated. Avoid at all costs the clique formation and any power trips that keep people out of the 'chosen few'.
- Listen to the volunteers. If they call with a question, they should get answers quickly and feel their concern has been heard. If you don't have answers, tell them you will get back to them, and then follow through.

- Step back periodically and observe how the different age groups are working together, how newcomers are integrated into the group, and how minorities of any flavor are treated.
- Allow time and situations where volunteers can become better acquainted with each other. Providing a social setting for interaction is not wasted time. It is an important part of working together and developing community. Be generous with praise and appreciation.

Committee chairs must constantly keep the tension of tasks at hand balanced with the tension of looming deadlines and the interaction of their workers. Chair people must deal with the "we've-always-done-it-this-way" mindset. They must keep a balance between tradition and new, fresh, and untried ideas. Good leaders listen to the folks in their group. They seriously consider other ideas and ways of doing things. They value others' input. They might even change their opinion on a subject after hearing more. They listen, they are flexible, and they aren't afraid to make decisions after they have looked at the possibilities. The leaders can't put on the event by themselves. *This is a team sport.* Working together breeds success. Working together builds community.

Creating Community Events

Community happens at many different levels. When I began the Medieval Fantasy Festival, I envisioned people from the businesses, the libraries, the schools, the arts groups, civic organizations, the city, and churches all coming together to work on a common project. This kind of cooperation gives more than one result. An obvious result is that the base of participants and volunteers is enlarged. More people will know about the event and have some investment in it. Attendance increases, as it is promoted through more organizations. On top of those positive effects, a deeper sense of community begins to blossom. One's circle of acquaintances and friends begins to grow.

Even without that goal of many different groups within a city working together, there is a real potential for growing community through your event:

- One level of community is among the core group which will probably include citizens from different groups. Close friendships may grow as people work together.
- Even if friendships are not the natural result of working together, your associations in the community expand. Respect for others and their contributions are important outcomes.
- Another level is interaction between groups we don't normally associate with. We tend to socialize with people just like ourselves, those with the same outlook, the same ages, and the same educational background. An

event may find teenagers working with senior citizens, both gaining a new respect for each other.

- Another level is found among those who attend more than one similar event in the region. Shared experiences and interests develop among craft vendors, among attendees, and among leadership within the events. One worker put it this way, "You have given us another sand box to play in."

What is community?

I am not a sociologist, but I have discovered the importance of community and I have learned that events "grow" community. It is a by-product of persons and groups working together on a project to reach a commonly-held goal.

In your event there will be people who support each other and people who care about each other. There will be people that you know by name and people who listen to you and to whom you listen. They share common goals and ideas, which may include making the city they live in safe, having good educational opportunities for their children, and nudging the citizens of the earth to live a green and sustainable lifestyle. They will work together to meet those goals.

10. Working with Your Community

The Building Blocks of Your Community

Prepare a list of all possible associations and institutions that are the building blocks of your community. The purpose of this list is to think of how they might participate. How can both you and the community group you are considering mutually benefit from the interaction?

How might these groups be helpful to your event? They may be able to:
- Provide volunteers
- Be a way of publicizing the event through individuals, newsletters, or meetings
- Be a source of entertainment possibilities
- Participate in your event by providing a booth
- Provide a source of vendors
- Provide an activity
- Allow you to use their facility, resources, or equipment for your event
- Provide in-kind support or sponsorship
- Facilitate community-building goals for your event

- Help you draw a bigger crowd
- Provide positive recognition and authenticity by association with event

Adding community groups may bring all this and more that is good for your event. It might also add more challenges as you deal with more leaders, another bureaucracy, personalities that may clash, different ways of perceiving goals, and possibly more rules and protocol.

To encourage high quality, *major* participation of a particular group, plan to donate a portion of the proceeds to the group after the event. If you plan on having the Boy Scouts take responsibility for security, recycling, or another significant task, make it worth their time. Draw up a contract with them, or at least a plan in writing, laying out the responsibilities on both sides.

Here is a list of groups to get you started. It is just the beginning of possibilities. Consider your community and your event, and put down all that might be remotely related. Add more as they occur to you. Put down their contact information and the leaders who can help put you in touch with that constituency?

Groups that make up your community
- Ethnic segments
- Large employers
- Military bases
- Retirement communities

Sport-related groups
- Walking clubs, bicycle clubs, softball leagues, bowling clubs
- Horse-riding clubs, dog-training clubs
- Sports-instruction businesses

Cause or special interest groups
- Green groups, land trusts
- Cause-related nonprofit groups
- Political parties
- Health, nutrition, exercise-related
- Singles, parenting groups
- Branches of national groups, e.g., National Audubon Club

Educational institutions
- K-12 public, private, and parochial schools
- Pre-schools and child care businesses
- Community colleges and universities
- PTAs, PTOs, booster clubs
- Businesses in tutoring, instruction

Groups with a religious affiliation
- Churches, synagogues, mosques
- Men's, women's, youth groups within the above
- YMCA, YWCA

Youth related groups
- Boy Scouts, Girl Scouts (all levels)
- 4-H, FFA, FHA

Hobby groups
- Quilters, model-train enthusiasts, stamp collectors, knitters
- Chess club, garden club
- Motorcycle, car clubs

Promotion of the Arts
- Performing Arts—drama, music, dance
- Fine Arts—painting, sculpture, photography, etc.
- Writing, literature, poetry
- Crafts clubs
- Businesses involved in instruction and support of the arts

Organized civic, social, and fraternal organizations
- Rotary, Kiwanis, Lions Club
- Moose, Elks, other lodges. Masonic groups
- Employment-related groups, veterans' groups
- AAUW, Soroptimists

Institutions
- Libraries, museums, historical societies
- Hospitals, HMOs

Government institutions
- City, county, state
- Community classes and events
- Senior or youth centers and their programs
- Departments within a city, e.g. Parks and Recreation

Business promotion groups
- Downtown associations
- Chambers of commerce
- Tourism bureaus

Ideas for Working with Local Businesses

If your event is hosted by a downtown association or a chamber of commerce, you might already be fortunate enough to have in place a block-captain system of reaching businesses with information. (In this system, the geographical area needing the information is divided up into blocks, with one person in charge of contacting businesses in each block. Neighborhood Watch programs and telephone trees are similar examples.) If not, you or your volunteers will have to resort to pounding the pavement to get your information out. Take heart! It is good exercise. You also get valuable feedback from those you talk with.

Keeping the businesses informed is very important. You don't want visitors wandering into a business during the event and hearing, "Oh, is there an event today?" or hearing a hassled manager trying to cope with an unexpected crowd while muttering that if he had known, he would have brought more people into work.

Listen to the words of praise and complaint from the business community. Write down their problems concerning the event, and see if you can find solutions or ways of minimizing the drawbacks. You will not be able to solve everyone's problems, but you can make them believe that you care about working with them. Work with the business owners to come up with solutions. Here are potential concerns that might arise.

Parking

For a street fair, you might find that one big hassle is parking. People want to park right in front of their destination, even if it is the gym where they are going to get exercise. Business owners might complain bitterly about event parking taking up customers' parking spaces even when those same owners and their employees park in front of their businesses all day, moving and rotating their cars where there are time limits on parking.

You don't have much control over where the public chooses to park, but you do have leverage when it comes to volunteers and vendor-parking areas. Save the close parking for customers and the public.

Closed-off Streets and Lack of Access

Blocking off street access to a business is another concern. Some businesses have access from a rear parking lot that could be used. Suggest that businesses plan ahead with their customers and find their own ways of solving problems. Suggest that a beauty salon tell its customers about any event planned on the day of their appointment. Offer special deals and coupons to be used for another day's visit to the area. Point out the positive aspects of the event. You are bringing much more foot traffic to the area. Craft ways of turning those people into potential customers.

Competition from Vendors

- Make a point of choosing vendors that do not duplicate what your local merchants carry. Bring in vendors with unusual and handmade items. If all of what a visiting vendor has is too close to your merchant's inventory, let your jury process keep them out.

- Be careful where you place particular vendors; keep them away from businesses that will object. Don't put a puppet vendor in front of a toy store that carries similar puppets.

- If restaurants are concerned about competition from food vendors, they might consider advertising box lunches to go at a set price. The convenience of this would appeal to craft vendors, staff, and volunteers. They might appreciate the alternative to the food vendor choices. Workers at an event are usually under time constraints and cannot be away from their posts very long. An enterprising, nearby restaurant might even send an employee around to the vendors early with the choices, the prices, and a phone number to call. Delivery would be appreciated as well.

- Another way of addressing restaurant concerns is to suggest they offer specials are related to the theme of your event. You can promote their participation in your publicity, and in turn they help advertise the event.

Lack of Visibility and Loss of Foot Traffic

- Another concern is vendor booths blocking visibility of businesses. Look for solutions. Maybe an aisle can be left in the row of vendors for easy access to the business. In front of permanent business, put open, see-through booths with no backs to avoid blocking visibility.

- Often people who come to a street fair focus solely on the booths. They don't even see the stores in the area. Some store owners appreciate an organized attempt, planned by the event, of getting visitors into their businesses. Make it fun.

- Anything you can do to increase their foot traffic will most likely be appreciated. A good way of advertising and getting visitors into stores and businesses is to create an event passport. (See Chapter 17 for a description.)

- Offer free or greatly-reduced rates for businesses to have booths in the vendor line in front of their stores. They can promote their business in many ways. Suggest ways of tying in with the theme of the event—you still want appropriate décor and merchandise. Businesses that are hard to tie in with a theme (such as a bank or insurance company) might sponsor a children's activity booth in front of their business. Find ways of getting the name and visibility out there. This idea could also be utilized by businesses not in the immediate area who want to be noticed.

- During the event another way of getting visitors into businesses is to distribute a little quarter page with several spots on it to rubber stamp. There should be space for the name and contact information of the visitor. When the visitor goes into a business, the clerk stamps a spot. When they have gotten all the stamp spots filled, they turn it in to a central location. At the end of the event, names are drawn for raffle prizes. This is a win-win-win situation. The visitors are introduced to area businesses, they get a chance at a nice prize, and the event producers get names and contact information for future events.

- Find creative ways of using your event program to offset the concerns. How can you structure the information to make the event attendee into a potential business customer?

Make participants, not outsiders

- Make a window decoration contest one of the activities of the event. Window decoration contests are another way of getting the public to notice businesses. If your program has a map, note the participating businesses. Star the winners. Encourage visitors to enjoy the creative efforts of the business.

- Include a costume contest for employees. Make them a part of it, not grumbling outsiders. The public will see that they are part of the celebration and may interact with them more easily and positively.

- Have a fun contest (or a contest division) only for businesses and their employees. Talk it up. Make sure that the media is aware of it. Include it in your program and press releases. The prize could be something business related, like a promotion on the event or chamber website, special newspaper coverage, or something else that appeals to business owners.

- Set up a roulette wheel in a central location. Involve merchants in the process. Set up guidelines, such as a free spin for every receipt dated during the event over $2. Receipts totaling $100 might get a premium – a shirt, tote, or whatever. Sponsors could be solicited for prizes. For some spots on the wheel, a promotional, name-dropped item from one of the participating merchants might be given—a pen, keychain, or letter opener. Worthwhile event-special coupons might also be given away as prizes for one spot. A person whose spin landed on this spot

- might be able to choose a coupon from two or three businesses. If they can make a choice, the coupon has more value to them.

Working with Agencies

You may have to deal with city, county, state, or perhaps even federal agencies as you conduct the business of your event.

You may be working with those who have the power either to shut you down or to promote your event. It might mean dealing with the police department, the county health department, or the city. It may mean dealing with someone from ADA to make sure that your event is wheelchair accessible. It may mean dealing with a state regulating agency like those responsible for alcohol beverage control.

Find out as much as you can about the hoops you must jump through to comply with the rules and regulations. Take them seriously and get your paperwork done neatly and in a timely manner. You want to be seen as being cooperative. You don't want any red flags posted on your event.

From the beginning, you should plan to treat those in agencies as allies, folks who are there to help you create and sustain a successful event. Avoid forming an us-versus-them climate. Cultivate a network of people in these agencies and get to know them by name. Attend civic events where they may be. Cultivate a reputation as one who "plays well with others." Lay your groundwork carefully.

Sometimes you may run into an individual whose zealous adherence to the rules creates roadblocks. Your network may help solve the problem—especially for an event with longstanding community tradition.

If you do run into a road block from an agency, here are some helpful thoughts:
- Face-to-face meetings may work better if there are bumps in the road to smooth out. Emails are good, but cannot communicate on the same level.
- Very rarely use the opportunity to "go over someone's head," and only then after great thought.
- Be very prudent. Choose your words well.
- Approach the person in authority diplomatically. Seek their guidance on handling the situation. Remain in the cooperative mode.
- If it is appropriate, you may even thank the person who presented the difficulty for doing their job well and trying to keep the event safe and within the rules.
-

Keeping the Public Happy

You are on your way to success if you have chosen a location that makes your event easy to find, if your signage is good, parking is plentiful, and you can deliver on your promises. If you have been conscientious about letting your public know what is going to happen, where it will happen, and when it will happen, you have taken major steps to have a happy public.

Make sure that the expectations created by your promotional materials are realistic. Include a clear schedule as to what happens when. Because plans go awry in ways you can't predict, add the caveat, "Subject to Change".

Deliver what is promised. If you have a tomato festival, work to have as satisfying an area as possible for tasting, educating, purchasing, and exhibiting. Be realistic about the number of vendors expected in your advertising.

If an event is advertised as free, the public should not be charged for the major focus. If you advertise free, make it very obvious about any special portion that has a fee. Don't bait and switch.

In your volunteer training, inspire volunteers to create a pleasant atmosphere for the public. Be sensitive to what their day may have been like already. John Q. Public may have been in a traffic jam on the freeway, had trouble finding the event, had trouble finding a parking place, and now has waited through long lines at the entrance, at the toilet, and at a food vendor. He is already hungry and testy. He does not need to be corrected in his pronunciation of the food item he has chosen before being told they are out of that item. He will not remember the event fondly, he will not be back, and he will tell 20 people how bad it was!

As best you can, try to minimize the negatives that the customer might experience. Work diligently on your signage and logistics. Otherwise the public may remember only the frustrations, not the marvelous entertainment, the beautiful sets, the variety and quality of vendors, and the whole experience of the event you have worked so hard to produce.

11. Sponsors and Support

A Tough but Necessary Job

Many folks do not like to ask for money. It is outside their comfort zone. This task takes a special kind of person. Because they will hear the word "no" so many times, they should also be a resilient person. Some say they would rather face oral surgery without anesthesia than go after sponsors.

The reality is that there would not be events without sponsors—businesses and individuals who give of their cash, goods, time, and talent. It costs a lot of money to put on an event. Just think. The average wedding in the United States costs about $25,000. That's only a party for two extended families, and you want to throw a party for a community? The insurance, the porta potties, the chairs and tables, licenses and fees, not to mention the publicity, all cost an arm and a leg. Then you add entertainment, décor, and venue rental to the list. That money has to come from somewhere.

For a large event with major expenses, laying the groundwork well in advance is important. Bring corporate and community sponsors in at the initial planning stages of your event. This foundation will help the rest of the planning go more smoothly and give your event more authenticity.

Events need both cash sponsors and in-kind sponsors (those who donate a service or product). If you can get some of your amenities and publicity for free, that stretches your dollars so you can afford better quality entertainment, more activities, and more profit for your cause. If you can get raffle prizes donated, that is less of your budget you have to spend. ***Your job here is to cover as many of your event tasks as you can with other people's money and make them pleased to give it.***

It helps when you realize that it is a two-way street. Correlate the need for cash, goods, and service for your event with the needs of a business:

- Businesses need to get their name known by the public, to be visible to the public.
- They have new products to introduce to the public.
- They need to grow a larger market share.
- They want to be seen in a positive way by the community.

Your need and their need can match, and both can benefit. By putting sponsor-seeking in this light and giving concrete ideas to aid your search, the task will be less intimidating.

Seek Out Possibilities; Borrow from Other Events

Begin with the basic ideas that you have in your head about what you need from sponsors. Jot down businesses and individuals that you think might be a good match and be willing to give to your cause. Think about how you can reach these folks and also how they might benefit from supporting your event.

Then pay attention to other events and donation requests you receive in your business, in the mail, or see in the media. Which ones impressed you? Did you feel positive or negative about the request? Why? Were they impersonal or pushy? Was the cause important to you? Were they unrealistic in their expectations?

Look at event programs and event newspaper ads. Who are the sponsors? How are they recognized? Look at the size of the print and the logos included. How are the sponsors related to the event, and what do you imagine they plan to gain from their sponsorship?

Do an internet search. Check out event websites and look at their sponsor pages. How do they attract potential sponsors? Who are the sponsors they do list? What types of businesses become sponsors? If you look at an event in your area and learn who sponsored it, you may find that these businesses might be willing to work with your event as well.

If you look at events similar to yours in different areas and find out that many of them list restaurants as sponsors, that may be a hint for you to contact restaurants for your event.

How does the event website ask for sponsors? Do they have a "come-on" letter? What do they give in return or in recognition of the sponsor? Does the event break down the support given into different levels? Then ask yourself, what ideas can you take from all that you have seen? How could these ideas be adapted for your particular event? What would work best for you? What do you want to avoid? Did the process give you any new insight into a new, creative idea for a sponsor?

Talk to other event organizers. See if they will share some of their experiences on how and whom to contact. A word of caution, some event producers in your same area may not want to give away any secrets about their best contributors or share their insights. If you are talking to another event chair from your same parent group, they may offer help and ideas, but want you to stay away from *their* sponsors. They do not want to put their sponsor income in jeopardy. If you are talking to event organizers in a different region, they may not feel threatened at all, but they may be willing to share their experiences.

Your state or your parent group may be a part of a larger association which might have a convention with classes or sessions on certain topics, like putting on successful events. If you are from a tourism group that meets with others in similar roles from a wider region, there may be a round table discussion group that allows you to share ideas and learn from each other.

After all of this study and preparation, go back to your original notes and draft your plan, including what you have learned.

Promotional Folder

Put together a promotional folder to for potential sponsors. Be sure to include:
- Newspaper clippings and positive letters to the editor about your event.
- Copies of your newspaper advertising showing sponsors.
- Postcards, programs, fliers,
- Photos of fun, educational, or heartwarming activities.
- The stated goals of your event.
- If you are raising money for your nonprofit, add what will tout the good work that they do in the community. Show how great the need still is.
- A sponsor packet with letter, menu, and application.

Show pride in your event and what you have accomplished. With this folder, the potential donor has more information about your event, and you have opportunity to talk it up.

Support Letter

Draft a support letter and donor record sheet. These letters can be used for smaller donations where the official sponsor packet is not necessary. The support letter will be used for items such as raffle prizes, children's game components, items that are used in making décor, or snacks for your volunteers.

Sample Green Festival Support Letter

Third Annual Green Festival in Downtown Opswatch
April 18, 2015

Dear Friends,

We are inviting your business to support the Third Annual Green Festival in Downtown Opswatch, IZ. It will be held April 18, 2015. This festival is hosted by the Downtown Opswatch Business Association, a not-for-profit 501 (c) (6) corporation. (Our ID# is 12-345-678.) We expect to draw 4000 people to this festival, building on the popularity and success of the previous years. There is no admission fee.

The purpose of this letter is to ask for your support. Here are some ways you can help:
1. Donate items and gift certificates to be used as prizes for games and contest winners.
2. Donate refreshments and bottled water for our volunteers.
3. Provide small promotional items to be used as prizes for children. Items like pens, rulers, key chains, and toys with your company imprint are fine.
4. Please ask for a sponsor packet If you wish to be a sponsor of the Festival.
5. Volunteer help from your business, your employees, family, friends, or charity groups of which you might be a member.

This Festival will have music, green vendors, arts and crafts vendors, and food. There will be activities for the children, speakers and workshops for adults on environmental themes, and a plant identification contest.

The Green Festival is designed to be family-oriented. All kinds of businesses in the downtown—the Carnegie Library, Old First Church—and volunteers are working together to make this possible. For more information you may call the Downtown Opswatch office at (111) 333-5555. Thank you for your support of our Festival. Your help is greatly appreciated.

Sincerely,
George Green
Green Festival Chairperson

The support letter should be appreciative and it should list the tax ID number of your organization for the donor's tax purposes. The letter and your record should have the item listed and its dollar value. Your donor record sheet should have a place to record the name of the business, the person with whom you talked, what they are donating, and any arrangements to pick it up. The record sheet should get all of the information you need to send thank-you letters.

When you are pounding the pavement seeking sponsors, take this letter and record sheet as well as the sponsor packet with you. Use the letter rather than the more formal sponsor packet, if it is appropriate.

Sponsor Packets

Put together your Sponsor Packet. This has three sections: the letter, the menu with different levels of benefits, and the application form.

Sponsor Packet Letters

Your brief letter should accomplish these things:

- Include an invitation to support the event.
- Tell them when the event is, what the event is about, and what the group will do with the funds raised. If you want to elaborate more on the goals and the event, you may include a page just for that purpose.
- Talk about the benefits that donors will receive.
- Give the information on how to sponsor and give the contact information. List your website so they can visit.
- Include appreciation of their time and generosity.

Menu or Different Levels of Benefits

Sponsors wish something in return for their gift to your event. They are looking for prestige, for exposure, for recognition, as well as for new customers. They are looking for ways to stand out from their competition. They look for opportunities to introduce new products and for customer goodwill in return for their support of worthwhile causes.

Since we usually think of businesses when we look for sponsors, be sure not to overlook *individuals* in your community who might be glad to sponsor your event. Some will do it just because they believe strongly in the cause. Some will do it for the personal prestige they get for their support. To be seen as a patron of the arts gives them an entry into the world of the arts. Individuals, as well as businesses, should receive benefit from your sponsorship menus as well.

Lots of organizations use the platinum-gold-silver-bronze categories. I have seen some list friends of the event, champions, pro team, community partners, and benefactors. I think it is good to find names that add to your theme. For a green event, choose names like energy wizard, polar pal, and green thumb.

Make a list of all of the possible benefits they might receive from you. When you set up your menu with different levels of sponsorship, plug in what you can afford and what they may find attractive. Here are some ideas.

Levels of Benefits for Sponsor Menus		
Low Level	**Medium Level**	**High Level**
Name in program as friend of festival	Name in program as sponsor	Name and logo in program as sponsor
Name on website as friend of festival	Name on website as sponsor	Name and logo on website as sponsor with link to sponsor's own website
General admission tickets - vary the number of tickets		
	Acknowledgement at event with audio announcement	Stage time to make awards
Name in print advertising	Name and logo in print advertising	Name and logo in print advertising and on banners
		Exclusive vinyl banner on display during event
Event T-shirts, commemorative wine glasses, mugs, complimentary beverages Vary the number.		
Preferred or valet parking, on-site parking. Vary the number of passes.		

Other ideas for benefits for sponsors

- Tent cards on tables with friends of festival and sponsors. Pre-event promotional tent cards may be placed on tables in supporting restaurants.
- Free exhibit or vendor space. New products can be introduced or sampled, new programs highlighted, and coupons distributed. Some exhibitors will use this as an opportunity to develop mailing lists, for example, in their enter-to-win spins and raffles.
- For events with catered dinners and entertainment, offer tables in a preferred area.
- Name on stage, major venue, or activity. There is a reason why we have the Eukanuba® Dog Show, or why the ice skaters at a competition perform in front of boards covered with State Farm® logos, and why race cars are covered with logos.
- If your event has a race, the name and logo may be displayed at the finish line. If the event has contests, the name and logo may be displayed where the winners are announced and photographed.
- Access to VIP area with hospitality, goodie bags, snacks, beverages, comfortable seating, and shade.

- Ad space in program. Size of ad increases with donation size. Prime spots are covers, centerfold, or anything in color in an otherwise black-and-white program.
- Invitation to thank-you party for volunteers, sponsors, and supporters after the event.
- Special performances for sponsors, coffee hour, meet-and-greet, or dinner with the speakers or entertainers. Autographed copy of author's book or musician's CD.

TIP   Check with current tax law dealing with sponsors and donors as you set up your menu for your sponsor goodies. There are rules about donors, money and in-kind service they give, and what the donor can and cannot do.
They may be able to write off a gift as a charitable contribution or as promotion or advertising. Donors may have to declare the value of goods received like T-shirts and tickets. Sometimes donors may not be able to accept anything in return except acknowledgement and thanks. Federal and state tax laws change. *It is beyond the scope of this book to give tax advice. Be aware and do your research.*

Draft your Application Form

The form gives you a record of the sponsorship and its level. It gives you the contact information and the information that you need to meet your obligations and say thank you with as little hassle as possible.

A sample Sponsor Packet from the Green Festival follows.

Green Festival in Downtown Opswatch
An Earth Day Fair with a Future Flair, April 18, 2015

Dear Friends,

We are inviting you to support the Third Annual Green Festival in Downtown Opswatch which will be held on April 18, 2015. This Festival is hosted by the Downtown Opswatch Business Association, a not-for-profit 501 (c) (6) Corporation. (Our ID # is 12-345-678.) We expect to draw 4000 folks to this home-grown Festival, building on the popularity and success of the first two years.

The Green Festival is a family-oriented Earth Day Fair. We will have music and entertainment, activities for the kids, contests, food, and fun. Adults will find food for thought from our very interesting workshops and speakers. We will have vendors with art and craft items and vendors of eco-friendly merchandise. We hope to inspire our residents to live more healthy, eco-friendly lives, promote stewardship of our natural resources, and promote a greater appreciation and understanding of the natural world around us.

The reality is that there would not be events without sponsors—businesses and individuals who give of their cash, time, and talent. At our Green Festival the entertainment and activities are free. The porta potties, the insurance, the chairs and tables, licenses and fees, not to mention the publicity—all this costs us an arm and a leg. That money has to come from somewhere. Your donation makes it possible. Your generosity helps us create an opportunity to build community, enjoy a fun fair, and become better stewards of our earth and her resources. We welcome your contribution.

We have included a list of our levels of sponsorship – Green Thumb, Polar Pal, Earth Champion, and the Energy Wizard. We appreciate your generosity. We need help on all levels so that we might have more entertainment, amenities, and attractions helping us grow a truly wonderful festival.

If you have any questions, please call our Downtown Office at (111) 333-5555.

Thank you,
George Green
Chairperson, Green Festival

2015 Green Festival in Downtown Opswatch
Sponsor Menu – What we can do for each other!

We greatly appreciate your help.
Without your contribution our Festival would not be as successful.

Green Thumb level – Any amount from $20 to 100.
- Your name will be added to the Friends of the Festival list in the Festival program.
- If you fill out the sponsor form, you will get a free ticket to our special donor's raffle drawings.
- One Festival tote bag.

Polar Pal level – Cash, goods, or services up to $101 thru 500
- Your name listed on the program and on website as a Friend of the Festival.
- If you fill out the sponsor form, you will get 5 tree tickets to our special donor's raffle drawings.
- One Festival T-Shirt and one tote bag.

Earth Champion level – Cash, goods, or services up to $1500.
- Your name listed as a sponsor on our website.
- Your name on our print advertising, in our program, and vinyl banners.
- Small ad in program.
- Two Festival T-shirts, 2 Festival tote bags, and 5 free tickets for special donor raffle.

Energy Wizard level – Cash Goods or services up to $1501 and up.
- Your name with logo listed as a Sponsor on the Entertainment Stage, in the program, on our print advertising, vinyl banners and on our website.
- Preferential seating at the band gazebo music performances.
- "Meet-and-Greet" Happy Hour with the John Denver Tribute Group.
- Four Festival T- shirts, four tote bags, 5 free tickets for special donor raffle, and a beautiful, plush, dated "Eco-Bear" souvenir.

Additional Sponsorship Opportunities
- Children's Activities $200 each activity
- Program Sponsor $200
- Speaker or Forum $200 each speaker
- Gazebo Music Entertainment $400

Underwriting the cost of these activities will put your name on them and give you further publicity in our program, print, and media advertising. First Come, First Choice!

To qualify for any of these listings, the sponsor form must be received by April 1, 2015. For maximum exposure, respond early to take advantage of our advertising and our website traffic.

2015 Green Festival in Downtown Opswatch Sponsor Form

Yes, we would like to support the Green Festival in Downtown Opswatch to be held on April 18, 2015

Company Name _____

Contact Person _____ Date _____

Address _____

Phone _____ Fax _____

Email _____

Website _____

Amount – Please enter dollar amount of the cash, goods, or services you wish to donate.

_____	**Green Thumb**	**(from $20 – 100)**
_____	**Polar Pal**	**(from $101 – 500)**
_____	**Earth Champion**	**(from $501 – 1500)**
_____	**Energy Wizard**	**(from $1501 and up)**

We will contact you for your logo, shirt sizes, etc. Please list the contact person and the best way of reaching him or her for this information.

Contact _____

The deadline for your gift to be listed is April 1, 2015.

If you wish to sponsor a specific activity, please list your first and second choice.

1. _____

2. _____

Please make your check out to DOBA (Downtown Opswatch Business Association) Mail to: Green Festival, 110 Library St., Opswatch, IZ 90000. If you have any questions, please call George Green at (111) 333-5555.

Recruiting Sponsors

Now that you are armed with all of this material, you are ready to begin your search for sponsors. It is many months yet away from the event. You could mail out your sponsor packets to some potential businesses, and you might be fortunate enough to receive a positive reply. Most of the time, however, you will have to get out there and approach them in person. You can read all the fundraising books you want, but eventually you will have to meet potential sponsors face-to-face.

Asking businesses that already know you...

Start with the easy ones first. If you have never done this before, it is good to practice on them. Begin with businesses that are on your board of directors. Branch out to businesses and institutions that you already do business with. If you know the people on the decision-making level, that will help.

If there is a supplier that you use again and again for events or that you and your committee members patronize regularly, check with them. They may be able to add some extra to your order at no charge, or supply beverage cups, vinyl banners, or tote bags. They are already in relationship with you and are more likely to help.

Getting sponsors is not the job of a sole individual. Ask others on your committee to approach businesses and individuals with whom they have contacts. Divvy up the businesses and individuals you want to approach. Put some thought into the best volunteer for each. Make a chart that lists who will contact which businesses so that there is no duplication or oversight. It looks more professional to have one individual work with a business from start to a (hopefully) successful conclusion.

Approaching businesses you don't know...

Choose your targets and try to find

- Businesses or individuals that will likely benefit from the event.

 The Green Festival approached the local utility company as a partner and sponsor. It made sense: many of the programs on conservation and alternative energy already in progress with the utility dovetailed extremely well with the festival goals.

- Businesses or individuals that have supported similar events in the past.
- New businesses that are looking for a way to increase their visibility.
- Alumni from a school, if the event is hosted or sponsored by that school.

While you may never have asked for donations before, big corporations see hundreds of requests. Many corporations plan their budget with sponsorship dollars built in. They may have set policies about giving back to the community where they have their business, and you can bet they have set aside a certain amount in their budget for charitable works, public service, and donations because of the tax breaks they get. Sometimes they will put their sponsorship policies on their website. Look for the procedures that must be followed. There might be an application form on line.

This money will be doled out to those they find worthy during the year. For many corporations, the process is quite elaborate and must go up the chain of command, probably to someone outside your region. Give them enough time to carry the process through.

Part of the learning curve for those who seek sponsors is finding out about the processes and timelines that different businesses follow. For example, Business A needs two months to process sponsorship opportunities. Business B needs almost a full year for sponsor requests to go up the ladder to the decision-makers who weigh many requests before they let you know. Business C has vested the responsibility in their assistant manager, Sam Dollar, who takes appointments on Thursdays. Business D will only consider requests at a certain time of year. Take notes and keep records for each potential company sponsor. It will help when you do this again.

 Get all donation agreements in writing. You may find later that an individual with whom you made arrangements has had a change of job duties.

In some instances the wording of the request might make a difference. A business wants to be able to write off their gift as an expense. They may not be able to do it as a charity donation, but some requests may actually qualify as advertising or promotion. Some of these decisions can be made by folks lower down on the corporate chain and usually in much less time. Businesses may use some of their marketing and promotion budget if they get a spot in the program to recognize their donation or if the master of ceremonies verbally gives them a plug.

Small mom-and-pop stores also receive many requests. For their self-preservation, many have developed their own policy about giving. Some will give only to certain charities—like sports or music in the public schools—that resonate with them. They might have set a monthly budget. Some have decided what type of help they are willing to give, for example, product—not cash or gift certificates. Don't take it personally if your request is brushed off. They may be suffering from donation fatigue. Some businesses may be experiencing financial difficulty. Their sympathy with your cause may be high, but their pockets may be empty. Think of ways that you can help them as well as ways they can help you. Even if you hear a "No", not all is lost. You are growing relationships that may bear fruit at a later time. You are spreading the word about a worthwhile event. Invite them to come.

Many times businesses are not willing to give cash, but they will help you out with in-kind support. This is great. If the sanitation company is willing to donate the garbage toters to your event, you can use your cash for something else. If your local newspaper is willing to give you free advertising space, that means your money will stretch even further. If the local hotel can provide a room for your entertainer, you may afford to have better quality entertainment.

Ask both the in-kind sponsors and the cash sponsors to fill out the forms. Make sure they get the credit and the perks they deserve with the level of their donation of goods or services.

A sample Donor Record follows.

Donor Record

Name of Business _____

Address _____

Phone _____ Contact Person _____

"Thank you" goes to _____

Type of Donation _____

Received   Yes   No

Pick up on Date _____ Best Time _____

Person to ask for _____

Date picked up _____

Value _____

Notes:

_____

Some businesses may be very interested in special kinds of sponsorships. You might look for someone to sponsor the wine and beer glasses, any trophies or prizes that will be given out, staff T-shirts with sponsor logo on back, barricade covers, or chairs with a cover over the back with the sponsor's logo.

TIP   When you are looking for raffle prizes, don't overlook the suppliers that you or your committee members do business with. When I owned a gift store, I would attend gift shows to order merchandise. When I placed an order, I would say we had a festival coming up, and would they be willing to donate something for a raffle prize. I would give them a flier about the festival, and often they would be quite generous. They have samples, overstocks, and discontinued items that they may be very happy to write off in this way. One toy company donated a huge box of small toys that we used for children's prizes. All we had to do was pay the shipping. Sales reps who came to the store would often donate some of their samples or tack a prize on to our order, free of charge. Suggest to businesses in your organization that they try that. It is a painless way of getting raffle prizes for your event.

Creative ways of obtaining sponsors and support

Now that you have all of your sponsor packets and charts done, don't close yourself off to other ways of getting support:

- Don't overlook manufacturers in your internet search for in-kind support. Some will give away free products or samples that might be included in goodie bags or used as one stop on a roulette wheel spin. Make sure that you have a legitimate use for the items before you go ahead and make the request.

- If you are selling tickets, perhaps a business can buy a block of seats or a table at a dinner.

- Some businesses may be willing to loan items to your event. Those ficus trees or silk floral arrangements may be just what your décor committee needs. If you can get the loan of a portable stage for your entertainment, you can use the money you saved on renting one for other needs or for profit.

- You will find businesses with a plan in place to support causes by sharing profit. Some pizza or other food chains will give a percentage of their sales during a certain time period as a fundraiser when customers specify the nonprofit. Restaurants aren't the only ones with a plan in place. Check with other corporations, such as Barnes & Noble. Find out what their policies are and follow the guidelines. They win because you have drawn in more customers who make purchases. You win with the percentage of sales; the more people you have encouraged to participate the more you will make. Both of you win from the added promotion, visibility, and good will.

Taking Care of Sponsors

Give credit where credit is due. Someone should be assigned with the task of making sure that the sponsors get the credit and goodies they deserve and that all are properly and publicly thanked.

Sit down with your sponsor menu and organize who gets what. As these responsibilities are fulfilled, document what has been done.

It doesn't hurt to make sponsors feel special. There might be a VIP tent where they can relax, sit, and have access to coffee or water. If your menu promised special VIP treatment of sponsors, think about goodie bags for them. Goodie bags would include stuff to make the day more comfortable, more educational, and more meaningful. Sponsors may appreciate sun block, a fan, water, a visor, program, raffle tickets, or coupons at nearby or participating businesses. Samples from manufacturers can be included. Area tourist fliers, snacks, rain hat, flashlight, and key chains are other possibilities that you might be able to collect.

Applying for Grant Funding

It is hard to believe, but there may be foundations and corporations willing to give you money for your event. Some foundations were started by large philanthropic gifts. The interest these funds generate is granted to groups or individuals who apply and win. Foundations usually try to award grants to those working for the greater good, to improving life in the community. Some foundations are set up to fund specific areas such as environmental education, arts programs, and peace building.

Why pursue grant funding? Knowing the money is available to defray costs can alleviate a lot of headaches for the event planner. It may save you time, too. The time invested in writing a grant is less than the legwork to dozens of small businesses to solicit donations or goods. But it takes advance planning—at least a year in advance.

Grants are available for both nonprofit and for profit organizations. Always read your potential granting institutions guidelines before starting the process. See if your organization qualifies under their policies.

Be aware that some grants are only available to non-profit organizations. If you have a repeat event that increases community involvement, consider forming a nonprofit—a "Friends of..." group. It will take several months to obtain your nonprofit status, but then your organization can apply for grants in collaboration with your own for-profit organization. Foundations appreciate groups collaborating together to produce an event.

If you are starting a new event, begin by asking local institutions for support. Most granting institutions like a detailed accounting of what their money will be used for: special band, added security, venue fees, and so on. Be very specific in what you are asking for. That said, some institutions *will* donate funds for start-up projects and are less specific in their requirements.

Always prepare a budget very early in the process for the event if you are pursuing grant money. A note to the event organizer, keep records of volunteer hours for your event. Prepare a sign-in/sign-out sheet for volunteers to make it easy to record volunteer hours. These are like gold coins in grant writing, as volunteers provide in-kind donations and also highlight the community aspect of your event. If your event in any way builds community and fosters communication and education, you have your "foot in the door", so to speak.

Most community events can be seen as building community and as such are potential recipients for grants. If you are in doubt, call up the granting officer of the institution and talk with them regarding your event. Be prepared to give projected numbers of attendees and what the benefit to the community would be. If you have numbers of volunteer hours from previous years, this is another indicator of community involvement to the granting institution. Also, be prepared to discuss what the benefit would be for the granting institution.

How to find grants? As mentioned above, start locally. Banks, large national chain stores, community foundations, healthcare institutions, and other nonprofits all are potential donors. Ask other event organizers or check the websites of potential granting institutions. If you have an event that is long-standing, then you might want to pursue federal funding. But you really need to have accurate records from past events. The best place to start is with an internet search using the words "community event grants" as your key words.

With any grant, be prepared to devote several days to write and edit your grant proposal. What are the benefits to the community of your event and why would the granting agency be interested in sponsoring the event? The best piece of advice that I have received regarding grants is to establish a working, personal relationship with the granting officer of the institution. They can guide you past potential "potholes" and can assist you in crafting your grant proposal. They can also be an advocate for your event with the grant approval committee.

If you are new to grant writing, you can investigate by taking classes or go-it-alone and check out a book from your local library. Some classes are pretty pricey, so be selective. That said, don't get discouraged if your first (several) applications are turned down. Always call up the grant officer to thank them for their time and to get their perspective as to why your grant was not funded. You will soon learn the process and the language.

If you do receive grant funding, your work is not done. Make sure that you keep accurate financial documents as where, when, and how the grant money was spent. Most granting institutions require a budget submission after the event has occurred. These financial records will also help you if you re-apply for additional funding or pursue a new source of funding.

Part III
Execution of the Plan

You pull together your activities, entertainment, vendors—all that the public will come to see and do. Convince the public to attend. Celebrate the event!

Chapters

12. Art, Craft, and Merchandise Vendors

Vendors in this guide are the craft, food, and merchandise sellers. They are the exhibitors at a home and garden show. Vendors can pay for the bulk of your event expenses. They may be the reason that many people will come to the event and are considered by some to be *the* entertainment. The visiting public will judge the quality of your event by the quality of your vendors.

In event-planning books geared to corporate and other business events, the term "vendor" often refers to those folks hired to do certain tasks such as catering and floral designing, or from whom equipment is rented. That is *not* the definition meant in this guide.

In this chapter you will learn how to find the right type of vendors for your event, set fees, draft applications, mark the booth spaces, and much more.

Setting the Vendor Fees and Deadlines

Look at other events in your area. Check their websites to see what kind of fees they are charging. Bounce these figures off your committee members. If you are doing a two-day event and have to pay for overnight security, be sure to factor that cost into your fee. If you have to pay a fee to your health department for having food vendors, and if you also have to rent a greywater tank, the food vendor's fee should be higher than the fee for merchandise vendors. Make the food-vendor fee high enough to cover the costs and still reach your goal.

For a start-up event, it might be smart to keep the cost low and work especially hard to make it a great event for your vendors. They will be happy to return the second year and not quibble about the higher fee.

Options for setting fees

Charge a flat-rate fee for vendor booth space. Booths will all be the same size. If a vendor needs a larger space, give them two booths for slightly less than two individual booths.

- If your event is inside, charge per table. If you are supplying the tables, be sure to factor in their rental cost.
- Charge by the foot. Begin with a ten by ten space, for example, for $150. For each foot over 12 feet charge $10. So if they want a 20' space, you would charge them $150 + $80 = $230.
- If you sell the space at 10 x 10 feet, but actually give them 12 feet, the vendors aren't going to be on top of each other, making better neighbors.
- Vary your rates by deadline. If it is important that you get all of the vendor fees and credentials early, you might structure the fee with a carrot-and-stick approach. For example, the fee could be $150 if received by December 1st for an event the following April. After that it would go to $200 until March 1st, when it would increase again. Depending on the situation and the desirability of the vendor for the event, these fee changes may be waived by the committee.
- Charge a lower rate for vendors that sell merchandise directly related to the theme of the event, and charge a higher rate for a separate area of non-related merchandise.
- Charge a lower rate for crafts made by the vendor and a higher rate for manufactured or imported items.
- There are some amenities that vendors will pay extra for. If they want a corner space, charge a fee like $25, first come, first served. Request that amount as a separate check. That way, if you run out of corners before their application arrives, you can simply return the $25 check and not have to write a refund check to them.
- Vendors may also pay extra for tables, pop-ups, chairs, or electricity, if you can offer these amenities. They may also be asked if they want to advertise in your event program.

- Nonprofits applying for a booth may receive a drastically lowered rate, especially if they fit in with your stated goals.

- Some events, especially established ones with stellar reputations, charge a small application or "jury fee" of $5 to $25. (See glossary.) This jury fee is submitted on a separate check and is non-refundable, even if the vendor is not accepted and you return their vendor fee. Such a fee is not advisable for a small or a start-up event.

- Divide up potential booth space by the total amount your vendors need to bring in. If you have space for only 60 vendors and you need to make X amount of dollars from your vendors, divide 60 into that amount. If you would like to have a little fudge room, or if you know there will be nonprofit booths that will not be charged the fee, divide 50 into that amount. Then you will be able to meet your X financial goal.

- Some events charge a minimal booth fee plus a percentage of sales. This method may appeal especially to beginning vendors. Bookkeeping and paper work increase with this option. There may be varying degrees of honesty in reporting sales from your vendors as well, so be forewarned; maybe you don't want to go there.

- It is your prerogative to negotiate or change the fee structure for individual vendors. If they are providing more interest to the consumer by demonstrating a craft, or if they provide components or helpers for you, or if they constitute a very high draw to your event, you may waive all or part of the fee.

Setting Deadline Dates

There is a tension among all of the major players involved with vendors when it comes to setting deadlines. Much of this has to do with the documents that vendors are required to submit. These documents may include proof of liability insurance, a copy of the vendor's driver's license, a copy of their seller's permit (sales tax), licenses from the health department for food vendors, and, of course, the check for the vendor fee. *If any of these are required for some events, but not received, the vendor will be unable to participate, even if they show up.*

As the event planner, you will have the challenge of seeing the work is organized so that everything goes as smoothly as it possibly can. You may have to struggle to keep the following folks happy:

- **Vendor chairs or office staff**. They will have to chase documentation from the individual vendors and also have to meet their own deadlines of reporting to their board and to the city.

- **The vendors themselves**. They are the attraction for the public and are also paying the bills of the festival. Some vendors are better artists than they are business people. Some wait until the last minute and stretch the terms of the deadline. You need them, and they really do increase the quality of the festival, so they should be kept happy, even if it means they're a little late.

- The city or **those with the responsibility of permitting the event**. They work with a layered bureaucracy and set out demands. They may believe they are in charge.

This leads to an interesting balancing act for the folks who are organizing the festival. It goes back and forth. Festival organizers are caught in the middle, and neither vendor nor bureaucrat is completely pleased with the organizers. The answer is to keep at the vendors; be diplomatic and diligent in your quest for credentials. Make sure all of the parties are aware of all of the deadlines involved *long before* they arrive.

Consider these thoughts when setting deadlines:

- When you choose your deadline dates, don't hide them around holidays (for example, January 1st). People will be very busy and will not be focused on festival applications. They will likely miss the deadline, and rather than being annoyed at themselves, they will blame your event.

- Understand the vendor's calendar routine. Many are busy every weekend in summer and some through Christmas or Hanukkah. After the season is over, they probably break for rest and relaxation, evaluation, and creating more inventory. The optimum time for that first round of emails or letters seeking vendors might be when that evaluation and productivity time comes for the next year. You don't want your application buried during the holidays under a geologic layer of "look at someday". You don't want emails to be forgotten and lost in cyberspace.

Vendor Liability Insurance

Many professional vendors already carry liability insurance. It may be the wave of the future. If you have requested proof of liability insurance from your vendor, more than likely it will come to you from their insurance carrier on a standard industry form—an ACORD 25. Make sure that *your* requested wording is used.

Have someone on your committee find the best company for the vendors to buy the insurance at a decent rate. You can recommend that company in your application materials or suggest they call you for a recommendation.

If your city or permitting organization requires liability insurance, check with your own insurance company. Perhaps they can add individual vendors for a fee of $25 or so in their coverage. See if your city has an insurance plan that vendors can tag onto. Include the cost of providing this in the fee you charge vendors.

 One of the biggest surprises and setbacks in our first year of planning for the Medieval Fantasy Festival was discovering that our city required all event vendors to "provide a certificate of general liability insurance naming by endorsement to the policy 1. our city and, 2. our downtown business district as additionally insured in the amount of $1,000,000."

Dealing with this resulted in our vendor applications being sent out only a few months before the event. The little mom-and-pop vendors balked because it was too expensive. They also thought it was a ridiculous request since most other events and other cities did not require it at that time. We scrambled to find sources to recommend for this insurance. Our event was fast approaching and we had very few merchandise vendors who had applied. Finally we made the decision to waive the vendor fees entirely, except for food vendors, just to get vendors to sign up. Some of the vendors from the Renaissance fair circuit who had already agreed to participate talked their friends into coming. We did pull it off and everyone had their insurance.

Sales Tax

Be familiar with your state's sales tax rules. Ask for each vendor's sales tax (seller's permit) number on your application. You may be required to submit a list of the vendors and their sales permit numbers to your state. If so, your state official should check the vendors on your list and let you know if all is in order. They may refuse any who have outdated information or business names that don't agree with their records. The possibility of not being able to participate may make those vendors hustle to jump through the hoops to obtain a current sales permit before the event.

Composing the Application Packet

An application packet generally has three sections.

1. Event overview and invitation to apply—the enticement letter

The first is a letter that says what the event is looking for. This letter should generate excitement about the event and get the potential vendor interested. It should tell about the event and where they can find more information.

2. Rules and regulations

The second, which may be on the reverse side of the letter, is a list of all the rules and regulations. Now that you have the vendor "hooked", you can give them the boring stuff. (If you do it in the "come-on" part, it is deadly.) If your event is outdoors, you may wish to state that it will happen "rain or shine".

You might also establish and include a refund policy. Some events say a full refund up to 60 days prior to the event, 50 % up to 30 days, and no refund after that. You might think that is harsh, but it is hard to replace the lost income from vendor spaces on short notice. When a vendor says they are coming, it means that you are holding a space for them. Also, you still have expenses of security, porta potties, advertising, and so on, that don't go away if vendors back out.

 **TIP**   Life happens and is uncertain. You need a Plan B for vendor cancellations because of hardship—accidents, major illnesses, or a death in the family. This does not have to be stated on the rules page, but can be handled on a case-by-case basis as you wish.

3. Application form and disclaimers

The third is the application form. Do not put the rules on the paper they send back. You want them to keep the rules and abide by them, not mail them back.

A Sample Vendor Application Packet follows.

Sample Vendor Application Packet

2015 Green Festival in Downtown Opswatch, IZ
An Eco-friendly Future Fair

Dear Friends,

Enclosed you will find the *Rules* and a *Vendor Application Form*. This form may be used for green, eco-friendly vendors or arts, crafts, and merchandise vendors or nonprofits for the Third Annual Green Festival in Downtown Opswatch. This festival will be held on Saturday, April 18, 2015. This is a very unique and exciting, family-oriented festival sponsored by the Downtown Opswatch Business Association (DOBA).

The green vendors will have ecologically-friendly products such as electric cars, solar-powered products, organically-grown cotton clothing, and other products that use our world's resources responsibly. With your participation we are going to showcase products, organizations, and ideas to delight and inspire us as we begin to move together out of the petroleum-based energy era into the future of alternative energy. In our jury process we look for variety and an awareness of green, eco-friendly standards.

The arts, crafts, and merchandise vendors will be chosen by our jury for quality, variety, and appeal. We reserve the right to choose vendors that fit in with our theme from among the applications we receive. Note: we want to *augment*, not duplicate what the downtown businesses carry. Made-by-exhibitor merchandise will receive priority.

If you would like to be a part of the Green Festival, please fill out the vendor application and ***return with all of the requested documentation*** with the appropriate fee as soon as possible to reserve your space for April 18, 2015. Spaces are limited, so we encourage you to apply early.

If you have any questions, please do not hesitate to call the Downtown Opswatch Business Association (111) 333-5555. You may contact us by email at info@downtownopswatch.com. For additional festival information please visit our website at www.downtownopswatch.com .

Sincerely,
George Green,
Festival Chairperson

2015 Green Festival
GREEN, ECO-FRIENDLY, ARTS & CRAFTS VENDORS, AND NONPROFIT BOOTH
RULES AND REGULATIONS

1. Please provide information about what you will be showing / selling. Photos or a write-up will suffice. These will not be returned. Returning vendors may skip this requirement.

2. Spaces are 10' x 10' and are assigned on a first come, first served basis. The **vendor fee for the Green festival is $90.**

3. If you need more space, add $10 per foot after the first 12 feet. We will consider special requests for locations where possible. For a corner space **please include a separate check for $20.** If we have no more corners when your application arrives, we will return that check.

4. Make out checks to DOBA. If you must cancel, a full refund may be given up until 60 days before the event. Up until 30 days, a 50% refund may be given. After that date, no refunds will be given. This event will be held rain or shine. *The deadline for applications is April 1, 2015.* Your booth location will be emailed to you with your acceptance.

5. We reserve the right to limit the number of vendors within each category and to accept only those applicants which we believe are compatible with our theme and purposes.

6. **Please note this wording: You must provide a Certificate of General Liability Insurance naming by endorsement to the policy 1. the City of Opswatch and   2. the DOBA as additionally insured in the amount of $1,000,000.**
   The liability insurance is not an option. Provide the insurance documentation 60 days before the event. We can suggest a source for it, if you don't already have this insurance.

7. Insurance required by # 6 in no way limits the vendor's liability. Any injury to the vendor arising out of, or resulting from, participation in this event is the responsibility of the vendor.

8. The hours of the Green Festival are 9:30 a.m. to 5:00 p.m. on Saturday. You may begin setting up at 6:00 a.m. on Saturday.

9. You are responsible for your own tables, chairs, canopies, etc. Vehicles not used for display purposes must be removed from the event area prior to 9:30 a.m. Use of your vehicle for display must be pre-approved. No Exceptions. If your vehicle is to be used as part of your display, you must include proof of insurance (declarations page) with your application.

10. Vendors must collect and pay their own sales tax. A copy of your seller's permit must accompany your completed application.

11. All packing materials must be removed from your exhibit space prior to the time of opening. All additional trash, zip ties, empty containers, and packing materials must be removed when you leave. Please flatten empty boxes. Lay them in the designated area by the porta potties. The Opswatch Boy Scout troop will empty that area periodically. You may **NOT** dispose of ice / water or other liquids into planted areas or storm drains.

12. Vendors are responsible for providing and arranging all necessary labor in set-up and tear-down. Vendors shall not store or display materials on benches, planters or other architectural surfaces.

14. If you are a nonprofit group and will be handing out information only, please contact us to negotiate your vendor fee.

15. Breakdown for the event begins *no earlier* than 5:00 p.m. Saturday. *All spaces must be vacated by 7:00 p.m.*

Vendor Application and Agreement Form
Green Festival in Downtown Opswatch - April 18, 2015

Check one: Green _____   Arts, Crafts _____   Nonprofit _____

NAME (please print) _____

BUSINESS NAME _____

ADDRESS_____

CITY_____ STATE _____ ZIP _____

BEST PHONE (day) _____(eve) _____ (fax) _____

WEBSITE _____

E MAIL _____

Driver's License _____ SELLER'S PERMIT # _____

Please provide a description of the items you plan to sell or promote (required):
_____
_____

Will you be bringing a canopy?_____   Booth size needed _____
Remember to enclose the following:
     ___photos of your merchandise   ___photo copy of your driver's license
     ___copy of your seller's permit   ___proof of auto insurance (if required)
     ___certificate of liability insurance
     ___check for the vendor fee made out to DOBA
          _____ $90 - for 10' X 10'
          _____ $10 each additional foot after 12'
          _____ $20 additional for corner space (separate check, please)
          _____TOTAL ENCLOSED

AGREEMENT
As the main contact, I am responsible for any others that are working at my booth. We may be subject to scrutiny by the DOBA, the City of Opswatch and/or Police Department.

I have read and agree to observe the 2015 Green Festival Vendor Rules and Regulations as set forth in this packet. I do hereby agree to indemnify and hold harmless the City of Opswatch, Downtown Opswatch Business Association, and their respective officers, agents, underwriters, individually or collectively from all fines, penalties, liabilities, losses, claims, damages, and expenses including court costs and attorney fees incurred or suffered as a result of, or relating to, my participation in the event known as the Green Festival in Downtown Opswatch.

_____   _____
Authorized Signature   **Date**

Please mail to: Green Festival, 110 Library St, Opswatch, IZ 90000

Setting Quotas

List all of the types of vendors that you could possibly have in a well-rounded group consistent with your theme. (There is a sample of a "Category and Quota List" for the Green Festival in the Appendix.) What types of vendors would you really like to see? Think of the amount of foot traffic that you might be able to draw. Too many selling the same thing will not keep vendors happy. Lack of variety will also diminish the excitement for the customer. You will generally get lots of jewelry vendor applications. List the possibilities for each category of merchandise you can think of. Allow only one or two of each kind, or more if you believe a category warrants it.

Consider home-based businesses (such as Tupperware®) which may apply as vendors. In favor of their participation—the vendor fees they generate, what they sell may fit your theme well, and they are eager to take part. Against including them—some apply to any and all events and may be in the public's eye everywhere with the same jewelry, cosmetics, and candles. Do you want your event to be unique? If they or another type of vendor present a problem for your event, think about setting quotas. Think about setting a higher fee for these commercial resale booths than for exhibitor-made item booths. It depends on what you want at your event.

Nonprofit Booths

Decide early on if you will allow political or "cause" booths. The bylaws of some organizations dictate that they must remain non-political. When this is the case, candidates for office cannot have booths. There can be no blatant support for causes that might be divisive. This includes booths for any competing-cause groups that trigger emotional needs from the public to take sides.

You will want to include some nonprofit booths, especially if they are related to your theme. These booths can help you reach your goals. If your event is promoting enjoyment of nature, it gives more quality, depth, and value if you bring in Audubon clubs, Master Gardeners, native plant societies, and state conservation agencies.

Sometimes nonprofit booths will add to your event by providing an activity that the public will enjoy. They might have a children's game or a contest. In a health-related event they might provide blood pressure screening or have interesting displays like comparisons of the amount of sugar found in several popular drinks. They might provide important information and demonstrations that will fascinate the public. It is not uncommon for many agencies to have public outreach money budgeted for these types of events.

If you are having trouble selling those last vendor spaces, rather than let them be vacant space for the public to walk by, offer the spaces to nonprofit groups. It is good public relations.

For-Profit Information Booths

You will probably get requests from real estate businesses, travel agencies, banks, and other businesses that want to have a booth at your event. There are several reasons either to allow them or not to have them present.

Reasons to include them:

- If your event is a chamber of commerce or downtown event and the application comes from a member, it must be taken seriously.
- You need the money from the booth fee.
- If the applicant is putting up sponsor money, you will want to encourage them. If this type of booth is not generally permitted in your event, in order to justify it, set the sponsor dollar amount significantly higher than the regular booth fee. Here is an opportunity to coordinate this with your sponsor menu. If a certain dollar amount gets them a free booth, then they are in as a vendor.
- If they are related somehow to your theme, or if they increase the value of the event to the public, accept them.
- It may make a difference if they are giving away appropriate "premiums". On a hot, muggy, airless day it might be nice to have a freebie paper fan with a bank's name on it.

Reasons not to include:

- People who travel from craft show to craft show find commercial information booths boring to walk by. If they see a number of the information-type booths, they begin to think, "There isn't much here."
- Their goals or offerings conflict with your theme and goals.
- They detract from the overall ambience. (Conversely, their booth décor and staff in costume might add to the ambience.)
- If they are not related to your theme, they detract from the quality of your event.
- If past experience tells you these folks just sit there, put in their time, and do not try to engage the public—or on the other end of the spectrum, they are over-eager and in the face of the public to the point of being obnoxious—you may not want them at your event.

Chasing Vendors

Vendors are the backbone of most festivals I have worked on. Not only did vendors draw attendance, the vendor fees paid for all of our logistics, décor, and entertainment. A good vendor-chaser is always on the lookout for high-quality folks to add to the event database. You will need a good-sized database. If you want 50 vendors at your event, you may need to invite 500.

TIP   When you put together your promotional material for seeking vendors, be honest in your expectations and with your facts. I talked to a promoter one time about the advertised 200 vendors at an event that I knew would have only 40 vendors. He said that the public would turn out better if they thought there would be 200 vendors. More people would come, but never again if the event didn't live up to their expectations!

To find vendors in your area, do an internet search on craft fairs in your state. Check a site that gives listings of fairs and events within a certain number of miles from a zip code, and by month. (Some sites are listed in the Appendix.) You or others on your committee should plan to go to several of these events and seek out vendors. Some sites will have more event information available to you if you become a subscriber.

When you approach vendors at an event, look first at their merchandise. Is the merchandise appropriate for your event? Will the merchandise sell in your community? Will the prices work well with your local pocketbooks? Is the booth attractive and interesting?

When you strike up a conversation with the vendors, be sensitive to the customers they are talking to. Customers come first. Tell the vendor you are looking for vendors for an event coming up and where it is. Plan ahead of time and have a flier to hand them. It should give the name of the festival, date, location, what types of vendors you are looking for, and where to go for more information. If you have a website, make sure that is included. It is helpful and expedient if they can download applications from the website. In any case, the flier you give them should have the contact information for any questions they might have.

We found it was helpful to use programs and postcards from the immediate past festival with a sticker on each one giving the dates for the upcoming festival. Potential vendors can glean a lot of information and taste the flavor of a fair by looking at the program.

Collect business cards or other information from the vendors you are interested in:
- Write the name of the festival and the year on the card.
- If you wish, give the vendor a rating according to gut level reaction or criteria you have established earlier. Some will be just perfect for your event. Note that!

- Check to make sure the card has the contact information you need, including email.
- If it is not obvious from the card what type of merchandise the vendor has, make notes. Jot down enough to bring this particular vendor to mind later. You will never remember which card was from the best of the ten fused-glass jewelers with the best stuff at the best prices unless you make notes.

Invariably there will be several who forgot their business cards. Ask them for their contact information. Some festivals have wonderful programs that give the names and contact information of the vendors. (You may also find this information on the festival website. This is a gift which allows you to plan your strategy ahead of time.) You will still want to make helpful notes on your program.

A particular vendor with high-quality merchandise may not fit in with your theme, but take one of their cards anyway. Maybe the organization you are a part of will decide to do a chili cook-off. That barbecue-apron vendor who wasn't appropriate for the medieval festival might be perfect for the chili one. Collect outstanding vendors. Grow your database.

You may also take note of vendors that you don't want to invite. If you see a vendor to avoid, one of poor quality, one with tacky or offensive items, note that. If they should call you one day and want to be a part of your festival, you at least have a "heads up" warning.

The vendors will have questions as well. They will want to know:
- When and where
- How many years the festival has been running
- What kind of attendance you expect
- What your vendor fees will be

You will find that some won't do one-day fairs or start-up events. The more established your festival is, the easier it is to attract quality vendors.

If you take pictures of a vendor's booth, don't do it without their permission. Some artists are very sensitive to that. They don't want anyone to steal their ideas.

Contacting and Securing Vendors

1. Put all of your vendors into a computer database. Include their business name, the contact name, type of vendor, how you found out about them, and contact information.
2. Organize or rate your database of vendors into three categories: most wanted, solid or good, and backup.
3. Develop an outline of the types of vendors you want with a quota system.

4. Organize your vendor binders. I like having my vendor information on hard copies in binders. Each vendor business has its own page. A sample vendor record is included in this section. This is where I write my notes about "most wanted" and so on. Communications with vendors are jotted down. If I have communicated with them by email (other than standard vendor emails), a copy gets clipped to their information sheet. When they apply, I move their papers into a "coming" binder. Their application form then is clipped in front of their other papers.

 Emailing may be one step in greening your event. Emails save postage, they save paper, and nobody has to drive them to the post office. If you don't have an email address for a vendor, do an internet search before you send off that paper packet through the mail.

5. Send out personal emails explaining what, where, when to all vendors. Attach the appropriate vendor application. Refer them to your website or suggest they call for an application, if that would be more convenient for them. For the vendors who are not computer-savvy, and for whom you were not able to find emails, send an application packet through the regular mail.

6. Send a second email and/or phone them. Introduce yourself and say, "I am calling to follow up on an email sent earlier with vendor information for our event." Determine who should have received the information and their title. Did they get it? Double check their email address. Tell them what address it came from and the date if they are interested. (If they were not familiar with the sender, or the subject line didn't grab their attention, they probably deleted it unopened. This is especially true if there was an attachment.)

Say, "I found out about your business from … and believe that you would be a good fit for our festival." Give the event website address and suggest that they check it out. Do they have any questions? Do they need more information? "Does it sound like something you would be interested in?" Find out if there is a convenient time you could call back to follow up.

Give them any appropriate incentives. If they have to travel a very long distance and I really want them, I could waive or reduce the vendor fee.

A Vendor Record form is included on the next page. It is a good way of keeping track of your interaction with vendors.

TIP   One thing that you will learn very soon is that you can't complete something with just one phone call, email, or visit. Invariably the person you need to speak with is not in, or they can't tell you an answer now, and so you play phone tag. Sometimes you get an affirmative answer from the vendor, only to find out that their spouse or partner is not at all thrilled with participating. However long you think it will take to do something, multiply it by four. If you are dealing with a bureaucracy, multiply by ten.

Emails are a great invention, but some people don't check their email regularly. Some of your messages may end up in a spam folder. Some vanish into cyberspace and are never seen again.

Vendor Record

Business Name _____Date of 1st contact _____

Source of contact _____

Contact Name _____

	Invited	Came	Year
	_____	_____	2013
Phone (best) _____	_____	_____	2014
	_____	_____	2015
Phone (cell) _____	_____	_____	2016
	_____	_____	2017

Website _____

Email _____

Address _____
Crafts Vendor _____ Green Vendor _____ Nonprofit _____ Food Vendor _____
Entertainer _____ Speaker _____ Other (specify) _____

Merchandise category (jewelry, pottery, etc.) _____

Rating – Scale of 1 – 10 _____ Comments _____

Concerns / Red Flags / Comments _____

Items Description (also attach business card if possible)

Record of Communication :

Jury Vendors

To *jury vendors* means you have some criteria in mind and will choose only the most appropriate. A jury also implies more than one person doing the choosing— usually a small group. In this context, jury does not mean a twelve-person panel as in a criminal trial.

The function of this jury is rather like a gatekeeper. Set up your vision ahead of time regarding the type of vendors you want for your event, and share this with your core committee or with whomever is acting as the jury. You want the vendor to fit in with your theme, you want to have quotas on different types of vendors, and you want the vendors to be of high quality. Otherwise you will end up with lots of jewelry vendors, boring information booths, junky flea-market stuff, lots of imports and very few handcrafts, and probably a few high-quality vendors you will never see again after that year. The jury process can be as formal or as informal as you like. By setting up the criteria and quotas ahead of time, a couple of people can serve as jurors and choose vendors to accept. If they need more input to decide on certain vendors, they can take it to the larger committee.

Marking Vendor Spaces

Outdoor spaces

If your event is on closed-off city streets, plan ahead and make a to-scale map of each street on graph paper. Each square on your graph paper should represent two feet of real space. Put in crosswalks, light poles, and landscaping that juts out into the street. Put in access locations for electricity and water. Mark the beginning and end of each business. Use a rolling street measurer to get the distance. (The gadget that we used was by Trumeter™ and is listed in the Appendix.) When you get done, double check it. Tape the sections together. Laminate each street map.

However you set up your vendors on a street, you will need to begin with enough clear access for fire engines and emergency vehicles. Your fire department can tell you how many feet of clearance you need.

If your street has no curb areas that jut out into it, you might consider having the vendors back-to-back in the center (or slightly to one side). The vendors would face existing businesses which appreciate more visibility and access. Pedestrian traffic would move between the vendors and the businesses. If your street is set up with interesting curb projections and landscaping, you are probably stuck with having the vendors against the curbs facing the center of the street. The customers would go down the center of the street. They would have to go out of their way to reach existing businesses. You might plan breaks within the line of vendors.

Your laminated street plot is a useful tool that can be used for other years and other events. For each vendor, cut a Post-it® to the scale size of the booth and place it on the map. Use dry-erase markers on the lamination for space you want to keep open, space for certain activities, and location of certain amenities. Tack the street maps to the wall. As each vendor applies, add their Post-it. Use a different color for "pending" booths. You can note where the porta potties and hand-washing stations will be. Visually you can track how many more vendors you have room for. Some vendors request corner spots and pay more for the privilege. If you mark those spots on your map, it is easy to keep track of how many corners are still available

We did the space assignment emails to the vendors while consulting the maps as well. We said something like, "Your space is on Main Street in front of Sow & Sow Nursery". The Post-its with vendor names and the storefront names were right there on our maps for convenient reference.

I found that when we actually assigned the vendor their space, it was a good idea to add a little tape to the sticky note, avoiding accidental dislodging. We rolled up the maps and took them with us to mark the actual space on the streets a few days before the event. Armed with the rolling street measurer, our laminated maps, a spray can of marking chalk, a big piece of cardboard (for protecting any parked car), rubber gloves, and some sidewalk chalk, we began marking. We put a chalk line over the curb with the spray chalk. Experience taught us to wear old clothes for this task.

Then we printed the name of the vendor on the curb with sidewalk chalk. Sidewalk chalk is what kids use. It will not last through any kind of rain. If it rains between your marking and the event, your names will be gone. You might have to go to Plan B and print out vendor names in big letters on your computer, put them in plastic page protectors, and fasten them with duct tape to the space.

If you have uniformly-sized spaces, you may choose to number them and not chalk the vendor names on the street. Vendor assignments are easy to do by number.

Marking chalk comes in spray cans, available at your local hardware store. It is designed for temporary use and is removable. (The kind we used is listed in the Appendix. Look for Aervoe Industries®.) The spray can claims that the mark will naturally disappear with water, traffic or other abrasions, but will remain visible up to three weeks. Some of our marks were still visible a year later when we went out to mark the next event. They claim also that the marking chalk can be used on soil and turf without damage to the grass.

After the event was over, we moved our sticky notes from the street side of the line on our laminated maps off to the side where the businesses were named. We taped them in place. Since many of our vendors wanted to be in the same space as they had been the year before, this made it easy to find their old spot and plug them in.

Marking space in an indoor facility

For indoors, writing on masking tape or blue painter's tape (which is touted as not leaving residue) would probably do the trick. You might ask the folks at the facility what they recommend. They should have experience and know what works. Whatever you decide to do, try it ahead of time. I can't imagine a worse nightmare than using duct tape and learning, after the fact, that when you pull it up, the floor wax or the continuous-filament carpet also comes with it. Yikes!

Use your computer to print the name of the booth and its number on separate pieces of paper. Tape these to the booth-space floor.

You might choose to plot out your spaces and number them. This plot can be used from year to year. Assign the spaces by giving the vendor a number. They could be listed in the program by number as well.

You could still do the "to-scale" layout of the room on graph paper. You might find that instead of the rolling-measurer gadget, you can count floor tiles. It is possible that if you are renting a facility, they will have a floor plan that you can enlarge and use. Double check first, though, before you plug your vendors in. Don't assume that the facility has done an accurate, to-scale job.

Confirmation and Space Assignment Letters

Your vendor confirmation and space assignment letters should go out to vendors one to two months before the event. For later applicants, they should go out as soon as you decide to accept them. If possible use email to save postage costs. Attach a copy of the confirmation to their application form in your binder for your records.

These are the basic items to cover in the letter:
- Congratulations on their acceptance.
- The location of their space and how it will be marked.
- If they still have any outstanding credential obligations, for example, certificates of liability insurance, you can note that. The wording may then be "pending receipt of such and such, you are accepted as a vendor in our event."
- In this computer age, it is good to give the cross streets or the street number for the location of the event. When vendors get driving directions from the internet, they need that information.
- You may wish to highlight some of the vendor rules in this letter.
- When can they begin to set up? Where and when will coffee and/or water be available?

- If appropriate, remind about overnight security. You might use a disclaimer, "It is advisable that you take any valuables with you. We are not responsible for any items that are stolen or damaged."
- The location of vendor parking should be included.
- Ask if they need a list of hotels and motels that are offering special vendor rates. If so, the list can be sent via email or fax.
- A phone number to call if they have questions. Give your event website. Tell them if a program or schedule is posted.
- Any last-minute changes in the event.
- Thank them for participating.

Keeping Vendors Happy

Your street bosses should be on the location from before the vendors arrive until they leave. They will help vendors find their spaces, answer questions, and deal with any problems that may arise.

You may want to make suggestions to your vendors in dealing with the weather, especially if you know they are newbies. For an outdoor event, it is essential that they think about protection from sun, rain, and wind.

- Sun is easy—a pop-up.
- A little rain probably won't keep the public or most vendors from participating. Remind them to bring something to keep their back stock inventory and accoutrements off the ground. Puddles may appear. If the booth is on the street, backed up to the sidewalk, remember why they call it a gutter. The surface of the street is curved to carry the water away from the center and to the storm drains. Don't impede it!
- A crafter's real nightmare is wind. Pop-ups cartwheel down the street, and displays blow over. If you have a pop-up, you will need weights on each leg. Some vendors fashion leg-sleeves—sand-filled, canvas pads wrapped around the pop-up leg, going high enough to cover and brace the joint in the leg. You can tie cement blocks to the leg. One vendor brought empty five-gallon jugs, filled them with water at the site, and used them to anchor his pop-up.

Streets are one thing; dealing with muddy ground is another. If you know it is going to be bad weather and your event is in a field or park, your logistics person might plan ahead with bags of wood shavings. Check with your event-site owner beforehand to see if that is a solution they recommend. Orange cones or barricades may help the public avoid some muddy and dangerous areas.

Vendor Evaluation Forms

You will want to collect information from your vendors as to how they did. Information and feedback from them will aid you in drafting your forms for the following year and in crafting a better experience. You can learn both from positive and negative vendor experiences. A sample evaluation form follows.

Vendor Evaluation Form Green Festival 2015

In order to improve our festival, we would like you to fill out and return this form. We hope that you had a profitable experience as well as having fun!

Name of Business _____

Circle your category: Green   Arts & Crafts   Food   Nonprofit

Did you do well enough to want to come back?   Yes   No   Perhaps

Comment on the organization of the Festival. Include what we should consider changing and your comments on ways of improving. Use the back if necessary.

Were the rules that the vendors were required to follow clear?   Yes   No

Were the directions on finding your space clear?   Yes   No

Did you receive an email about your space and other information?   Yes   No

Were you well-treated by event staff?   Yes   No

Can you give us suggestions on where we should advertise to bring a larger customer base to you?

What other vendors could you recommend – either a specific vendor, or a category of vendors?

Other comments:

Please give this completed evaluation to one of the festival staff or send it to Green Festival, 110 Library St., Opswatch, IZ 90000. If you wish you may answer the questions with an email and send them to info@downtownopswatch.com.

Thank you.

13. Food Vendors

Food is a vital component of any special event. The type, quality, and quantity of food vendors are very important to the customer and may increase the length of time and the amount of money they spend at your event. The variety and type of food adds to the customer's perception of the ambience of the event and their overall satisfaction.

Options for Providing Food at Your Event

- **Food vendor**
  You charge them a booth fee. You apply to the county health department or whatever entity in your area is responsible for making sure that food served to the public is safe. The vendors do all of the work, handle their sales; the financial risk is theirs, and they keep the money they made.

- **Catered meals**
  You arrange with a business to take care of the food. You pay them for a certain number of meals, select the menu and they prepare it, serve it, and clean up. You might consider charging the public or selling tickets to

get your money. Any financial risk would be on your part because you were not able to sell enough tickets.

- **Arrange with a nonprofit group to handle the food**

  Before you do this, find out about your health department rules. You might contract with a school, church, or a service club (such as Rotary) to handle the food. Some organizations make their money by putting on a barbecue, a spaghetti dinner, or a pancake breakfast for an event. They do the work, provide the food, and some even use their own equipment. They take the risk and keep the profits.

- **Bake sales**

  Check to see if these are regulated by the same county health department that is responsible for food vendors in your area. They may or may not be. Cookies and brownies may not be considered perishable foods, and bake sale regulations may fall under a different regulatory agency or none at all. Stay away from cream or custard pies, anything that needs refrigeration, or anything with mayonnaise.

- **Do it yourself**

  Your event committee may decide to prepare the food themselves and make the meal the centerpiece of the event. If you have folks with experience in serving large groups and sufficient volunteers to help, this may work. If you represent a school or church with a commercial kitchen and you have folks who are experienced at this, it might be a way to make more money for the event. You would have to have a large enough body of volunteers to pull this off. This scenario has the committee doing all the work, taking all of the financial risk, and reaping all of the profit.

Some events are planned so that the public can move through them fairly quickly. An example of this event would be a job fair or one providing information for seniors. The public doesn't need to have food provided, but the people working the event are stuck. If there are no food vendors at your site, plan ahead to make sure that your captive audience of presenters, booth personnel, and event staff has meals, beverages, and snacks provided. Find a sponsor who will foot the bill or let the folks know ahead of time what the charge will be.

Finding and Choosing Food Vendors

You find good food vendors the same way you find other vendors—you go to lots of events. Take note of which vendors have long lines; it may mean their food is very popular. Ask those you see eating the barbecue, pizza, or snow cone if it is good. Do they recommend it? Choose a likely vendor and try it yourself. If most of your lunch ends up in the dumpster, put that vendor on your "NO" list. Some vendors you will see again and again, year after year. They are probably doing something right! If you are having trouble convincing the food vendors to go along with your theme, nudge them there little by little. It takes time. As your event grows and vendors compete for spots, you have more leverage to bring them into your theme.

For choosing food vendors your criteria might include:
- Type of food or menu appropriate for the event.
- Variety of menu—beverages, main course, snacks, dessert.
- Both vegetarian and meat choices.
- Healthy, low-calorie, low-sodium choices.
- Your expected attendance may determine how many vendors you need and their variety.
- Are there restaurants in the area that will be impacted or could be used to advantage?
- Are there members of your organization that must be offered first priority to become vendors?
- Cooperation and track record of vendor.
- What will the weather be like? Hot soup or snow cones?
- Avoid having more than one vendor with the same menu items. Vendors stay happier.
- Health department criteria. Does your permit cost vary with the number of vendors? Do they count vehicles the same as tents?

> **TIP**   In our county, even pre-packaged commercial food is considered to be under the auspices of the health department. That means that if a vendor wants to sell sodas, candy, tea bags, or pickled asparagus, they will have to jump through the same hoops as the regular food vendors. The rules aren't as long and the fees not as high, but they must comply.

Considerations for Placement of Food Vendors

These may be:
- Space needed for cookers and smokers.
- Fire department and health department requirements.
- Prevailing wind and smoke. Don't put a clothing or textile vendor downwind from the barbecue. They will be very unhappy.
- Physical features of the site—curbs, trees, and so on.
- Vendors that must be next to each other for personal reasons.
- Distance from porta potties and hand-washing stations.
- Size of tents and awnings.

- Electrical outlets and noisy generators.
- Whose application and credentials were received first?
- Customer expectation: "The popcorn guy has always been here!"
- Vendor preferences and requests.

> **TIP** If you are doing tasting—for example at a chili cook-off, find out what the rules are before you get too involved in planning and promoting. The rule might be that only judges can taste, not the public. This makes a tremendous difference in how you advertise the event. If you were planning on selling tastes to raise funds, it is important to know the rules first.

Food Vendors Go Green

Greening your food vendors begins with the jury or process of choosing. Think about the ideas expressed in Chapter One in the Event Design—Practice What You Preach. Practically speaking, in a smaller community your choices may be limited. It may be very unusual, for example, to have access to a coffee vendor that serves only fair-trade coffee.

Go with your best options, encourage your chosen vendors to be green where they can, and plant seeds of encouragement. Let them know about your goals of greening the event. Put together a sheet that tells about carbon footprints, fair trade items, and other going-green ideas. Support even small steps of accommodation to your design.

Find out about and let your vendors know of companies that sell biodegradable flatware and recycled paper napkins. Suggest they use squeeze-mustard jars rather than the little, individually-packaged pouches. Suggest they use cardboard rather than foam containers. Ask vendors to consider how they serve the food.

> If it is important to your theme to make a green statement, consider having the event buy green products for serving food and provide them to your vendors to use. They will appreciate the convenience. Determine what they need for food service. Set your food vendor fee high enough to cover your cost. Add the cost as a budget item. Set up a central condiment table in your food vendor area with flatware, napkins, ketchup, etc. Assign a volunteer to keep the area clean, stocked, and to make sure vendors have the supplies they need.

Your food area should have plenty of trash, recycle, and possibly compost containers. Label the toters with large, easily-seen signs. You might even use pictures as well as words. The easier it is for the public to find the right toter, the better cooperation you will receive in separating types of waste.

In planning for providing food for your event, avoid or be sensitive to:
- Anything that is wasteful
- Anything that uses excessive packaging
- Anything made of virgin petroleum products
- Any waste that cannot be recycled
- Bringing in items from long distances or out of season

The Davis Whole Earth Festival in Davis, CA, sets up their food vendors in an admirable way. The festival is set in the university quadrangle. The food vendors are grouped in two areas. When you order your food and drink, it is given to you using cafeteria-type plates and glasses. You pay a deposit of one dollar for each plate or glass. When you are finished, you empty your food scraps and biodegradable napkin into a bin for composting. You return the dishes to one of the conveniently-located dishwashing stations where the attendant gives you your deposit back.

Visitors are encouraged to bring their own water bottles. There is a freshwater tank truck where you can fill your container free of charge. The whole festival generates very little waste. Their ways are worth emulating.

14. Entertainment and Speakers

Entertainment is one of the major components of your event, both for your expense budget and for the experience of the public. It is the reason many people will come, will stay, and will come again.

Functions of Entertainment

- **May be the main course of the event or one of the main purposes**
  Many events revolve around music. The musical performances may be central with all the other activities playing a supporting role. For an event to raise funds for a school music program, the public would expect to be treated to student performances.

- **Draw and keep a crowd**
  Music says, "Something is happening, something is going on." People will come and they will stay if they like what they hear. When a group becomes known for its excellence, their fans will attend as many of their concerts as they can, and they will spread the word.

- **Provide ambience**

  Any ethnic event cries out for music from that culture. Who can imagine an Oktoberfest without a German oompah band?

- **Enhance theme**

  For a themed event, the appropriate music is almost obligatory. Tradition says that John Philip Sousa marches belong at a patriotic event. Jazz at a Mardi Gras event is expected.

- **Set the mood at the beginning**

  Excitement is built at the opening ceremonies of any event with a heraldic trumpet fanfare. A bagpiper and a drummer draw attention to the stage entrance of the entertainers or the master of ceremonies.

- **Move people from one area to another**

  If you have more than one stage or area of entertainment in your outdoor setting, people will move naturally from one area to another, following the sound, the sight, and their program schedules to experience it all.

What Type of Entertainment Do You Need ?

Begin with your purpose and theme. List all of the possible entertainers that you can think of locally and regionally that might fit. Start your wish list. Put down an estimated dollar amount needed by each of your choices. What length of time do you have to fill with entertainment? What kind of budget do you have?

These are some of the entertainment questions you might consider:

- Will you have entertainment after dinner? A band for a dance? Are you selling tickets for a concert where people will sit and listen? Do you need a string quartet or harpist playing background music, adding to the ambience while people mingle and munch on hors d'oeuvres from the buffet, or while they study the works of art on display?

- Who is the entertainment for? Children? Teens? Seniors? A general audience? Determine who your target audience is.

- Think about variety within your theme—solo performers, ensembles, and larger groups, vocals, instrumentals, dance, and drama. Don't overlook comedians, jugglers, and other variety acts. If your event has an educational aspect, use speakers, forums, or how-to demonstrations.

- If you are planning an event with many days of entertainment to fill, such a Festival of Trees, consider inviting choirs from your community's churches and schools. If you are having a black-tie gala with the tree auction, save the best and most impressive entertainment for that occasion.

For some events canned music with a DJ would be appropriate. Though most of this chapter deals with live entertainment, recorded music should be in the list of options.

The Green Festival committee in Opswatch struggled with what kind of entertainment would be appropriate, affordable, and memorable. There was nothing that said "green" to them about different music styles, so they felt they could use a wide variety of music that drew good crowds.

They thought about the intended audience—the folks most likely to come to an event like this. They chose a variety of entertainment to appeal to their target audience and to the age ranges that they expected. The results were

- A group that put on puppet shows with a green theme.
- Two speakers were scheduled. One spoke about planning meals using local produce. Another gave a presentation on water-wise gardening.
- A local grade school choir with music selections of patriotism, peace, and the great outdoors.
- A John Denver tribute folk group that included songs with a family, earthy, nature feel.
- A Native American flute, drum, and dance group.

They did draw attention to the fact that their stage and sound system were powered by a mobile solar generator provided by Opswatch Power and Light.

Choices for Entertainment

Staged Music, Dance, Drama

As seen in the entertainment functions above, music is probably the first thing that comes to mind when you think of staged entertainment for an event. Within the infinite variety of genres, musicians, and songs, you can find moving, totally enthralling experiences for your event! Let your theme point the way to perfect performances for you.

Within your region, there may be a wide variety of dance groups and schools, from ballet to tap, modern dance, square dance, belly dance, and various ethnic contributions—Irish, Scottish Highland dancers, Hawaiian groups, and Ballet Folklorico. These groups look for positive ways to gain exposure, to gain experience, and to perfect their performances.

The drama possibilities range from skit and melodrama to full-blown theatrical presentation. Coordinating your event with a local theater company's production might bring out the best possible crowds for both.

Music, dance, and drama can be combined into a variety show or an event that stands alone.

 The Will C. Wood High School in Vacaville, CA, has a well-known choir, the Sylvan Singers. Their Madrigal Dinner event in early December is an eighteen-year tradition of music, dance, and drama set in the mythical court of a duke. Each year there are repeat performances, and tickets are often sold out. A restaurant caters the dinner staged at a local banquet hall. Guests are seated at round tables surrounding the dais where the court sits. An open space is provided for dramatic action and dance. A new script is written each year with different characters and settings. Depending upon the talent of the current students, choral, handbell choir, and ensemble selections are chosen. Dances, such as the sword dance or Morris dance, are performed. All of the performers are in costume. The Sylvan Choir Boosters hosts this dinner as one of their major fundraisers for the year.

Storytelling can be yet another possibility—one you might not have thought of for your entertainment. This can simply be an individual with carefully selected picture books reading with great expression to children. It can also be a costumed individual who has created a character and who is doing a live performance—almost like a one-person play. An example of a performer who combines music and storytelling is the Celtic harper, Patrick Ball, who gives his audience folk music and folk tales from Ireland. Check for performers and storytellers in your area that might put on similar types of shows related to your theme.

Walkabout

These are folks who are not scheduled in one place at a particular time, but move throughout the event, gathering a crowd, and performing at will. Jugglers, magicians, musicians, and character skits are only a few of the possibilities. Costumed characters who interact with the public and folks who make balloon critters for children are also walkabout entertainment.

Walkabout entertainers should be given guidelines to work within, schedules of the staged entertainment, and the opportunity to meet the other walkabouts. They need to have an area out of the public eye for breaks and preparation. They should:

- Be willing to work with others to give good coverage of the scope of the event.

- Be sensitive to any area which needs quiet.
- Be active in creating good customer draw throughout the entirety of the event.
- Remain in character while in the public view.
- Know if they are allowed to pass the hat. (Sometimes their performances are called "hat shows.")

Some of these roving-entertainer hat shows have a shape to their performance. The first part of their show is gathering the biggest audience they can. The last part of their show is convincing the audience to be generous when the hat is passed. They don't like their performances interrupted by a parade or some other happening. You can schedule their performances and avoid such interruptions. Or you can let the performers know when and where scheduled parades and activities will be happening. They can time their show accordingly. You want them to be financially successful.

Consider solo musicians, such as accordion players who might fit into your event both theme- and budget-wise. They might be walkabout or staged. They could be performing while the stage is being readied for the next group.

Guilds

Guilds are a marvelous invention that I am including here with the walkabout entertainers. I first associated guilds with Renaissance fairs and the SCA (Society for Creative Anachronism), though they show up in Civil War re-enactments, Scottish games, Colonial events, and living farms of days gone by. A guild is a collection of people who share the same interests, usually about an historical time and culture. It might be the Queen's court, a rag-tag bunch of traveling merchants, a peasant group, pirates, or a group trained in fighting with weaponry of an historical period. Some guilds have created formal nonprofit groups dedicated to teaching history through interaction. Some guilds are local, small groups of like-minded people who just enjoy acting out a certain historical period.

Guilds usually meet periodically to learn about and promote their interest. They attend events and interact with the public. Their event "home base" might display authentic tents, furniture, cooking utensils, and weapons. It is common for individuals within a guild to create a character for themselves, complete with costumes, personal histories, and ways of speaking. Their character interacts with other guild members and with the crowd.

Guilds bring with them their own set-up and activity, greatly enhancing the ambience. A good guild provides authentic entertainment that you don't have to pay for, create, or worry about. They are often helpful in other ways as well. They can add to any processions or parades through your event. They can alert the event staff to problems and security issues.

> **TIP**   Though most guilds work in a very professional manner, it might pay to do some research before asking particular ones to participate in your event. Find out about their goals, other events they have been in, and how they were perceived by other guilds and the public.

A "walk through history" can be created using many guilds from different time periods. The public enters the area where the most ancient history is portrayed and moves through to the most modern. Skills, pastimes, clothing, weapons, furnishings, banners and flags of the different periods make a very interesting, informative event.

If your event is at all related to history, to a museum, or to old-time skills, look at the possibility of finding appropriate guilds to help you. If there are none available, take a lesson from the guild concept, and have interested volunteers create living history for you. Start small with costumes and demonstrations of skill and grow with the guild idea.

Parades

Parade in this context is not a major, close-off-the-streets parade with floats and marching bands. Parades here are processions walking through the event, adding color, pageantry, and drawing attention to some aspect of the event. They might lead folks to an activity. They might showcase the winners of another activity or contest. They may represent different teams walking with their own banners. If you have acting troops, costumed characters, or guilds at your event, you might suggest or require that they become part of your parade.

Demonstrations of skill

Demonstrations have a high entertainment value. They are not just for old-time skills and events with a history theme. Modern-day crafts and arts can be demonstrated as well. Sport or athletic skill can be demonstrated. If you are having an event that is themed with fiber arts, find shearers, carders, spinners, weavers. Set up a sheep-to-shawl contest. Feature sheep dog trials.

> **TIP**   Check with local city regulations regarding animals at festivals and city events.

If your event has a food theme, have cooking demonstrations. Celebrity chefs and 4-H demonstrations may captivate your audience, heighten the educational impact of your event, and raise the entertainment value.

These demonstrations can be placed in line with your art and craft vendors, have a section by themselves, or even be scheduled at certain entertainment areas at different times. The entertainment value of demonstrations of skill can increase if they become something the public can participate in, not just watch.

Speakers

For some events, "talking heads" are a natural. It is good to add a serious or an intellectual dimension to an event. We get tired of fluff and frivolity. Some events can offer a balance—more strokes for more folks.

Among the possibilities are lectures, forums, panels, debates, PowerPoint presentations, and round-table discussions. Your event committee goals will guide you in the choices and format. What information are you trying to impart? Who are the *bona fide* authorities that you might get to participate?

Choose wisely. Have you or any of your committee heard the speaker before? How did you hear about them? Who recommended them? Where else have they spoken?

Pay attention to the logistics of this portion of the event. Can the speakers be heard? Can the visuals be seen? Is the room too bright, too dark? Is the audio-visual equipment adequate, and do the people running it know what they are doing? Is the presentation ready to go at the appointed time, or must the audience twiddle their thumbs while the equipment is tried, adjusted, and tweaked? Has the operator reduced any computer snafus as far as humanly possible?

Is there someone in charge who is not afraid to get things going on time, keep the speakers to their allotted time, and end the discussion? Has that person given thought to introducing the speaker or panel members? Is the introduction accurate and succinct? Have they thought of a good way of eliciting the best questions, perhaps by having the audience submit them on cards to a moderator? Is there water available for the speakers?

Vendor Musicians

Vendor, in this instance, means musicians who are performing in their own booth through the duration of the event and selling their CDs. These vendors are usually in the same area as the other vendor booths.

Because these musician vendors are such a specialized group, you may or not decide to charge them a vendor fee. They should be juried along with the other vendors.

Look for high quality and enhancement of your theme. You will need to coordinate their location with the other entertainment venues. They will be happiest where their sound does not compete with other music or noise.

Finding the Right Entertainment

For all of the following groups, you will find that quality varies, so choose carefully. Within each group are some that are of outstanding quality, some that are ho-hum, and some that are dreadful.

Talent from within your committee
- You may have the talent within your committee or volunteer group to create special entertainment, such as a skit, expressly for your event.

Local groups
- Might be willing to buy into your event and volunteer for the cause.
- May negotiate with you on their fees.
- Might have a public following that will attend.
- May be ecstatic to precede or follow a bigger, name-draw performance.
- Local and school groups may merit good coverage from local media.

School and Student Groups
- Elementary, secondary school, and beyond—all the way to college level.
- May be willing to perform as volunteers for the experience and exposure.
- For school events and some civic events, they may *expect* to be invited to perform.
- Student performers will bring their parents, friends, and extended families to swell the audience.
- May include some surprising, outstanding talent.

Bigger Name Professional Entertainers
- Require a higher budget, but offer a bigger, regional draw. If yours is a ticketed event, a musical group with a regionally-known name will sell more tickets.
- If someone on your parent board, your committee, or a major sponsor has a relationship with the potential entertainer and is willing to set up a performance, going through them may be the way you want to go.
- Check out the entertainers' websites for booking information. Look at their schedules. Are they available? If they are not booked on your event date, are they performing in your area on adjacent dates? If so, you may be able to afford them. Sometimes these are called B list performances. If they are going to be in your area anyway, their agents might want to "backfill" those dates.

- Hiring a celebrity or a famous group may require going through a professional agent and producer. Terminology, rider requirements, and large-scale productions are not for the faint-hearted or the novice. Stars bring with them a whole retinue of support folks whom you also may be expected to pay for. Stars will also bring other logistical issues to your event, such as the need for greater security.

Where do you find the right performers?

Set up an entertainment binder like the one that has been recommended for potential vendors. You can use the same vendor record sheet as is, or adjust it to your entertainer needs.

- Read the entertainment section of your local paper and keep an eye out for upcoming events. Look at different events and see whom they advertise as entertainment.
- Do an internet search. Look for general local musicians, bands, and groups. Also look at the internet sites that list available vendors and entertainers. Look at other events on the internet and see who they have chosen.
- Ask among the committee members, ask your friends, ask your local music teachers. Word-of-mouth is one of the best ways of finding good entertainment.
- Go to events in your region. See who is popular, who draws a good crowd. If the crowd you see matches your target audience, maybe you have found a good match. Get the business cards of likely performers.
- Check street performers in your area. That juggler who entertains the crowds waiting outside movie theaters may be just the right choice.
- In one of your initial press releases, put out the word that you are looking for entertainers.
- Some entertainers will find you. Some performers, looking for other venues in a geographical area in which they are booked, may contact you out of the blue. Check to make certain they are affordable, suitable for your theme, and of good quality and reputation.

Contracts with Entertainers

Contracts may be as simple as applications or be long, complicated documents with rider stipulations regarding hospitality. A contract should include legal language to limit the event's liability. It should state the performance location, the time of load-in or set-up, equipment supplied by event or the performer, the performance length and times, and the break-down time. It should state whether or not they are being paid. If they are to be paid, it should state how much and when they receive their compensation.

A sample of the Green Festival Entertainer Application is shown here. Those entertainers whose applications are accepted will receive an Entertainer Confirmation Email, which is also included.

Entertainer Packet

2015 Green Festival in Downtown Opswatch
Entertainers, Musicians, Actors Packet

The Green Festival Committee is seeking entertainment for Saturday, April 18, 2015. The Festival will have one main entertainment area and several walkabout entertainers to give maximum life and color throughout the festival. We are seeking entertainers in these categories:

1. **Staged performances** to be done at a particular time and place. The main stage will be at the Park Gazebo. Bands, dance groups, singers, and performances requiring a sound system will be featured there.

2. **Walkabout participants** who develop a character and personality— musicians, actors, jugglers, mime artists, and other entertainers. They move through the festival, in character, in costume, and add to the overall ambience. They interact with each other and with the customer. The characters chosen may be invented by the actor or they may be mascots of eco-friendly organizations.

3. **Performer-vendors** who will perform at their own booth where they sell their CDs. These entertainers may request a time slot at the main stage as well.

In almost all cases, these entertainers will be volunteers. Performers unknown to us may be asked to audition or supply video or references. We do not charge an admission fee for our spectators. The hosting Downtown Opswatch Business Association is a nonprofit organization.

All performers must register and sign the City of Opswatch's liability policy form, included in this packet.

If you are interested in any of the above, or have any questions, please call the Downtown Opswatch Association office at (111) 333-5555. For additional festival information, please visit our website at www.downtownopswatch.com.

We thank you for your participation.

George Green,
Chairperson of the Green Festival

2015 Green Festival in Downtown Opswatch (page 2 of 3)

Entertainment Application and Agreement Form

Name/Name of Group _____

Contact Person _____

Address _____

City _____ State _____ Zip _____

Phone (best) _____ (alternate) _____

Email _____ Website _____

Type of entertainment offered

_____

_____

How many people are there in your group? _____

How large of an area do you need? _____

Time frame requested _____ (Circle) AM   PM   Either

Needs (check what applies) ___electricity ___ sound system ___changing room

Other needs _____

Most of the Green Festival entertainment is done by volunteers. Passing of the hat is permitted. Please call (111) 333-5555 if you have any questions.

All entertainers must read and sign the two agreements which follow. This is required by the City of Opswatch, the Downtown Opswatch Business Association and the Green Festival Committee.

Agreement 1: This is a family-oriented event and there can be no profanity or sexually explicit language. Performers cannot be under the influence of drugs or alcohol. Appropriate attire must be worn at all times. As the main contact you are responsible for any others that are with you and may be subject to scrutiny by the DOBA and the City of Opswatch and/or the Police Department. There may be pictures taken of performers for use on the DOBA website and for publicity on this and future festivals.

Signed _____ Date _____

Agreement 2:

NOTICE: The Green Festival, the Downtown Opswatch Business Association and the City of Opswatch do NOT provide liability insurance for the protection of persons, organizations, businesses, groups, spectators or others who may participate in the Green Festival. In exchange for permission to participate in the Green Festival event and any and all related activities (collectively the "Event") THE UNDERSIGNED, on behalf of the below listed organization, business or group, including their officers, employees, and volunteers, and/or myself, my personal representatives, heirs, next of kin, family, relatives, guardians, conservators, executors, administrators, trustees and assigns, ACKNOWLEDGES and AGREES to the following:

1. I HEREBY RELEASE, WAIVE, DISCHARGE AND COVENANT NOT TO SUE: the Downtown Opswatch Business Association and the City of Opswatch, other participants, operators, officials, or any persons, sponsors, advertisers, owners and lessees of premises used to conduct the Event and each of them, their officers, officials, contractors, agents, employees and volunteers (collectively the "Released Parties"), from any and all liability to the undersigned, for any and all loss or damage, and for any and all claims or demands for injury to person or death or damage to property of the undersigned, whether caused by negligence or other legal fault of the Released Parties, arising out of or in connection with the undersigned's participation in the Event.

2. I HEREBY ASSUME FULL RESPONSIBILITY FOR ANY AND ALL RISK OF BODILY INJURY, DEATH AND/OR PROPERTY DAMAGE due to the negligence of other legal fault of the Released Parties, arising out of or in connection with my participation in the Event. I expressly acknowledge and agree that participation in the Event may be of a hazardous, strenuous, and/or physical nature, and may involve interaction with other participants.

3. I HEREBY AGREE TO DEFEND, INDEMNIFY AND HOLD HARMLESS the Released Parties from and against any and all liability, loss, expense (including reasonable attorneys' fees and expert witness fees) or claims for injury or damages arising out of my participation in the Event, but only in proportion to and to the extent such liability, loss, expense, attorneys' fees and/or expert witness fees, or claims for injury or damages are caused by or result from the negligence or other legal fault of the undersigned. Acceptance of required insurance certificates and policy endorsements does not relieve undersigned from liability hereunder and shall apply to all damages and claims of every kind suffered, or alleged to have been suffered, by reason of undersigned's negligence, misconduct, or other legal fault regardless of whether or not such insurance policies shall have been determined to be applicable to any of such damages or claims for damages. These provisions shall survive any termination of the Agreement.

4. I FURTHER EXPRESSLY AGREE AND ACKNOWLEDGE that the foregoing Agreement is intended to be as broad and inclusive as is permitted by law, and that if any portion of the Agreement is held to be invalid, the balance shall continue in full force and effect. I HAVE CAREFULLY READ THIS AGREEMENT AND FULLY UNDERSTAND ITS CONTENT. I AM AWARE THAT THIS IS A RELEASE OF LIABILITY AND A BINDING CONTRACT. I VOLUNTARILY AGREE TO EACH OF THE TERMS AND PROVISIONS HEREIN AND SIGN THIS AGREEMENT OF MY OWN FREE WILL. I FURTHER AGREE THAT NO ORAL REPRESENTATIONS, STATEMENTS OR INDUCEMENTS APART FROM THE FOREGOING AGREEMENT HAVE BEEN MADE.

Signature _____Printed Name _____ Date _____
Please mail or fax to (111) 333-5555, the completed, signed application to:
Green Festival, c/o DOBA, 110 Library St., Opswatch, IZ 90000

You can have agreements about their use of language, dress, behavior, and not smoking in public, if these are important to the committee of a family-friendly festival.

Entertainers need to know:

- What style of music you expect so that they can tailor their performance to the theme. You can negotiate some music selections to enhance your theme.
- Their place in the schedule, how much set-up time and tear-down time they have. They should have time to set up and test their equipment.
- Let them know ahead of time if they are allowed to push their CD sales, who is responsible for sales, and where those sales will take place.

The contract may spell out the following:

- **Sound system details**. Who provides it? Who will be there to run it? If the event producers are supplying it, what type of sound system do they have? How many amps are provided or needed? What numbers and locations of speakers, monitors, mikes, and so on are needed?
- **Stage**. What is the size of the stage space? Is there a need for a stage plot where all mikes, singers, the drummer, and so on are located?
- **Performance space**. Is there a need for a special floor? How about band shells and choir risers? Will there be a backdrop or stage sets?
- **Will the performance be recorded?** By whom? What restrictions are placed on the use of the recording?

All entertainers should receive a confirmation email or letter telling them what they need to know in order to be at the right place at the right time. This information should arrive separately from the contract and arrive in plenty of time.

Entertainer Confirmation Email

Entertainment Confirmation Information   Green Festival, April 18, 2015

Your assigned performing area is _____

Your assigned performance time is Saturday at _____

You may begin your set up on the Gazebo stage at _____

(For Walkabout players)   When you arrive on Saturday morning, please check in at the Information Booth on Main St. near the Carnegie Library or give George Green a call on his cell phone at (111) 987-6543.

As per our agreement you will be paid the amount of _____.

You may pick up your check from George at the Information Booth after your performance and before 5:00 p.m.

(Or— depending on who is getting the email—)

As per our agreement you will be volunteering for this event. You are allowed to pass the hat.

If you have any questions about sound or electricity needs, please call George at the Downtown Opswatch office at (111) 333-5555.

There will be an unloading and loading area of parking reserved for entertainers on Main Street between Park Ave. and McMeen Ave. Please respect the entertainers that need this convenience and don't leave your vehicle there longer than necessary.

If you need a list of hotel vendor rates, please email us back or call as soon as possible, We can fax or email this information to you. If you have any questions, please give us a call. Thank you for participating in the Green Festival.

George Green, Chair of the Green Festival

What Else Do You Need to Know?

Compensation

Sometimes your will to compensate performers is greater than your ability to do so. Generally entertainers are open to negotiation. Professional performers depend on what they earn at events to pay their bills. That being said, some performers do very well by passing the hat. If you find folks who are willing to perform for free, it does not necessarily mean that they will bring low quality, amateur work that brings your event down. Sometimes you will find amazing professional acts that will thrill your audience for free. A great deal depends on geography, timing, and what the entertainers are looking for in experience. Sometimes you are lucky.

Audience space and seating

If your event does not take place in a venue that has fixed seating, you will have to decide how you want to accommodate the audience. Will they stand? Sit on hay bales? Should they bring their own lawn chairs? Will they sit on the grass? Will you provide chairs and tables?

Do you have to pay royalties to use copyrighted music and songs?

Technically, any time licensed music is played in public, it is subject to royalty payments. The performance rights organizations that are involved with this in the United States are ASCAP (American Society of Composers, Authors, and Publishers) and BMI (Broadcast Music Incorporated). They license the work of songwriters, and pay royalties to the copyright owners. The producers of the event are usually the ones who must initiate contact with them and pay the costs. For further information on this, do an internet search. The contact information for ASCAP and BMI has been included in the Appendix.

Lighting

For evening performances, you not only need adequate lighting, but you want lighting that enhances the performances. Bring in someone that knows what they are doing, either because they have worked that venue before, or they have the experience and the equipment to do you proud. Ascertain ahead of time that you have the proper electrical support that their equipment requires. Blowing circuits and having everyone wait, or leave, is not good entertainment.

Another lighting consideration for evening performances is safety. Lighting should be adequate to lead people safely back to their transportation.

Master of Ceremonies

Do you need a master of ceremonies? What will that job look like? Will that role need to be figured into your budget? List the possible choices for this person. Look at their qualifications, their experience, and their suitability for your theme.

Scheduling

Block out the schedule for each entertainment area. If any of your event activities, like a costume contest or impersonation contest need stage time, plug those in. How much more entertainment do you need to fill the time? Decide what your prime times will be, and put your best entertainers where they will receive the maximum audience.

 In the Medieval Fantasy Festival we learned about coordinating the activities the hard way. At our outdoor stage we had a Celtic rock band. Inside the library on the other side of the parking lot, we had scheduled a speaker. The Celtic rock band was heard just fine—in both places—even in the library behind two sets of doors. The speaker was not heard at all and was not pleased. The next year, the speaker in the library was coordinated with the Costume Contest on the outdoor stage. Both activities went fine.

Having more than one entertainment area is a good vehicle for getting the public to move through all of your event space. If there is more than one stage, they must be coordinated and spaced to avoid an obnoxious cacophony of sound.

Don't schedule one band going off stage at 1:00 and another one starting at 1:00. They need time to break down and set up. You might have some acts in mind that can be done during this transition time. Some transition acts only need a small piece of the stage, and some can even be in front of the stage. They might mingle with the audience. If nothing else, you might wish to resort to canned music. Plan ahead and your schedule will work more smoothly and not get farther and farther behind as time goes on.

Logistical Needs of Performers

These are some of the possible amenities that your performers may ask about. Some of these have been mentioned, but now think of them in relation to each of your entertainers and the contract:

- **Dressing rooms, green rooms**
  A place to change clothes, to put on stage makeup. Performers also need a secure place to store instruments, street clothing, and other personal belongings.

- **Preparation space**

  Musicians and other performers need a place to warm up and to tune up away from distractions and other sound. They need opportunity to mentally prepare themselves to give their best.

- **Stage requirements**

  What size space is needed? Do you need to allow space for a juggler's flaming or sharp objects? Do you need to rope off an area surrounding the stage to keep fans back from performers?

- **Sound requirements**

  What kind and how many amplifiers, microphones, and speakers are needed? If the performance is being recorded, what type of equipment is needed and who will run it? Will there be adequate time to set up and tear down each performer's equipment?

- **Lighting requirements**

  Do you need lighting for nighttime performances? Will the power available at your stage location be adequate or will you be left literally in the dark?

- **Risers, chairs, music stands, props**

  Who will provide them and set them up? Where will they be stored when other entertainers are on stage?

- **Dance floor**

  Ballet groups, Irish dancers, belly dancers, and square dance groups will have requirements of different-sized floors and surfaces.

- **Background set or décor**

  Should there be a backdrop or stage set for ambience, as well as to hide stage assistants and paraphernalia behind the scenes? Will the performers have their own stage set or backdrop? Will this work in your space? Does its setup require certain fixtures or hardware? Even if the backdrop is as simple as a flag, how will it be hung? Does the venue have any landscaping, furniture, or built-ins that must remain in place but that may interfere with the entertainer's décor?

- **Inclement weather or Plan B**

  Will you need shade for hot sun, or a cover for rain or snow? Are your sets secure for windy conditions? Will your performers need cold or hot drinks?

- **Information about expected weather**

  If your groups are performing outside and they are not familiar with your area, what kind of weather can they expect during the event dates? Be aware of changing weather conditions during your event. Think not only about how the performance can continue safely, but about the safety of the audience, should the weather become nasty.

- **Technical and production crew**
  Is the set-up elaborate enough to require this? Or can this be done by the performers and volunteers?
- **Parking, loading and unloading**
  Adequate space must be blocked off ahead of time. Are entertainers expected to move their vehicles within a certain time after their performance? (Some may decide to leave their vehicle there and go and enjoy the event.) Who monitors this area?
- **Signage needed**
  Who is performing at present? What is the schedule for this location? Who is sponsoring the stage or performance?
- **Selling CDs of performers**
  Where will this take place? Will the performer handle this or will the event staff?
- **Audience seating / shade / food / amenities**
  If the audience is comfortable they will likely linger. If they are not, they will leave.

Helpful Language and Terms

Here are a few of the terms you might run across in your dealings with entertainers.

Back Line

Instruments and accoutrements that the musicians don't want to haul with them. They want the event to provide them. Typically these are bulky, heavy items like drum sets and bass amplifiers. These needs would be spelled out in the rider requirements.

Contracts

Basic contract with the where, when, load-in time, and compensation details. Parties agree to follow this firmly.

Cover Music

Cover music is music that was previously recorded by someone else. Popular songs and oldies-but-goodies are cover music. The opposite of **cover** is original by the performer.

Rider requirements

Negotiable and required details about amenities and hospitality. Sometimes this is a wish list from the musicians. Many of these items may be negotiated.

Sets

A set is a group of songs or pieces about 45 minutes long. A set is usually followed by a 15-minute break.

15. Smorgasbord of Activities

This chapter is a lengthy, annotated list of possible activities to start the brainstorming process. Choose what is appropriate for your theme, for your intended audience, and for the time of year. Adapt the ideas for your event and let them inspire you to create new activities. Check what will be appropriate with local city regulations and what is compatible with your liability insurance.

Vary your type of activity. There will probably be a lot of things to *see* at your event, but make sure there is also something to *do*. Having the public participate actively—contests of skill, contests of knowledge, races, new experiences—may also breathe new life into an event that might otherwise become stagnant.

Many of the following activities can be designed to create income if your committee chooses. Use your imagination to find ways to have fun *and* raise funds for your cause. This list is intended to jumpstart ideas for your enjoyable and creative event:

Food-related
Vendors with all possible creations of your theme food—from deep-fried, to ice cream, to smoothies, to casseroles; eating contest, cooking contest, canning or

preserving exhibit or contest, cook-offs, cake decorating, community pancake breakfast, community BBQ, pie-eating contest, pie-throwing contest, soup supper, watermelon seed-spitting contest, pumpkin chucking with a catapult, auction of boxed suppers.

Vendor-related

Arts, crafts, imports, hand-crafted merchandise, green, eco-friendly vendors, vendors who can demonstrate their skills, vendors who have a hands-on activity like dipping candles, a "make-and-take" activity.

Décor-related

Window decoration contests, banner making, store or business decoration, employee costume contests.

Holiday-related

A festival of trees, pictures with Santa, holiday boutique, tree lighting, living crèche, Mardi Gras bash, haunted house, trick or treat, scarecrow contest, Jack-o-lantern carving, Easter egg hunt, May Flower baskets, Martin Luther King, community service day, sleigh rides, New Year's dance or Halloween ball.

Festival of Trees

A festival of trees is a very good money-maker at Christmas time for a charity such as a children's hospital, homeless shelter, or the support of a local symphony. There are many variations on how these festivals are organized.

Basically, decorated and lit trees are donated by individuals, groups, or businesses. Guidelines are set by the festival committee for tree skirts, tree type and size, lights and so on. Some donated trees even include props, gifts, and toys. A space allotment is given for each donated tree. Decorations are wired on or fixed securely. A day is scheduled for groups of volunteers to set up and decorate their trees. At the end of the event, trees are auctioned off and delivered to the buyers.

If community building is one of your goals, set up your festival with volunteers or groups supplying and decorating the trees. School classrooms, churches, individuals, and civic organizations plan and prepare their trees. These volunteer creations have charm and beauty, are satisfying, and are worthy of great pride.

Some festivals of trees go in a different direction. They have designer-decorated trees which are sponsored by corporations for a healthy donation price. Professional decorators work their magic. Traditionally these trees, too, are auctioned off.

A festival of trees will require an exhibit hall or large area with reliable electrical power. Volunteers sign up for either mini- or full-sized trees months before the event to begin planning their theme and decorations. Some festivals provide the trees, some don't. Some festivals have added divisions of decorated wreaths, miniature trees, or gingerbread houses.

Other activities like a Christmas boutique, a bake sale, pictures with Santa, and entertainment, will bring in more donations and volunteers for the cause. One unique idea is to have a food-tree raffle. This tree is decorated with food donations and gift certificates donated by local grocery stores and restaurants.

To make their money stretch as far as it can and make the most money for the cause, festival producers seek sponsors and donations to cover space, publicity, tree delivery, and programs. Some festivals do charge admission to view the trees.

Be aware of tax laws regarding write-offs. Because the money goes to charity, you might think that the whole check, written for the tree being auctioned, could be deducted. That is not necessarily so. The creators of the tree should provide the cost of the tree and the decorations for the purchaser. If you have questions, consult a CPA or tax person about your responsibility for needed information.

For more information on activities surrounding a festival of trees and planning one for your area, do an internet search for Festival of Trees. You can read the stories of other communities' festivals, gain information from their press releases, and perhaps even view their guidelines and applications for a tree.

Demonstrations
Blacksmithing and other old- time skills, skateboarding, gymnastics, Border Collie sheepherding, ballroom dancing, fiber arts skills, chain-saw sculpting, square dancing, roping, jousting, fencing, archery, ice skating, hawking.

Exhibits
Students or classes highlighting activities and learning content; 4-H displays to highlight club and attract new members; shows of historical artifacts from theme of celebration; displays of low-water-use landscaping.

Children's activities
(Also see Chapter 16.) Commercial carnival with rides, fish pond, bowling, diaper derby, pitching pennies, egg-on-a-spoon race, relay races, storytelling, pony rides, face painting, make a flower garland for the hair, apple bobbing, hat or ring toss.

TIP   Try different things for the children. We discovered that, while the children might be interested in an Earth Day activity booth with science experiments, the parents were looking at their watches impatiently, saying that such and such entertainment was going to be starting in a few minutes. Many adults weren't willing to stay with their children for the activity, so they all had to move on.

On the other hand, the Maker Faire goals included hands-on activities. (See Appendix for Maker Faire.) They had great participation in these "learning skills" booths for both children and adults. Some even charged for the privilege.

Other amusements

Haunted house, human chess or checkers, mazes, labyrinths, door prizes, dunk tank, pillow fight, poker rally, wine or beer tasting, fireworks, word search puzzles, crossword puzzle on event theme, scavenger hunt, treasure hunt, tree identification or similar hunt, white elephant exchange, film festival, showing a movie related to your theme, guess the number of objects in a container, a fifties sock hop, mud-wrestling.

Theater entertainment

Punch and Judy show, melodrama, plays, skits, impromptu theater, comedians, pantomime, community theater production.

Walkabout entertainment

Jugglers, stilt walkers, clowns, mimes, magicians, storytellers, bubble fairies, costumed characters, one-man band, Keystone Cop routine, character skits.

Contests

Whisker contest, trivia contests, spelling bees, essay contest, poster contest, scarecrow contest, pumpkin carving or painting contest, hairy foot contest, watermelon seed spitting, Ratapult, costume contests, rodeo skills, dioramas, science projects, whistling, hog calling, kite flying, poetry, photo contest, fishing tournament.

Art activities

Art show, art contest, chalk art, poster or postcard photo contest, art gallery walk.

How to do an art contest or show

Make arrangements for a location which either has good wall space for hanging art work or room for several panels for hanging art. An indoor location is best, as wind, sun, and inclement weather are not art-friendly. The size of location will help determine how many pieces you can accept.

About five months before the event, send out a "call to artists". This call should state that your event will include an art show with a particular theme. You may say all media is accepted. If your space is limited, you may wish to put a size limit for each piece or limit the number of pieces each artist can enter. State when art is to be submitted. Send fliers to art groups, put the notice on your website, and do press releases. The call to artists should name the person to contact for more information.

About two months before the event, send out reminder fliers with the information. More detailed information that doesn't belong in a press release can be given here. You may wish to say that all two-dimensional art must be ready to hang, framed and wired. All art must be original by the artist, photographer, or sculptor.

An Art Show Agreement form is included in the Appendix. You may wish to state that "Every possible care will be taken to protect the art during the show. The (name your event) cannot assume any liability for any loss or damage to the art. Artists assume all risk and are responsible for any insurance they might desire."

The day before the event you will hang the show. Set a particular time period to check in the art and have the artists register their work. They should fill out a form with their name, address, phone number. The form will need spaces for the title of the work, the media used, the price that the artist has put on the work, and the artist's signature. If the work is not for sale, use NFS (not for sale). Assign a number to the form which will be repeated on the tear-off stub on the bottom. The stub on the bottom should have the artist's name and the title of the work. It should give the time when artwork must be picked up. This must be presented at the end of the show to reclaim artwork.

The event staff or committee can reserve the right not to show a particular work of art if it is not family-friendly, if it does not fit the theme of the event, or if it is a political statement when the rules have said that those would be unacceptable.

Some art shows are judged by a panel of judges or artists. Some have the public determine the winners by voting. The attendance may be bigger at the show if people are aware that they can vote for the winners. If you decide to let the public vote, have a table with ballots, a box to deposit them, and signage giving directions. Prizes may be ribbons, art supplies, or gift certificates.

You may state that unless arrangements have been made previously, all unclaimed art will be subject to a daily storage fee if it is not picked up during that time. After 14 days (or however long you want to put) it becomes property of the event and may be sold or disposed of as the organizers see fit.

On the day(s) of the show make sure that at least two people are present at all times to answer questions and watch the art. They may point out the directions for voting on the welcome table.

At the end of the show when people are picking up their art, match stub with art and return the work. Have enough people so that it goes smoothly.

With all of the information you have collected, build your database for future shows. Keep a record of buyers as well as artists. Contact them about shows at subsequent events.

Talent Contests
Impersonation contests, *American Idol* take-off, talent show with a theme.

Shows
Cars, motorcycles, quilts, dog show, Christmas trees, fashion show, costume show, flower show.

Pageants
Beauty queen, king and queen for event, junior pageant.

Health-related activities
Free blood pressure check-up, tour of emergency vehicles, CPR demonstration, fun run, healthy-eating-menu giveaways, stretcher or gurney race, wheelchair race.

Activities involving animals
Animals draw attention and fascinate people of all ages. Pet parade, educational exhibits with birds of prey, spiders, bats, or snakes, pony rides, petting zoos, cow plop bingo, draft horse exhibits, blessing of the animals, dog agility demonstrations.

If you are doing an ethnic event or one related to a country, have animals on hand from that area—Scottish animals or South American animals. If the event is from an historical period (for example, the Old West) have horses, longhorns, a rodeo. If your event is about textile arts—have sheep, angora goats, llamas, angora bunnies, and silkworms. Find a craft person who knits with dog hair for a very interesting, informative exhibit. Many dog breeds lend themselves to this art.

Just think of the animal-related success story of Punxsutawney, PA, with Groundhog Day. Yearly they receive national recognition and publicity from what they do with the old-wives' tale. They have made the event into theater with tuxedos, top hats, and a well-trained groundhog. Create your own animal idea, borrow one from mythology, or choose a well-known fable and do a spoof on it.

Musical entertainment

Bands, ensembles, choral competition, barbershop quartet competition, accordions, song-writing competition, choir sing-a-long, Karaoke. Put together a community choir, rehearse for several weeks, and do one or more concerts.

A choral society may have a summer sing-a-long evening that functions as a fundraiser and as a promotion to gain new members. They choose a major work, arrange for a location (usually a church), and for an organist and soloists. They borrow music scores from churches and college music departments. They invite singers from church choirs and other community choirs in the region. The charge is low (perhaps $10 for general and $5 for seniors) to sing that one evening along with the choral society members. The turnout for the sight-reading sing-a-longs might be 200-300. The evening consists of warm-up, practicing some of the more challenging spots in the work, and a complete run-through of the work followed by coffee and refreshments. This social gathering afterwards has prominent tables with opportunities to learn more about the choral society, sponsorship opportunities, and to buy the society's CDs.

Parades

Costume parade, main street parade, pet parade, decorated bicycle or tricycle parade, theme parade like the Pasadena Tournament of Roses Parade®.

For a model on parades, do an internet search of City-of-Plano-Parade-Planning-Guide. You should find an interesting PDF file that lays out parade planning in detail. Since this document is done by the city's risk-management division, it is helpfully skewed in the direction of safety concerns.

Races, tournaments and athletic activities

Sack races, tug of war, three-legged races, Dachshund races, 5K run, Olympics, horse riding, obstacle courses (maybe precede one race with a "Blessing of the Feet" ceremony), bicycle races, jumpathons, marathon, bikeathon, triathalon, walkathon, rockathon, danceathon, golf tournament, tennis tournament, shuffleboard, dart tournament, rubber duck or turtle races (Heads up—these might have to follow raffle rules in your state.), billiard tournament.

TIP If you are using a walkathon or another event to raise money, you will need to draft a pledge sheet. The name and date of the event along with a space for the participant's name should be on top. There should be spaces for the pledger's name, contact information, how much they are pledging (per mile or flat rate), ceiling amount, total amount due, when the pledge was paid, and if paid by cash or check. It simplifies collection matters if the flat-rate pledge is collected when pledgers sign up.

Money-making

Jail fines for folks not wearing an event button, raffles, 50-50 raffle, photo-ops with celebrities, showing a popular film, create a cookbook with event theme or an ethnic or cultural recipe book, rummage sale, used-book sale, wishing-well fountain, silent auction, handyman skills auction, roulette wheel, auction of donated items, catered dinner, home tours. (A brief description of how to do a silent auction is given in Chapter 17. Samples of paperwork for it are included in the Appendix.)

Grad nights

Many communities have adopted this idea for an all-night graduate party, keeping seniors safe and sober. Resources abound on the internet for entertainment, interactive games, and contests. Grad night committees work all year on their theme, activities, and raising funds.

Wine Strolls and other alcohol sales events

See Chapter 17, Fundraising Activities for ideas and discussion.

TIP Be careful with liability. Limit your risk with careful planning. Research your local regulations and policies.

Educational, serious, thoughtful
Speakers, Bible study, forums, panel discussions, debates, lectures, documentary film showing, book fair, book discussions, essay contest, job or career fair.

Pre-event events
Activities to do ahead of time to make money—design commemorative mugs, glasses, design T-shirt, tote, collect recipes and sell cookbooks.

Planning ahead for contingencies is smart. For the Medieval Fantasy Festival and the launching of a new activity, the Ratapult, planning ahead really paid off. (The Ratapult is described more fully in Chapter 17.) We had promoted the Ratapult heavily. We had presold hundreds of dollars' worth of entries. There was a great deal of excitement about the debut of the Ratapult in which we planned to launch toy, stuffed, costumed-puppet rats from a catapult on Saturday and a trebuchet on Sunday. I had made arrangements for both siege engines to be there both days.

What I didn't expect at all was the traffic accident that wiped out the catapult. On its way to our event at 4:00 a.m. on Saturday, the catapult was hit by a driver who ran a stop sign. He creamed the catapult and its trailer, damaging the van hauling it as well. The catapult was totaled. (I would have liked to have heard the conversation between the driver and his insurance company: "You hit a what?") We pressed the trebuchet into service a day early and the event went not only smoothly, but was wildly successful. The moral of this story is to always have a back-up siege engine!

Activities built around the strengths of your organization
Museums may have walking tours of places of historical note in the area; art galleries may have an art gallery tour. The board of the local symphony might set up home tours with musicians (small ensembles or soloists) performing. For a school event, classrooms may display projects. Science fair exhibits could be held over for an Open House.

Green activities
Clean-up day for your school or church grounds, or the downtown area, or a creek or park area, planting trees or plants, beginning a community garden, green demonstrations: composting, plant propagation.

One community in a less affluent neighborhood had a marvelous idea for a green event. They had a neighborhood clean-up day. Children and adults were armed with garden tools, vinyl gloves, and trash bags. They picked up trash and got rid of weeds. At the end of the clean-up children were given a new school backpack filled with supplies. Kudos go to the organizers and sponsors. The children got the satisfaction of a clean neighborhood and some needed items for school. Participants come back from year to year for a job well done.

16. Children's Games and Activities

When you go to other events, make a point of looking for children's games and activities. When you go through the midway at a fair or carnival, look at the games and see which ones have the potential to be improvised and adapted to your themes. Which ones are the most popular and why?

Following are sets of game ideas that could be adapted to your event. You are only limited by your imagination. Use graphics and language to tie them to your event theme.

Don't try any of your games for the first time at your event. Experiment first. Try them out with children. Find out what works and what doesn't. What is fun, and what is challenging? Encourage new ideas. As you try out the games, make up the best set of rules. What wins? How many tries do you get? How far away do you have to stand when you throw an object? What is the prize you win? If you decide the answers to these questions in the experiment stage, your event will move more smoothly. Keep records of your rules and how the game is set up. The records will be invaluable to the person who is in charge next year.

Set the level of difficulty to the children who are playing. Be consistent and fair. Remember it feels good to win. Game leaders can hand out prizes for good tries, too! Plan ahead to get appropriate prizes.

Game leaders should have tried all of the games, had a chance to learn the rules, and answer the frequently-asked questions about each game.

Ideas for games

- Throw a ball or some object to knock over cans or other objects. The targets can be still or moving. They may be set up on shelves or on hinged uprights. They can be moving on a current of water.
- Roll a cabbage or ball against bowling pins or uprights of some sort.

 TIP   A handy hint—if you wrap your cabbage with plastic wrap and tape it with clear packing tape, you won't have as much mess to clean up and your "ball" will last longer.

- Throw a ring to encircle the target. The target can be an upright pole or series of poles, or it may be a narrow-necked bottle. It may be a rubber ducky moving on the water current. If you want more challenge, throw a Mardi Gras-type beaded necklace to ring an upright.
- Throw a dart to pop a balloon or to stick in a target area like a regular dart game. If pointy darts aren't appropriate for your event, use balls or beanbags with Velcro® to stick onto a target.
- Throw beanbags at a board with holes. The graphics on the board go with your theme. Different-sized holes would garner different points. Put the hole with the most points next to holes with minus points or a "game-over" hole.
- Throw smaller objects into various containers. Use plastic, gold coins to throw into a pirate's chest. Use marbles to throw into shallow bowls. The distance from the targets, the opening on the container, and the size and weight of the object will determine the difficulty.
- Use pennies to pitch onto a painted-target table. Get popcorn from your favorite kettle-corn person and see who can throw the most into a container several feet away. If you have a tub or wading pool available, throw objects into shallow, floating bowls. Sink an object. Roll balls into numbered slots. The slots will be part of a graphic that fits your theme.

At the Solfest, a green festival in Northern California, a very popular booth featured footbags (Hacky Sacks®) thrown at graphics of oil wells. The booth was about ten feet square with hanging fabric making up three walls. A barrier at the front kept the player at a certain distance from the targets at the back. The oil-well graphics were on one side of an L-shaped wood piece secured with hinges to a two-by-four board. There were maybe four or five such hinged wood pieces, about 4 x 6 inches in size, on each of three boards. These boards were supported by two stepladders set about seven feet apart. When an oil-well-derrick graphic was hit, it tipped on its hinge, bringing up a picture of an alternative-energy form. The fellow in charge of the booth kept up a constant chatter about the need to reduce our dependence on oil, and teaching about other forms of energy. When someone hit the target, it gave him more opportunity to talk about energy. The prize for the hit was a puzzle of the earth. He gave it to the winner with the admonition of helping put the earth back together. There was no charge for playing. You could play more than once, but after your turn, you had to go to the end of the line. It was surprisingly hard to hit the target. The dedication, personality, and patter of the game leader really made this game a great success.

- Set up a target area on the ground with about 25 squares, each square being about a square foot (12" x 12"). Number each square randomly from zero to nine, duplicating numbers until all squares have a number. Each player gets three beanbags and must throw all three, one at a time. The object is to land on squares so that the total number adds up to nine. Set the throwing line at a challenging, but not impossible, distance.
- Set up a memory-pairs game for wee children.
- Based on croquet or miniature golf, use mallets to make a ball go through a suitable obstacle course.
- Use small squirt guns to put out candle flames or drive a Ping Pong® ball or balloon in a wading pool along a course or toward a finish line. When the squirt gun is empty, your turn is over. Have two children playing opposite each other try to get the same balloon over their opponent's line. Play in an area where it is okay to get wet. Play only with parent

permission about child getting wet! Be careful with the candles and do not create a fire hazard.

- Throw beanbags onto a chalked-out target area on the ground.

 We did an adaption of this called Rat-Tat-Toe for the Medieval Fantasy Festival. We chalked out a large tic-tac-toe target. We used giant rubber squeaky rats—black and white—for the Xs and Os. On your turn, the object was to toss the rat into a chosen square as if you were marking an X or O. Play continued just like a regular tic-tac-toe game until the game was won. The challenge came when the rats bounced where one had not planned!

- Some children may enjoy coloring or activity pages that are themed to your event. Low, child-size tables and chairs are good if you want the children to stay and participate in this.
- Sidewalk chalk can be provided for children to create their own art on the streets.

 TIP   Some communities are very picky as to what constitutes graffiti. Before you schedule a chalk-art activity, make sure that it will be acceptable and not banned as graffiti.

You will notice that several of these ideas involve water. Use common sense where you locate them. If you want to try one of the games with a moving current of water, ask one of your local plumbers to help design and build the game and sponsor it!

17. Fundraising Activities and Merchandise

Activities That Become the Main Event

Activities at your event may not only provide fun, but provide income as well. For example, you might capitalize on hobbies or sports that are popular. These may become the bulk of the event itself. People will pay to do something they already enjoy. Some of these activities are:

- Running or walking
- Cycling
- Golf

Many groups use golf tournaments as fundraisers. Check with local golf courses and inquire about other local golf-tournament fundraisers. Are they successful in your area? Is it an idea that is overdone and therefore would not bring in as much money? Would the course be willing to share their expertise in setting it up? What kind of expenses would there be? What kind of entry fee would your market bear? Rather than charging players a fee outright, would it work better to have players get sponsors and bring in their own money?

One chamber of commerce held a Century Classic bicycle ride. This was a fun ride, not a contest. A pre-event event of a spaghetti dinner ($10) was held the night before. Pre-registrations taken here for the ride were $40. The chamber organized the course of 100 miles with rest, water, and food stops. For those wanting a shorter ride, a 100K (60 miles) and a 35-mile ride were offered. The chamber arranged for all of the permits, signage, food and drink, and logistics. Each cyclist paid $55 unless they had pre-registered. They got an enjoyable, scenic ride, and a great sense of accomplishment. They made new friends and contacts. At the end they enjoyed a tri-tip barbecue.

The Ratapult

The Medieval Fantasy Festival came up with a good idea we named the Ratapult. A crowd favorite, it connected two areas of the festival, enhanced the medieval theme, and made a lot of money for the event.

The festival committee had heard of great fun in pumpkin chucking with catapults and trebuchets (medieval siege engines). Along with the fun, though, came safety concerns. They didn't want anyone in the crowded downtown to get hit. They certainly didn't want to clean up the mess of smashed pumpkins. They didn't like the idea of wasting a food product, and anyway, pumpkins were not in season in the spring. Someone remembered that rats had been a huge problem in medieval times, spreading the bubonic plague known as the Black Death. Rats became the ammunition for the trebuchets.

From Folkmanis® the Medieval Fantasy Festival committee found a brown mouse puppet and decided this would be a marvelous choice for the Festival rat. (Information on Folkmanis will be found in the Appendix under Resources.) This puppet was cute, was priced satisfactorily, and manipulated well as a hand puppet. The festival sold them for $20. That price entered the rat into the costume contest and the launch. The committee presold rats to folks, encouraging them to make costumes for their entrance into the festival contests. There were some splendid creations. The rats were appealing enough so that parents and grandparents were buying them for their grandkids with no intention of bringing them back at event time. Profit from those sales also helped the bottom line.

The festival organizers knew that many of the folks at the event would not have heard of the costume contest ahead of time, but still would want a rat. The festival committee made little capes with numbers for rats, stuffed the rats with nylon knee-highs filled with split peas for weight, and sewed them shut. They sold them during the event as "Same Day Rats" also for $20. During the second year of the event, people who already had their rats paid only a $10 entry fee. Sales of the Same Day Rats were brisk.

Each rat was launched from both the catapult and the trebuchet. After each launch, two jesters ran out into the "field" and rescued the rat, placing him carefully on a small stretcher. The DJ added suitable sound effects.

The Ratapult had several different, related activities besides the launch:

- There were two rat costume contests. One was for the general public. The handlers walked with their rats on the red carpet, while the judges pondered their choices.
- The second rat costume contest was for businesses. The business rats were each given a number and gathered in a window display. The winner was determined by popular vote during the event.
- A Pied Piper Parade. This procession of handlers with their costumed rats followed a bagpiper through the streets of the festival.
- A competition (entry fee $20) for those who made their own trebuchets. (All of the local high schools have a trebuchet-building contest incorporated into their physics classes.)
- Rubber, squeaky rats were used in the children's activity called the "Rat Hurl". This was simply lining up children of about the same age and seeing who could throw their rat the longest distance. A local business had donated prizes of gummy rats for this free activity.

Beer and Wine Sales

For some events, serving alcohol is the primary money-maker. There is a reason why art and wine strolls, jazz and brew festivals, and Oktoberfests are so popular. They succeed because people are willing to spend money on alcohol at events: large profits can be made on drinks.

If you serve alcohol, you must follow your local and state rules and set up your logistics accordingly. These may be:

- Liquor license stating the total area of tasting stations. In some cities the license must be posted at all sales locations. Know your local and state regulations.
- Volunteers trained in serving alcohol and checking identification. They know what to look for and can tell when someone is close to over-

imbibing and becoming a danger to themselves or others. You and your servers should follow the rules meticulously. Keep your event safe from potential liability caused by accidents and folks under the influence.

- Contact wineries or stores to find donated wines. If they can also supply sales people or staff who know and can promote the wine, you will benefit from this.
- Determine the number of tastes and ticket prices. Know how many ounces should be included in a taste and where that amount comes to on a glass.
- Arrangements for glasses and cups. Some regulations require that different cups are used for soft drinks from the ones used for liquor.
- A main booth where tickets are purchased. At this location IDs may be checked and the purchasers given a bracelet or some proof (that can't be transferred from one person to another) that identity has been verified.
- Wine-tasting stations for each winery or group of wine choices.
- Wine-tasting stations need ice, large tubs or coolers, waste buckets, corkscrews, towels, and signage.

Think about the ambience you want to create. You want the public to be comfortable and stay a while. There is something satisfying about relaxing with friends, eating, drinking, and listening to good music. A beer garden may provide that. You may need to set the beer garden in a roped-off area. You may be required to contain the alcohol within that area.

If you sell alcohol at an event that is publicized as family-friendly, will it make a difference? If you serve alcohol, it may change the flavor of your event. Some scout troops will not be available to help as volunteers. Some venues will not allow alcohol on the premises. It may cut a little into a family-friendly ambience. You may lose a few folks on the socially-conservative edge and you may gain many more who enjoy the drinks.

How will your logistics be different if you serve alcohol? Will doing so provide more potential sponsors like wineries or brewing companies? Will you need more security? If so, make sure your security personnel know about checking IDs and the rules about serving alcohol. Don't believe that your volunteers will follow the rules. You must pay attention to what they are doing.

TIP   The rules for your paying sales tax on items sold, including alcohol sales, differ state by state. Be aware; find out what your responsibility is and don't be caught off guard with what you owe.

Wine Glasses, Brew Mugs

Serving alcohol gives you opportunity to make money from selling wine glasses and beer mugs. Find a sponsor to pay for the glasses. Charge the sponsor enough to pay for the glasses and give you a profit. Have the event logo on one side and the sponsor logo on the other side.

In some areas the liquor license or event alcohol-serving rules dictate the size of the glass that can be used. Know this before you order your favorite glass style.

Do you want the glasses engraved? Sandblasted etchings cut the design into the glass, giving it a classy look. Some companies offer imprinting directly on the glass. Look at samples and ask about pricing. Get all of the information from a few dealers before you make the decision.

If you are doing wine or brew tasting, the public likes a commemorative glass. Price the tastes and the glass as a unit. The customer receives a map of what wines are available and where, a schedule of any entertainment, the glass, and the appropriate number of drink tickets. You might offer a raffle ticket at the same time.

Food For Fundraising

Having a pancake breakfast or a spaghetti dinner could be the main event, one of your event activities, or it could be a pre-event affair to make money for your event. It takes a crew to decorate and set up, a crew to prepare and serve the meal, and another crew to clean up. A commercial kitchen will probably be needed—either at a school, church, or community center. Know and follow the rules of your local health department. Serving a meal makes more sense for your group if they have volunteers with experience, a venue without rental costs, and the equipment needed to serve large numbers.

The Heron Festival at Clear Lake State Park in California has an omelet brunch. The Festival involves a lot of physical activity—boat tours, birding, and hiking. The location is out in the boonies with few amenities available. Offering a scrumptious brunch of "create your own omelets" with a variety of fillings, a selection of fresh fruit, pastries, coffee and tea for $15 per person, is not only appreciated, it is a good fundraiser as well.

One of the good things about food for fundraising is that meals involve community. Drinking and breaking bread together have good theological implications. Some of my fondest childhood memories involve church suppers. They are legendary, as we know from Garrison Keillor and his Lake Wobegon stories. It is the time when all generations come together in the preparation, the meal, and the cleanup. There is a task for everyone. When the Lutheran church in our community had a smorgasbord as a fundraiser, there were a lot more than Lutherans eating together. When a church in Pennsylvania had a pot-pie fundraiser, they brought in big crowds and big money. If the Rotary Club sponsors a barbecue fundraiser after the Fourth of July parade, they can fund many of their programs.

Bake Sales

Many organizations use this idea to their advantage. Baked goods are donated. Reasonable prices are set and all of the funds raised are profit. A bake sale goes over well where people are congregating for other activities. Make a note of items that sell best. Suggest more of those for the next sale.

If the bake sale is tagging onto an event with food vendors, the health department may close down your bake sale if they see it. They have rules about commercial kitchens, how things are prepared, how food is protected, and how it is handled. On the other hand, some health departments have no jurisdiction over bake sales, especially if the food sold is non-perishable, such as cookies or fudge. Check to see what your local regulations are.

If a business or nonprofit organization would like to have a bake sale in conjunction with another organization's event, the polite thing to do is to ask the event organizers first. It is tacky and rude to just appear with a table of goodies, with no by-your-leave, and start selling, especially if the other event has food vendors.

Pre-Event Events

You might choose to have a pre-event activity to raise money and also raise awareness before your main event. A meal put on by your group may raise funds to cover the cost of the main event.

Another function of a pre-event is to educate folks and help them prepare for the main event. You might do a workshop on costuming or help contestants prepare for a contest.

If you have several bands or music groups coming for a weekend event, have a concert giving a teaser of each on Friday night. Make this Friday night part of the contract with your groups. You might sell tickets to the public. Use this preview concert to promote a bigger crowd at your event.

Passports

Passports are little booklets created to fulfill several functions.

- They provide a way of getting people on the street into the stores so they might become customers, while adding to the ambience of your event.
- Ads in the passport sold to businesses provide a source of revenue.
- They can be used to encourage participation in a variety of booths.
- A passport showing completion of certain visits or tasks can be turned in for a chance at a raffle prize at the end of the event. This is one way of getting names for your mailing list.
- If you sell the passport to the customer for a dollar or two, they provide even more revenue. If you decide to sell them, make sure they have value. Maybe they have a coupon for a free water bottle or a coupon for a free spin at a spinning wheel of prizes. Maybe they include tear-out forms for depositing at certain locations for raffle prizes.

The Passport created for the Medieval Fantasy Festival resembled a real passport. It was a small 16-page booklet, a quarter of a page in size. The cover was navy blue with gold ink for the logo and lettering. The passports, each with its own number, were sold for two dollars each. They contained the rules and listed the raffle prizes with directions for entering. Several of the pages had "visa" spots to stamp when raffle tickets were deposited or store coupons used. There were several redemption spots to be stamped. One was for a free bottle of water, one for a discount of festival T-shirts, one for a discount on costume ball tickets, one for free popcorn when a ticket was purchased at the local theater, and one for a free spin on the festival roulette wheel for prizes. The centerfold pages had a map of the downtown area listing the locations of all offers. The fonts chosen, the "visa stamp" boxes, the map and graphics were carefully done in the theme of the festival. The passport was accompanied by two regular pieces of colored paper that had all the coupons and raffle slips. The decision was made not to have to cut into the booklet. It was convenient, and the passport could remain intact as a souvenir.

A word of caution: We tried this the first year of our festival with great success. The passport was attractive and had lots of coupons and offers in it. We did it again the next year and the whole thing bombed. The public can be fickle. They want a new gimmick.

T-Shirts, Tote Bags

A good design is crucial to success in selling shirts. Start with a good design and work in your logo, the event name, and your location:

- Who are you targeting as buyers, and how old are they? If you want teens to buy the shirt, you might not have the same design or body style as if you want geriatric hippies to buy the shirts.
- Will you have children's shirts?
- Is your design aimed at men, women, or will it appeal to both?

Some events have had T-shirt design contests. You are at the mercy of the entering artists if you do this. You might get lucky and end up with a fabulous design. Or you might be stuck with a poorly-rendered "least of several evils" for a design. You can hardly change the rules at that point. Spend time and find good people to be responsible for the design.

Use good-quality shirts

This is not a place to economize with shrink-out-of-shape, cheap garments. You will have your name, logo, and design on them. You want them to hold up with pride. This shirt also advertises your event—a walking billboard. People will be wearing them out and about. Those who see the shirt may ask about the event. You will especially be aware of this if you wear the shirt to other events when you are looking for vendors and entertainers.

For green events, you might wish to consider these questions.

- Will your audience be offended by the use of mass market T-shirts produced overseas?
- Choose a product that is consistent with your goals. Is it important to avoid polyester and choose cotton, organic cotton, bamboo, or hemp?
- Will you want regular inks? Eco-friendly dyes? Soy-based inks or paints?

Other questions to answer

- Will you want only crew-necked shirts? Short or long-sleeve? Sweats? V-necks? Pocket tees? Scoop-neck tees for the ladies? Children's tees?
- Do you want the design printed on the front or the back?
- Do you want the year imprinted on the T-shirt for an annual event? If you do not put the year on your shirt design, leftovers from one year can be sold the next. This is the call of your committee.
- Do you want some shirts to be designated as staff, either by big letters or a different-colored shirt?

Other choices to make

Think about your community and your target audience when you are setting the size breakdown. Do not neglect the 2X and 3X sizes. The printer may have good suggestions, as well. You might start per dozen with one small, one medium, three large, four x-large, two 2X, and one 3X. Ask the printer where the price breaks are on quantities. Ask if you can mix shirt styles within the quantities (for example short-sleeved T-shirts and sweatshirts).

Before you decide on a shirt color, find out about its availability in the sizes you want. Not all colors and shirt styles are available in all sizes. Not all printing processes work on both light and dark shirts. Check with your printer before you set your heart on a certain color.

Can you add tote bags into the mix?

For totes, what style? Muslin, canvas, new recycled material, gussets or not, long handles, short handles? If totes are to be used at a convention where folks are walking and need to carry literature or purchases for a long period of time, over-the-shoulder, long handles are appreciated. If the totes are touted as reusable grocery bags, use short handles.

Printing processes

There are several ways to print shirts and tote bags. Talk with several printers. Find out what processes they use. Here are the options:

- **Silkscreen**

  This is the main stay of the industry. Each color is screened separately. There may be a set-up charge for each color. Not suitable for photos or many colored designs.

- **Silkscreen – CMYK process print**

  The ink used in this process is translucent. Overlaying the colors makes more colors— just like the colors produced by your computer printer. If the design is being printed on a dark-colored shirt, first a white under-base should be screened. This process has the potential of building up rather stiff ink areas.

- **Heat Transfer**

  The design is printed on special paper and then is transferred by pressure and heat onto the shirt. The transfer may have a tendency to crack over time. On the other hand, the design will not lose its sharp detail while the life of the transfer lasts. The design may have a plastic feel.

- **Discharge Printing Process**

  Uses water-based ink. The ink is made to de-activate the dye used on natural fabrics. In lay terms, it bleaches out the shirt color and puts down another color. The shirt will be soft because there are no layers of ink built up. The ink dyes the fabric. It works well on dark garments. It may not work on synthetic fabrics.

- **Full color simulation process**

  Good for printing photos or many colored designs. The design will not be as detailed as your photo. The knit T-shirt fabric cannot be printed with as many pixels as paper. The paint goes directly into the fabric. Over time, with wear and washing, the details of the design will become softer. As cotton is worn, lint comes off the fibers and your design loses detail.

  One advantage of this process is that the color can be tweaked on the computer before the design goes into the printing process. A sample can be printed and the color tweaked again. Brightness and dullness can be controlled.

- **Digital print**

  This will probably be the way of the future. The equipment is very pricey at present and the technology is new. The cost per shirt is therefore high. The advantage is that they can do one shirt only or a huge quantity.

For any of the processes, work with your printer. Ask to see samples of what the printer has done in the processes you are considering. Show the printer the design you are using and ask what the colors will look like when they are printed.

Size of the design

Find out about the size potential of the design itself. How big can it be on an adult shirt? On a child's shirt? If you are doing both adult and children sizes, you may have double screen charges and set-up costs. Check and negotiate. Don't assume that the printer knows what size you want the print to be on the finished product. You may be surprised when 244 shirts come in with a tiny 6" x 6" design when you expected full screen of 12" x 12". Specify the size before printing begins.

Programs

Printed programs have these functions

- Add to the ambience and theme of the festival
- Become a souvenir for attendees
- Congratulate winners of pre-event contests
- Educate about the event and celebrate its history
- Give tantalizing information on entertainers, workshops, and activities
- Highlight your cause
- Move people from place to place within the event
- Promote your downtown, your school, or your organization

- Provide list of performers, selections they are performing, and their photos
- Provide revenue by selling advertising space to businesses
- Provide space for rules of contests and activities
- Recognize sponsors and supporters
- Show a schedule with times and locations of activities

Programs can be as simple or as elaborate as you wish. They can be a one-page map and schedule of activities, or they can be glossy, full-color booklets. They can be free or you can charge for them. In this electronic age, you can even put them on your website for the visitor to print out before they leave home.

Think about the design of your event and find a suitable format that will coordinate with your theme, perform the functions you want, and remain within your budget.

If your program is to include advertising, somebody has to chase and sell ads, get the ads designed in the proper format, get them proofread, make necessary changes, meet the deadlines, and collect payment. This always takes more time than you think it will. In some cases you will have to chase back and forth between the advertiser and the printer to make sure the specifications are met.

If you know how much it will cost to print your program, how much of the area will be reserved for program content, and how much given to ads, you can figure what the cost per ad should be to cover the entire cost. To make a profit on your program, you may have to look at and adjust your choice of printer, printing method, number of pages, or your ad prices.

Set the ad prices high enough at the beginning to cover your expenses. Ad placement matters. You can charge more for spots on the inside and back covers and on pages that are referred to most often, such as the schedule page. If part of your sponsor menu includes a free ad in the program, you must allow for those free ads when you determine the purchase price of an ad. If the program is to pay for itself or even turn a profit, be sure to retain enough ad space for sale to make that happen.

If there is someone on your committee with graphic design and layout skills, you may be able to do the programs yourself and print them at a local copy place. If you need a printer that does offset printing or your committee does not wish to tackle printing on its own, check with several printers and get bids. See if any will be an in-kind sponsor, either for the whole program, or for the privilege of including an ad within the program.

Work with your printer to get the best quality program at the best price. Make sure that you understand enough of the technical language so there won't be surprises. What kind of format will your copy need to be in for the printer? If you want to include pictures, are there additional costs for screening them? Are there additional charges for folding, collating, stapling, and trimming? Don't forget to figure sales tax on the printing process in your budget.

 TIP   It is a good idea to have the ads that come in electronically sent to you as well as the printer. Request hard copies of the ads, too. You may not have the technical expertise, but you may be able to spot proportion issues and color-to-black-and-white issues. Keep on top of the process to ward off problems before it is too late.

If the program will have ads solicited from businesses, what do you need to know to get them right the first time? I absolutely hate to have a printer call me and tell me that there will be additional charges because some items weren't to their specification. The budget has been set, the bid awarded based on the dollar amount of the bids received, the event is a week away, and they have you between a rock and a hard place. It is far too late to change. You really are stuck with paying more, and it is very irritating.

Create an *ad sell sheet* in collaboration with your printer. On it put as much information as needed so the advertisers provide you with ads in the right size, the right resolution, and the right proportion. It is helpful to include a to-scale sketch of the layout of the program with the schedule, map, entertainer information, etc. blocked out. Number and price the available ad spaces on the sheet so the advertiser can choose the one that will work best for them.

It makes life much easier for the ad chaser, the printer, and the advertiser if the ad sell sheet includes the following information about the event:
- The 5 Ws— What, Why, When, Where, and Who
- Event contact information – who and how to contact
- Contact information for the person in charge of ads who will be able to answer technical questions

The ad sell sheet should tell what the program will look like.
- Overall size and format of program
- Number of pages
- Black and white, or full color

The ad sell sheet should give all of the information the advertiser needs to know to decide if this is a good place to spend advertising dollars.
- How many copies will be made?
- Where and how will they be distributed?

The ad sell sheet should give the advertiser all of the specifications the printer requires to make the final product look good:

- Specs for digital and hard copy submission should be included. You can charge a fee for ads not meeting specifications.
- Will there be any additional charges for services, such as screening photos or other conditions listed below?
- What are those services and how are they priced?
- The deadline for submitting ad copy.
- The email address for digital submissions.

Digital and hard-copy ads should comply with the printer's requirements. "Camera-ready" means nothing will have to be changed or adjusted. For example, the advertiser might hand you a business card and tell you to "put this in." All business cards are not created equal. Some will meet camera-ready requirements, but some will incur graphic-design service charges.

The following conditions in the original might present problems:

- If the business card they want reproduced is not done on white stock or has a background color, it will not look clean on the page and may need to be re-typed.
- If there is a gradient of light to dark.
- If the ad is in color and you are printing in black and white. For example, colored letters on a colored band are legible in full color. When you change everything to grayscale, the gray of the letter may be the same as the gray of the band and the letters disappear.
- If there is artwork or a photo—they generally require screening.
- If a business card is vertical but your spaces are horizontal.
- If size is out of proportion for the space of the ad.
- If the original copy has a low resolution, the final result may be pixilated.

If you can get the printer to look at each ad when it comes in and tell you what the problems will be, you are lucky. It will save time and grief in the end. Printers are busy with many projects. As ads and copy come in, they put them in a project folder. They probably won't look at them until they are ready to lay out the program. Then it is too late to go back to the advertiser for different copy. The deadline is past.

Billing for ads should be included in the process and not chased after the event is over. When a person commits to buying an ad, give them the invoice. When they see and okay the final proof, collect the money. The basic price of their ad size, placement, and any special features like color should be clear from the sell sheet and should be on the invoice. If their ad might need graphic services, the invoice should note that an up-charge of X amount of dollars may be incurred. It would be courteous to check with the advertiser before these services are performed.

> Help in greening an event may come from surprising discoveries. While working with a printer for a finished program of legal size (8.5" x 13"), I found they typically printed it on 11" x 17" paper and then trimmed it down to size. I had assumed that they would begin with legal size paper. This meant that the paper used was much more expensive, there was more labor, and there was a lot of waste involved. Find out what your options are, the reasons for them, and choose your printing options and your printer accordingly.

Proofreading the Program

Whether you do your own program or have a professional printer, more than one person should proofread the program when it is ready to run. ***Somebody other than the person who drafted the wording and laid out the program should proof it as well.*** They should go through it meticulously, checking spelling of names, phone numbers, and addresses in ads, and so on. Your printer may have re-typed the information on some ads with the intent of making the information neat, clean, clear, and legible. You don't know how the printer will use your electronically-submitted program data, either. In the computer world of copy-and-paste, PCs and Macs, and different desktop-publishing programs, there is lots of room for error. A printer might just re-format your copy, keeping all of your punctuation and spelling intact. On the other hand, they might re-type it, opening the door for errors.

Miscellaneous Ideas

50 / 50 Raffles

This is a simple raffle to set up. Sell tickets at a predetermined price. Use the type of ticket where one part is deposited in a container and the purchaser retains the other part. At the scheduled time the one winning ticket is pulled out of the box. The winner gets 50 percent of the total amount. The event keeps the other 50 percent.

As with any other raffle activity, check your state policy on raffles and gambling. Design your event accordingly. Sometimes the difference between being able to do a raffle or not has to do with what words are used to announce it or promote it. If you are inquiring about a 50/50 raffle, make sure that you indicate it is for nonprofit. Your state might have guidelines that would change the percentages allowed. Not following the rules could result in unpleasant audits and fines.

Silent Auctions

Items to be auctioned off may be donated artwork or items donated by businesses or individuals. You may ask your vendors for donations. Draft an agreement form for the person donating the item to fill out. Keep good records.

Items should be displayed attractively on tables. In front of each item place a sheet with the name of the item, its value, and what the starting bid will be. The suggested starting bid may be fifty percent of the declared value. Under that put spaces for name of bidder, phone number, and bid. Set a time for the close of bids. After bidding has ended the staff will announce the winning bids and take payment for the items. If the winners are not present, make arrangements to secure the item for them and call them for pick up. (A silent auction agreement form and a bid form are found in the Appendix under Other Event Documents.)

Educate and Make Money at the Same Time

Museums and theme parks have gift shops. People want items that will tell them about the history and how and why things were done. They want items with the logo or with the mascot on them.

 At one Renaissance Faire I attended, I thought the producers were missing out on a chance to make more money as well as provide more education about the Renaissance period. We got to the fair before it opened, bought our tickets, and proceeded to kill time for about an hour with a lot of other people. This was the perfect opportunity for the producers to have a booth with books that told about the Renaissance period, about their costumes, customs, and historical figures. It was the perfect time to buy postcards and T-shirts. It was the opportunity to buy sunscreen and bottled water. We really wanted a cup of coffee after driving for so long to an area out in the boonies where there were no amenities to speak of. A shopping area before the entrance would have paid handsomely. If your goals include making profit, strike while the iron is hot. Sell them some postcards and books! Have books for the children as well. Dover Publications™ does paper-doll, coloring, activity, and clip art books about historical periods. (See the Appendix under Resources for Dover information.)

Playing Cards

If your poster, logo, or shirt design lends itself to being put on the back of a deck of playing cards, that may be an opportunity to make money for your organization.

An alternative playing-card idea—if yours is a community event or deals with well-known people— choose 52 people to put on the face of the cards. Would it be a popular enough deck to sell well? Don't forget the jokers! Check into the cost effectiveness of this idea. How many decks would you have to buy to get a good price and make it worthwhile? Can you sell that many?

Costume Ball, Dance, Concert

A costume ball is much more fun with a theme. A period event or the Halloween or Mardi Gras season make this easier. People enjoy the chance to dress up. Require costumes at your event. Creative decorations will add to the festivities.

Balls, dances, and concerts potentially have large expenses but can be good fundraisers as well. It is very important to start with good financial information to build your budget. Investigate thoroughly and determine if there would be enough interest to attract the kind of crowd you need in order to succeed financially. Your ticket prices should be high enough to cover the cost of hiring a band or DJ, renting a facility, advertising, decorating, serving food and drinks, and all of your other costs. Your ticket prices should also be high enough to cover the money you need to raise for your charity.

Golf Ball Drop

If your venue is in a large, outdoor space like a golf course, you might have a golf ball drop. Each ball is identified with a name and number. They are dropped by a helicopter over a target. The one that comes closest to the target wins. I have heard of this being done with golf balls being sold for $100 each. A substantial prize was given. This idea makes more sense if the helicopter services are donated.

18. Logistics

Organize your event. Draw up a chart with all of the logistical needs, a timeline for their completion, and the person responsible for them. Chunk leaders might do a chart for their own activity as well.

When the event actually arrives, you may wish to have a very detailed chart with times, locations, tasks, and persons responsible. You may decide to do it in chart form or, like the Green Festival, an agenda form for their last-minute logistics meeting. (This last-minute logistics meeting agenda is found in the Appendix.)

This chart or last-minute logistics list is the working set of papers used as the festival gets underway. All of your core leaders should have copies. Prior to, or as part of your logistics meeting, it is helpful if there can be a walk-through of the event by the chair people and the street bosses. Visualize where things will go, how people will move from one element to another, and where there might be bottlenecks, need for signage, or something changed or added for safety reasons.

During the event, the committee chairperson should have his or her schedule cleared of all responsibilities. They should not schedule themselves for any tasks during the event because they will be very busy dealing with questions, putting out fires, dealing with the media, and observing how all of the parts and the whole are working. The chairperson will probably rack up more mileage during the event, start earlier, and end later than anyone else.

The Venue for the Event

If you have rented a facility, check it out well beforehand.

- Find out where the restrooms are, the light switches, the outlets, how to work the coffee pots, and so on.
- Do they have a person on hand or on call during the event to answer questions? What happens if the toilet backs up, the ice machine isn't working, or a circuit breaker goes?
- Who will have the keys? Who is responsible to open and lock up?
- Do they have any restrictions about what can or can't be done in decorating?
- When can you get in to set up?
- Find out where access doors are for deliveries, and note specific directions to pass on to delivery drivers.
- Who is responsible for taking out the trash? Where does it go?
- Think through all of the activities that will happen at the location and any logistical questions they suggest.
- Where is the best location for loading and unloading? Do they have a hand truck that you can use?

Legalities

Insurance

You will need to discuss with your insurance agent the kind of coverage you need for your event. If you don't have an insurance provider, check around, listen to recommendations, check the internet, talk with several companies, and request bids. You will need to be covered for accidents involving vehicles, anything that would present a danger by falling, anything that would make people sick, anything that would damage property, that would start a fire, or cause someone to trip. If you serve alcohol, you will need to covered against any alcohol-related incident or accident.

Check with your venue. Some venues allow the purchase of a rider on their insurance for the event.

 Plan ahead, structure your activities in such a way that safety is first, and do your best to be proactive to prevent any possible unfortunate occurrences. Then go ahead and get the insurance.

Some activities clearly are more dangerous than others. Pyrotechnics, carnival rides, glassblowing demonstrations, carriage rides, petting zoos, jump houses, jugglers with sharp or flaming objects, blacksmithing, pony rides, and rock-climbing walls are among the activities that carry a higher risk of an accident. You may require leaders of these activities to provide you with a certificate of insurance, naming your event, your parent group, and your city as additionally insured.

If your event will be held outdoors, you might look into the possibility of weather insurance and see if it would be cost effective.

Incident Reports

You should create a form, or copy one from your city, to be used as an incident report. (A sample incident report form is found in the Appendix under Other Event Forms.)   When an accident happens, when there is property damage, when someone is hurt or becomes ill, or when there is an altercation between folks at your event, you will want to document it. You can also document any incidents that didn't result in damage or injury, but had the potential.

Make sure that you get names and contact information of all of the parties involved and any witnesses to the incident. Your form should give you space to tell what happened and what anyone did about it. This is part of the common-sense protection for your event host and staff should any nastiness, controversy, or litigation follow. It also gives practical information in structuring subsequent events to avoid the same pitfalls. Your staff and volunteers should be aware of the incident report sheets, know where to find them, and know where to turn in completed forms. Inquire about city requests for copies of reports. If there is an incident involving injuries to a paid employee, you may have to deal with workman's compensation reports. It is a good idea to know what the process involves before the event—it may never happen, but at least you are prepared.

Working with police, city officials, and fire departments

Cultivate a positive relationship with these folks. An us-versus-them attitude with the fire, police, and city officials will not be productive. Treat these powers-that-be as friends, and assume that they are working with you in partnership to keep the event safe and ongoing. In this way you won't have grumbling going on behind your back. You might even see these very influential folks aiding in the promotion of your event.

Do you need to schedule a meeting with any of these officials? Are there any permits, business licenses, or other requirements? Who has to be in the loop: school boards, corporate boards, or city council? Who are all the entities who should be in the know to smooth the path for the event?

Some communities require a representative of the police department to review the event and its security plan. If you don't have security issues addressed in your plan, the event organization may be charged for additional officers and overtime.

TIP   Our City of Vacaville is typical in that it requires a Special Event and Temporary Use Permit Application if the event is open to the public and will take place on city property—parks, public streets, city buildings or other facilities. Depending on the event, there may be a meeting required where the event producers meet with representatives from the city, the police department, the fire department, public works, someone from ADA, and the city's risk management team.

Permits

What kind of permits will you need? Do you need a business license, a permit to sell alcohol, a permit to close streets? Find out what is needed for your particular event and put it on your timeline and your list of logistical responsibilities. Figure the needs into your budget.

To get an idea of a city's process of permitting for special events, do an internet search for "(name of city) special event permit application." You will find an array of different examples to check out.

Parking

You are very lucky if there is adequate parking nearby your event site. Visitors get one of their first impressions of your event by how hard or easy it is to park. It can color their experience. Good signage is of great importance here. It will direct folks where to park and where the event is located.

You will need parking for
- The public
- Staff and volunteers
- Vendors and entertainers
- Regular customers and employees of area businesses

If you are in a commercial area, the businesses will want to keep their regular customers from being inconvenienced. You want the public to find parking easily nearby so they will participate in your event. You want the vendors to leave the nearby parking spaces for customers, but not have to park so far away that they can't use their vehicles for extra storage of inventory. You will never make everyone happy, but you can increase the percentage of those who are.

Vendors may be assigned a specific parking area. Decide if and how you will enforce that assignment. Your street bosses can direct them to the proper area. Vendors arrive early enough to snag the best spots, but those with any business sense will leave the closest spots for the customers. Warn vendors ahead of time if parking in any of the areas they might choose is restricted by time during your event. They won't be pleased with your event if they get a parking ticket.

Check first before you tell groups of people where to park. For three years of the Medieval Fantasy Festival we had told vendors to park in a certain bank's parking lot with no problem. The fourth year we told them to park there again. Oops! New manager—and we had not checked. She said the vendors' cars would be towed if they didn't move them right away. Big interruption, major inconvenience for vendors, egg on our face, and unhappy people. In the end no one got towed, everyone moved, and we learned to ask first.

Your staff and volunteers should be most amenable to carpooling and parking at greater distances. They also arrive early enough to get the best spaces, but they should understand best why they should not take them.

Will you need remote parking? Where will it be and how will you bus the folks to the event? What will the schedule look like in order to keep waiting at a minimum? Who will direct parking at the location? What kind of security will you need and who will do it?

Solfest is an annual green event promoting solar living that takes place in Hopland, CA, far from the beaten path. They urge folks to carpool. They set up a SpaceShare on their website and have a free shuttle from their parking lot. They encourage visitors to bring their own plates, water bottles, and utensils. They provide facilities for composting and recycling. They provide free refills for water bottles. They lead the way in greening an event.

Street closures, barricades

If you plan to close off streets for your event, you will need barricades. Ask if your city's department of public works will supply the barricades at the same time you are getting permission to close streets. Ask about the procedure and timeline for getting and returning them. They are bulky and heavy. You may need to find a volunteer with a truck.

You may need other barricades or stanchions and ropes for cordoning off certain areas. Use barricades to hold signage for your event as well.

Security and Safety

You want the public to enjoy the event and you want them to feel safe. You want the vendors and performers to concentrate on doing their thing and not worry about theft or danger. You want the vendors to be able to sleep at night and not have to worry about their booth at the event. You don't want to worry about vandalism and extra expense, let alone the hassle.

TIP   During the event it is best for all those involved in logistics to be able to communicate with each other conveniently and quickly. At the beginning of the event, give a cell phone list to all of the people who are responsible for different areas. Print the list on a small card to fit in their badge holder or pocket. List the person, task, and cell phone number. (Do not include anyone's number without their permission.) Use two-way radios for those who don't want to share cell numbers or who don't have a cell phone.

Possibly your security can be handled by volunteers, school campus security, or a civic group. You might be fortunate to have a radio club or a scout group that is accustomed to handling daytime security at events. If you need security guards or bouncers because of liquor liability or requirements of the facility rental agreement, you might contact off-duty policemen. What is the customary arrangement in your community?

If you decide you must have professionals, contact event security companies in your region. Ask other events for a recommendation. For an outdoor, overnight event, this may be one of the major expenses. You need trustworthy folks.

If the event area is fenced off and you charge admission, you will need to have control over who goes in and out—door or gate control. You will need to monitor the perimeter.

Renaissance fairs have vendors, their employees, staff, volunteers, and entertainers "gate listed." Before the event begins, a list is created of all of the folks who need to enter. As they go in and out, their identification must be checked. If they aren't on the list, they must pay to get in and they are restricted from certain areas. Further checking is done if the fair has a camping area within the grounds for the staff and volunteers. Only those who are signed up for the camping area are allowed in. Tighter security is necessary for these areas where people must leave their belongings while they are working the fair.

Daytime strolling security personnel may or may not be in uniform or identified as staff. They keep their eyes open for problems, potential problems, drunks, lost children, shoplifters, suspicious activity, and other challenges. Some walkabout entertainers or guild folk may be used to aid in this function as well and will keep their eyes open and alert you to problems. Make sure that your volunteers and "eyes-on-the-street" know who to contact should they see a problem.

TIP   If your theme has the potential for people carrying weapons or including a weapon as part of their costume, you will want to have a policy regarding weapons. Most Renaissance fairs say, "All weapons must be sheathed and peace-tied". This means that swords, daggers and so on, are tied into their scabbards, preventing someone from trying to snatch them from the owner and brandishing them, and also preventing the owner from being an idiot show-off and swinging a sword around in a crowd. Vendors of weapons at your event should be aware of the policy, and in everyone's best interest, supply and do peace-ties for their customers and for anyone else. Your security team should know the policy, know how to do peace-ties, and carry a supply of them. If you have a pre-event meeting that involves the police department, let them know of your policy and steps to implement it.

You may have other weapons issues, too. If you plan to use black powder (for example, shooting cannons at a pirate event or Civil War re-enactment) or if you are having a skit with an Old West shoot-out using guns with blanks, these must be cleared with police ahead of time. Some demonstrations, like archery, will need clearance (double meaning intended) and forethought as well.

If you are charging your vendors for booth space (or not), you don't want unauthorized vendors strolling through, selling stuff without permission. Some are pretty brazen. We have even had people try to set up in someone's numbered space. When confronted, they told the volunteer that they had called the office and cleared it with them (which we knew wasn't true). Quick work by the street boss resulted in their eviction. Daytime security folks can escort these bold opportunists away from the event.

Anyone with a security or staff shirt will be fielding lots of questions. Help the event go smoothly by bringing these folks up to speed. They should know what is going on, and be familiar with the venue and the procedures for dealing with any possible problems.

For the Medieval Fantasy Festival we had overnight security from 6:00 p.m. to 8:30 a.m. We had three to four guards all the time. Between the hours of 11 p.m. to 2 a.m. when the patrons were leaving the downtown bars, we increased the guards by two. The vendors either cleared out their merchandise, leaving their tents and fixtures, or they completely closed their booth with sides and secured them. A few vendors who had made arrangements slept overnight in their booths. The security company and the police knew about the overnighters ahead of time.

Amenities

You may conduct internet or yellow-page searches for local sources for table rentals, portable toilets, security fencing, solar generators, imprinted items, grant sources, and security companies.

Porta potties

Generally you will need regular units, a smaller number of ADA units, and some hand-washing stations. How many people do you expect to attend the festival? The company you rent the facilities from will give you an idea of how many units you need. A more unbiased figure might be requested from the health department folks. They may have regulations about the number of units required per number of employees working at the food booths.

TIP   Your area may have several competing porta potty rental companies. You may contact each one and find out what they provide and what their costs are. Get bids for what you need. They may be willing to negotiate a deal with you, especially if you are responsible for more than one event during a year. It is worth a try.

Porta potties may be delivered the day before the event. You might wish to padlock them until the early morning of the event. This way they will be fresh and clean when the event starts. The rental company may give you extra paper and seat covers. Check periodically during the event to see if those supplies are needed.

TIP   Custody of the porta potty padlock keys should be given to a responsible person who will arrive very early for the event and who will not lose the keys!

If your event lasts more than one day, request and make certain that the units are pumped at night. At one of our festivals the company didn't pump. I don't know if it was from laziness, poor scheduling on the rental company's part, or a misunderstanding. Almost every evaluation we received said, "More porta potties!" The following year we went with a different company.

Garbage and Recycle Toters

Make sure you have ordered enough. Place them near food vendors, exits and entrances, restrooms, activity and entertainment areas. Think about the kind of garbage that will be generated and where the public might expect to throw it away. If your event is more than one day, you may want someone to shuffle the toters around in the early morning to get emptier ones where they are needed.

For events on public streets, you may want to think about not using the city waste receptacles already in place. If their use is allowed, they will be full. You can't move them, and they are inconvenient for volunteers to empty. Businesses in the area will not want overflowing trash receptacles waiting for a regularly scheduled pick-up several days after the event ends. I have seen this problem solved by covering over the city receptacles with plastic and tape. Right next to them are placed recyclable cardboard containers lined with plastic bags. These are easily emptied by event volunteers.

During the Medieval Fantasy Festival we added signs to the garbage toters. A rat with the words, "Litter causeth the Plague. Please use the trash bins," in an Old English font added to the ambience.

Electricity

Who is responsible for supplying power for entertainers and vendors? How will this be accomplished? Are you having night activities? Is the area well lit? Are there plenty of lights for the stage area? Will the electrical system in place support the amount of light and sound equipment needed? Is there a back-up plan?

 It may be possible to supply some of the power needed with mobile solar generators. You may be able to find a contractor or solar installer in your area that is willing to supply power to run a certain activity in exchange for an ad in the program or a free vendor booth. Check to make sure the power is dependable, how much power is generated, and if it could be conveniently located near where it is needed. Power by a mobile solar generator will be unique and interesting to some folks. It may also make a statement about greening your festival.

Water

Where will vendors get water for their food booths and for their animals? If you are depending on outside spigots, have you permission from their owners? Is there a special "key" to turn on the water? If so, who will be responsible for keeping the key and making sure that it is there when needed? Is the spigot considered "food-grade"? Is the supply enough? Does it get messy and muddy around the spigot? Plan ahead to deal with this.

Disposal of Greywater

If you are having food vendors this might be an issue you have to deal with. What do they do with their greywater (dishwater, the water and melting ice from their drink coolers, and their hand-washing water)? If you don't make it easy for them, they will dump it in the nearest flowerbed or down the storm sewer. Heaven forbid, they may even send it down the toilets and cause sewer problems! You can usually rent a greywater tank from the porta potty companies and they will take care of it for you. Be sure to include the cost of this rental when you figure your food vendor fees.

Tables, Chairs, Shade

People appreciate the chance to sit down after they have been at a festival for a while. You need tables and chairs—especially in your staged-entertainment areas, your beverage areas, and your food-vendor area. If the weather is hot and sunny, you may need to rent tables that have umbrellas. If the public is comfortable, can rest, has shelter from the elements, and is entertained, they will move from area to area and stay longer and spend more money at your event. If you don't take care of their needs and wants, they will leave much earlier.

Other Amenity Considerations

Think about how much time you want the public to spend at your event. What creature comforts must you consider to have them spend the whole day? What needs will the weather dictate to you? Do you have to think about sun, heat, cold, rain, wind, coat-and-bag checking, remedies for tracked-in snow, mud or water, blowing leaves, danger of wet floors, shade, ice, or bottled water?

Hospitality

First Aid

- Who will take care of it? Will you have a nurse, emergency medical technician, or a paramedic?
- What are their credentials?
- What supplies are needed?
- Where will the first-aid station be located? Is there appropriate signage? Is the location noted in the program?
- Are your staff and volunteers aware of the first-aid station?
- Is your first-aid kit or first-aid booth equipped to handle cuts, bruises, heat exhaustion, sun stroke, sunburn, CPR, dog bites, insect bites?
- Do you know what you legally can or cannot do?
- Don't be afraid to call 911. It is better to get the right response quickly in many situations. You might include the local police number on your cell phone lists. 911 cell phone calls may go to a different dispatch station than your local police and the response time may be longer.

Accommodations

Will you have speakers, performers, first-aid folks, or VIPs that will need lodging? Make these arrangements ahead of time, preferably when you first know they are needed. Double check close to the event to make sure the information has gotten to the right people and everything is in order. Be very clear about who is to be billed. If the event is paying for the room, you don't want the speaker hassled, charged, and the event embarrassed. You don't want to have to go through the process of reimbursing the speaker.

If the event is one where participants stay overnight in a campground, college dorm, hotel, or church, the hospitality chunk deals with all of the reservations, security, safety of the participants, and the related logistics this lodging will entail. For some multi-day events, vendors, volunteers, and performers may expect camping on site or a place to park their RVs. Check with local officials well in advance of the event to see if this possible.

 One of the important tasks of the Medieval Fantasy Festival hospitality folks was to provide the water wagon during the event for volunteers and vendors. We had a rolling ice chest full of bottled water. Periodically we would pull the wagon around, handing out water to the vendors and the volunteers. Some years when the weather was cold, we took around morning coffee. We were welcomed gladly, obtained a lot of information and feedback as to how it was going, and gained major appreciation from the vendors who were not used to being looked after at other events. The small amount spent on cases of water and ice was negligible compared to the good will generated.

Hospitality / Rest Area for Volunteers / Staff

If at all possible, set up a special area for volunteers and staff to take breaks. A place to sit down and put their feet up will contribute to their comfort. Shade, warmth, quiet, or whatever is needed will be appreciated. Water and maybe snacks could be provided.

If you are at an event without food vendors, you may need to provide snacks, drinks, and meals for your presenters and volunteers. Budget for this or find a sponsor who will be willing to cover the cost. Caution! To watch your bottom line wisely, you may want to provide tickets for food.

Welcoming

Making the public feel welcome and giving them the information they need to fully participate in the event are also the jobs of the hospitality people. They will be responsible for registration tables and information booths. If lodging is needed, they will have that information for the public. If accommodations are part of the arrangements with entertainers or speakers, they will take care of those details.

Physical Set-Up

Signage

Signs let people know what is going on, where, and when. It lets them find the amenities easily. Good, easily-read, well-placed signs keep your volunteers free to do other tasks. If signs are attractive, designed with your theme in mind, they add to the overall ambience and sense of satisfaction. They may even make people smile.

At some point in your planning, consider every activity and the signage needed. Plan to use some signs year after year, and create them with that in mind. Some could be laminated. Remember the logistics of storing signage.

Large, vinyl banners can be a good way of advertising your event.

- Sometimes one of your sponsors will offer to do banners for free. This could be wonderful, but you might have to give up control over the appearance and content of the signs. In some cases the emphasis is on the sponsor's product, not the event. Is it worth it?
- It is a good idea to ask permission before displaying vinyl banners. Highway departments don't care how much your beautiful signs cost. If they don't want them there, they will remove and dispose of them.
- Some cities have regulations about temporary signage. Be aware.
- You might find out about vinyl banners with changeable lettering so you can change the date and use them again.

TIP   Whenever a downtown establishment was going out of business, I would ask them about their A-frame signs. If they did not have plans for them, I asked if they would like to donate them to our downtown association. We were able to collect several at no charge over the years. With a fresh coat of paint (also donated), we had good sign boards.

Moving Stuff to Where It is Needed

On the day of the event, work begins before the sun is even up. If you have the luxury of setting up the night before in a secure place, you are very fortunate. If your event is a street fair, set-up begins as soon as the streets are blocked off. The challenge is to get everything where it is needed so volunteers can begin working their magic. Big stuff goes first.

The leader or leaders of an event need a fix-it kit available to them. If the venue is large, duplicate the kit and have kits stored in a secure place at the strategic corners of the event. The kit should include pens, pencils, scissors, notebook, duct tape, markers, safety pins, band-aids—anything you think you might need. A program and a list of your volunteers and cell phones are also handy. A fanny pack or backpack is also a good investment for the leader, who otherwise might set things down where they could be snatched or forgotten.

Setting up the event will be much easier if you have planned and organized ahead. For each activity your organization is responsible for, set up a computer check list of supplies, prizes, forms, signage, and equipment needed. During the week before the event, double check your lists, update them, increase the font size, print out each list on a separate page, and tape them to boxes. Collect the supplies in the box, checking them off as you go. As the lists are checked off, you will see what you might need to borrow or buy. If items like scissors are borrowed, mark them in such a way that it makes it easy to return them. Your activity leaders for each chunk should be responsible for seeing that all of their boxes get where they belong.

Make a list of Big Stuff as well, organized by where it goes. Big Stuff is defined as stages, and portable dance floors, as well as tables, chairs, pop-ups, sound system, big signs, cases of drinks, coolers—anything that won't fit in your activity boxes. Your Big Stuff list goes to the folks with the truck and the muscles to lift and carry. The list should tell them exactly what each area needs.

Moving Stuff List Sample

The following list is for the Green Festival information booth which has these functions:

- Distribution of business fliers and menus
- First aid, lost and found, city information
- Festival information and central command area

Sample Chunk Box - Green Festival

Information Booth Box - Location (Main Street near Gazebo)

_____ Markers	_____ 2-way radios
_____ Scissors	_____ First aid kit
_____ Table cover	_____ Table skirt
_____ Hanger w/ sample T-shirt	_____ Stapler, staples
_____ Sign with shirt sizes, prices	_____ Pens, pencils
_____ Cell phone list	_____ Incident report sheets
_____ Post-its	_____ Garbage bag
_____ Clipboard	_____ Serious (packing) tape
_____ Tape	_____ Bottled water
_____ Rocks (so stuff doesn't blow away)	
_____ Rubber bands	_____ Programs
_____ Business directories	_____ Ice bucket
_____ Paper clips	_____ Signage
_____ Duct tape	_____ Pad of city maps
_____ Merchant rack	_____ Merchant fliers for rack
_____ Information sign	_____ Mail list form
_____ List of upcoming events	_____ Schedule updates

During the evaluation process, review the lists and revise them. As activities change, they can be updated. You are well set for the following year!

Set-Up

All areas need enough help so that they are ready to function at the opening time. This takes a massive amount of coordination:

- All of the housekeeping needs to be done—company is coming!
- Décor, planned out ahead of time, needs to be put in place.
- Garbage and recycle toters need to be rolled into place.
- Information booth, stages, the T-shirt booth, the children's game area—all need to be set up. Porta potties need to be in the right places.
- In each vendor area, someone needs to meet the vendors as they drive in and tell them where their spaces are. (See *street bosses* in the committee section of Chapter 3.)
- Streets need to be blocked off, the barricades moved.
- Stage sound systems, shade structures, tables, chairs need to be set up.

For happy volunteers, make arrangements ahead of time to have coffee and snacks provided. The sun is not yet up, the restaurants and coffee shops are not yet open. People are much less cranky when they have their coffee.

Tear-Down / Clean-Up / Storage

Every year it seems, the clean-up crew is the chore of the dog-tired festival chair, a few loyal committee folks, a few spouses, and the executive director. If the volunteers for each activity are encouraged to clean up after themselves, that will be a major advantage.

TIP   If you are lucky you will have angels for the task. Angel, here, is defined as someone who is willing to take on the jobs of set-up and clean-up. That is their contribution to the event, and they are worth their weight in gold. People have a way of disappearing when the festival is over and the crowds leave. It always takes longer to clean up and for all the vendors to get packed up and leave than you think.

There is another part of the clean-up that is more invisible, but nonetheless important. It involves putting all of the stuff away, of organizing the storage, returning what was borrowed, paying the bills, collecting monies owed, making sure sponsor agreements are honored, evaluating the event and all of its parts, collecting and collating vendor evaluations, and saying thank you to all who helped make the event a success.

Storage

Many events have a collection of paraphernalia—children's games, signage, decorations—supplies that need to be organized and stored. If they are stored off-site, there should be a good, annotated, complete list of what is in storage so leaders can plan and so that purchases are not duplicated. Label boxes clearly with contents.

If you have "stage sets" to store, label each piece as to which set it belongs to, and attach directions on how it goes back together. Put any screws and hardware that goes with a piece in a clearly-labeled plastic bag and attach it securely to the set. This will make everything simpler when it is time to bring the set out again and put it back together. If everything is labeled properly and helpfully, then even if someone moves stuff around and separates the pieces, or inadvertently tears off the bags of hardware, you have a hope of putting each set back together. Perhaps the person who took it apart knew how it went, but they may be residing in a different state when the event comes around again.

19. Promotion - Getting People to Come

If you have done a good job with all of the previous chapters, you now have a marvelous event planned. It might be the best event ever, but if no one knows about it, it will fail. You need to grab the attention and interest of the public who must come and support it. Your time and energy will be caught in a constant balancing act—putting feet on the streets and filling the seats at your event versus providing a good experience for the public. You need happy vendors and entertainers as well as a happy public.

For clarity, I use the words **advertising**, **publicity**, and **promotion** in slightly different ways:

- **Advertising** is media attention that you pay for, such as newspaper ads and electronic billboards.
- **Publicity** refers to what you don't pay for—press releases, public service announcements, and feature articles.
- **Promotion** is the *total picture that includes all activities and marketing* designed to stimulate the public's interest in your event. It will include posters, fliers, T-shirts, your website, and advertising and publicity.

Keep a binder or scrapbook of all your promotion. Include paid ads, posters, fliers, press releases, and even letters to the editor about your event. This binder will be helpful in your evaluation and in making plans for promoting the next year's event.

Expectations

Your promotional material, press releases, and ad copy need to be written by someone sensitive to your goals and who knows the planned activities. Review what is written before it goes to the media and to the public. Avoid raising expectations for something you will not be able to deliver:

- Be sure to answer the who, what, when, why, and where.
- Does the name of your event signal what the public can expect?
- Does your promotion give clear information on the cost of the event?
- Is it clear what and when the activities will be?
- Do you state that the event will be held rain or shine?

TIP   Pay attention to how things are worded in your promotional material and ads. In the Medieval Fantasy Festival's first year, we announced that the festival would be April 7-10. We included a schedule of what was happening on what day. For example, the vendors and entertainment were on April 9th, the Troll Stroll and some contests were on the 10th. However, some people only saw April 7-10 and came expecting the vendors and entertainment to be there every day. They were disappointed. It never occurred to us that they wouldn't look at the schedule, or that they would expect each day to be a repeat of the one before. Our community has a different week-long celebration which has been around for more than 50 years. They post a schedule and every day is different. We assumed that people would read the schedule for our event as well. We didn't think of the fact that our event would draw from a different base. We learned to be very careful in our wording to avoid giving the wrong impression.

- If the event is promoted as free, are there sections or activities that will charge admission? Is that clear in your publicity and advertising?
- If your charity function has a significant ticket price, what will the people find when they enter? Will there be VIP guests that are treated to

obviously better amenities and privileges, making the folks who paid the ticket price feel like second-class citizens?

- Will anything in your promotion bring a short-term gain of dollars but result in a negative perception by the public?

Think about the weather possibilities when you promote your event as well. Give some thought to a Plan B for inclement weather. Is there a rain-date for your concert? Will you have to give refunds for ticketed events? Is your marketing to the public clear about possible changes because of weather?

Organizing Promotion

Sit down with your promotion subcommittee and make an extensive database of all possible local and regional ways of advertising and publicity. Include not only the obvious, like the newspaper and radio, but organizations that could be helpful. Include newsletters of various groups, related internet sites, and other events where you might have a promotional booth or other way to advertise. (Some sites that list events are listed in the Appendix under Resources.) Do some research to find out where people look for event information; make sure that you include those spots. Start with your database and build from there. Include name, email, address, phone, contact person, and costs for each possibility:

- ☐ Local newspapers, regional newspapers
- ☐ Advertisements on buses and public transport
- ☐ Arts, music, drama, sport groups
- ☐ Churches, civic and service organizations, senior centers
- ☐ Colleges and universities
- ☐ Community and library bulletin boards and kiosks
- ☐ Direct mail
- ☐ Family health clubs, swimming / tennis clubs, recreation centers
- ☐ Internet chat groups, social networks
- ☐ Links to other websites
- ☐ Lists on websites and periodicals that have event calendars
- ☐ Local and regional magazines
- ☐ Local, regional tourist bureau, chamber of commerce
- ☐ Other print media—penny-savers, community publications
- ☐ Posters in local businesses, schools, offices
- ☐ Pre-schools, day-care centers
- ☐ Public, parochial, and private schools
- ☐ Radio stations, television stations, cable stations
- ☐ Related-theme national magazines and internet sites
- ☐ Signage possibilities—vinyl banners, electronic highway billboards
- ☐ Your city's public information officer

Outside-the-Box Marketing

Be creative: find different ways of promoting your event beyond the traditional venues:

Through businesses

- Promote your event by having tent cards or tri-fold stand-up cards at local restaurants or bars. Design the tent cards to include your logo and the what, where, and when. Give tantalizing enticements for the planned activities. If your event has an educational aspect to it, include a question or quote to think about.
- If your event is targeted to families or children, prepare 11" by 17" placemats for children to color and supply them to restaurants. Include the name, date, location, and your logo with drawings of activities and characters found at the event.
- Develop a flier or postcard to use as bag stuffers for retail businesses. Ask your local utilities or professionals (such as dentists) if they could send out fliers with their bills.
- Ask businesses and civic groups to promote the event in their newsletters.

Novel ways of distribution

- Develop a tri-fold flier for chamber and tourist literature racks, libraries, and for waiting rooms at professionals' offices.
- Have a flier or mini-poster available as a PDF so that your committee members can email it to their friends and contacts. Some of them will print it out and post it—increasing your coverage.
- If appropriate, ask churches to mention it in their bulletins.
- Distribute or display information at regional businesses that may be related to your event. Try craft shops, costume shops, music stores.

Use other events to promote yours

- Enter a parade in another event with a float, vehicle, or costumed walkers carrying a large banner.
- Have booth, signage, or handouts at other local or regional events.
- Decorate a tree in the theme of your event for your community's Festival of Trees. This will help get the name of the event out to the public.

Other creative promotions

- Invite TV and radio stations to come to your event. Entice them with interesting activities. You may find your event on live news broadcasts.

Assign someone from your committee who is knowledgeable to track these invitations, be the spokesperson, and promote the event.

- Use your logo on reusable tote bags. Do an internet search on reusable, polypropylene grocery bags. (Several tote websites are listed in the Appendix under Resources.) If you find a reusable bag that you like, check the label or ask the company where they got it. Check with your local imprinter and look at their samples. Keep looking until you find one with a price, quality, and quantity that you like and can afford. You might partner with a sponsor who will cover the cost of the totes if their logo is included.

- Include award-giving in your event. Those being honored will likely bring their family and friends, increasing the attendance. Even if you don't have any awards to give out, one of your sponsoring corporations might.

- Run a coloring contest in your local newspaper. Display the entries at your event.

- Approach a business and offer to do a display window promoting your event. Make it eye-catching. It will bring attention to the business as well. If there is a vacant storefront strategically located in a good-traffic area, see if the owner will let you do a display window promoting your event.

- Offer a class at your local library. Create something for the event or learn about the interesting history of the period.

Press Releases

Local media will likely publish or air news of upcoming events. They depend upon you to let them know about the event with a press release. They will edit what you have given them and include it on a space-and-time available basis. They make no promises about when or if they will publish your releases. This is free publicity!

Find out from your local media outlets what the preferred format is for press releases. Do they have a length restriction? Do they require double spacing? Are emailed press releases acceptable?

Be sure to include the what, when, where, and maybe the why and who. Be sure to include the contact person and how to reach him or her for more information and questions. Direct them to your website.

Plan ahead for your press-release schedule. Keep the media informed about your event. Send out an "it's coming" or "date announced" or "volunteers needed for planning" type of press release several months in advance. As your plans and schedule become firm, send out more press releases highlighting the event. As different parts of the event come together, send out press releases about those segments as well. If an entertainer or vendor of special interest is coming, send out another press release.

Most radio and TV stations give PSAs (Public Service Announcements) to nonprofit groups for events at no charge. If you have to pay for event announcements, inquire about ticket-package giveaways in exchange for the advertisement price.

Paid Advertising

Sometimes you will want to insert an ad in your local paper. Use your logo, and design the piece to go with your theme. Proofread carefully. Make sure it has the what, when, where, your website, and a contact number to call for more information. Talk with your media sales reps and seek their advice about the best days to run the ads. Ask them about where to place your ad for the maximum visibility. Ask them what might help your ad stand out from the rest.

Most newspapers and other print media have their own graphics people who can design the ad for you. My experience is that this is usually included in the cost of the ad, but do check. You can help by sketching out what you want on your computer or with pencil and paper.

 TIP   The more often your ad runs, the more people will see it. If your event parent group has a long-term contract with the media outlet you are interested in, perhaps you can take advantage of the discounted rate. Other ideas for keeping your print media advertising costs down are asking your sales rep to let you know if there is unused space they need to fill before their deadline. That space may be sharply discounted. The media may negotiate with you for advertising in exchange for in-kind sponsor status. Also, they may be willing to match what you pay for with free advertising space, doubling your exposure, and gaining them as a sponsor.

When you design and proof your ad, remember to check to make sure any promised sponsor logos and names are included.

Posters and Postcards

A well-designed, attractive poster is worth a lot when it comes to promoting your event. It should be coordinated with the rest of your promotional materials. The what, when, where should be very obvious and easy to read. You want to portray your theme and give credit to the hosting organization and the sponsors.

Proofread the content carefully, and have more than one person do this. Look at what is actually there, not at what you expect to see. Unfortunately, Murphy's Law says most errors only show up when you receive 500 copies printed with your hard-earned money.

Print your posters on 11" by 17" stock. Ideally posters should be up a month in advance of the event. Brainstorm as to where they ought to be distributed. Print some in an 8.5" x 11" size. These will be ideal where space is limited in some shop windows or on corporate bulletin boards.

You can have an attractive flier or bag stuffer if you use your poster design to make postcards. Reduce your poster to postcard size, and add some wording on the back about the features of your event. Postcards can be used at retail outlets as bag stuffers or mailed to your collected list or to your organization's members. They can be given in quantities to the craft vendors that are coming to promote your event in other shows they do.

The Medieval Fantasy Festival used the same photographer for its posters from the beginning. She donated her time and talent and got credit on the poster. Her work was shown all over town, on postcards, and on the website. Though the theme, the logo, and the people are different in each poster, there was a uniform, elegant, keepsake quality to them.

Each year we bounced ideas around for a theme. We thought about people we might ask to be on the poster. We thought about the logo, costumes, props, and the colors. It became a tradition for the photographer, the costume designer, and the festival chair to go to the fabric shops with their ideas and shop as a committee for fabric. We shared our progress with the graphics team who created the logo. As soon as the photo was ready, the team ramped up the speed to complete the poster.

The graphics people worked in Photoshop, with the wording on the poster being in one layer. The serendipity of this process was that the photographer used her same backdrop from the poster, took photos of those who came to the festival in costume, added the layer of words, and sold the customer a Medieval Fantasy Festival poster with themselves as the subject.

If you don't do postcards, you can accomplish much of the same by doing quarter-page fliers. These can also be used in stuffing envelopes when your member organization sends out bills and so on. Retail stores will use them as bag stuffers.

 **TIP**   Before you put fliers under windshield wipers on parked cars all over town, find out about local laws. In some localities, this is considered littering. Each occurrence is punishable by hefty fines. Even if it is legal, some find it highly annoying.

Audio Logo

You have probably given thought to the graphics you use in your print media. You have a logo, consistent font, and a visual look to what you have been doing. Why not develop the same with well-chosen music and voice-over for your audio and audio-visual promotional pieces? An audio logo might also be of use on your website. Plan ahead.

It would be far better to choose your own music background than to let the radio folks pluck something out of their files that you may or may not like or find appropriate. Work with them. Folks quickly recognize a visual logo. They will pick up on a well-designed audio one as well.

Website

In the past ten years, having an event website has gone from unusual, to common, to absolutely essential. As you look at what other festivals are doing and as you search for vendors, keep your eyes and mind open while on their websites. Take note of features you really like and what you do not like. Note what is user-friendly, what is easy to navigate, and what is so obnoxious that you quickly go to a different site. Make a list of links for websites that you admire and whose features you would like to include on your own. The list will be handy in talking with your web wizard.

Choosing and registering your website name or URL needs thoughtful attention. Make sure your site is discoverable by search engines. Give your festival or event a name that has key words for search engines.

Name your links on the URL (web address) the same as the page title. The reason for this is that the search engine will crawl through your site looking for key words. It is not going to pick up www.yourdomain.com/e8974nnfou4j. It would rather see www.yourdomain.com/schedule.

Who will do the website?

Your website wizard should have the needed technological savvy, be easy to work with, and be able to give you the time needed to build the site and keep it current. This person is a real blessing. It is even better if they do your site as an in-kind sponsor or give you a lower rate in exchange for a website and a program ad. A current, active, user-friendly site is a good promotion for them and should motivate them to do their best for you.

Make sure your website wizard has all of the information and items needed to build the site in a timely manner. Provide a list of links (other sites you want to be connected to) for the wizard as well.

The site should have

- Your logo on all of the pages.
- Your home page should have an attractive come-on for all of the five W words—who you are, what you are doing, when it is happening, where it will be, and why.
- The "Contact Us" page should have the contact's name, address, phone, and email address. If your festival is big enough to have different leaders in charge of different areas, put them all there. Queries should go to the folks with the information needed to answer the questions.
- Drop-down menus should have vendor, food, and entertainer applications that can be printed out. An application for prospective volunteers can also be included.
- Other drop-down menus should have contest information, activity information, and new attractions.
- Ticket information, if needed. What is the cost, how does one get them, and what kind of payment is accepted?
- The schedule of events.
- When it becomes available, add an annotated list of vendors and entertainers.
- Coordinate graphics and fonts to the logo, poster and vision.
- Even if you don't sell promotional items from your site, you may show shirts, mugs, totes, and other items that will be available at the event.
- How much will parking be? Is public transportation available?
- Map showing how to get there and where to park. Include a physical street address in your directions so the direction search sites can find your event. A ten-mile-long major street with no number doesn't do it!
- Photos of the previous year's event add to the interest.

TIP Do you need a photo release to use a photo of someone in your promotional material and on your website? Is it okay to use shots taken in a public event in publicity?

Rules on this seem to be rather fuzzy. They have to do somewhat with the purpose of the photo. Is it to inform and educate? You will be less likely to get yelled at than if the purpose is commercial. On the public street, at a public event, people pictures are less of a problem. If the person is not clearly recognizable, there should be no concern. Sports complexes may consider themselves to be private property and therefore want to be in control of photos. You might consider it to be a public event, but they do not agree.

Err on the side of caution and get a photo release. If there are minors involved, be even more cautious. Better to be safe than sorry. A sample Photo Release is included in the Appendix.

Green your event by including information on your website about getting to your event using public transportation.
As an alternative, suggest that people carpool.

Links to related sites

- If you have a lot of links, you may have to categorize them.
- People follow specific vendors and specific entertainers. You want them to find your event with helpful links.
- Try to forge links to sites with related themes. If your event is about quilting, find out where other fiber arts folks get their information, and go there. If your event features jazz, link to jazz-related activity sites.
- Reciprocal links. You provide a link to their site; they provide one to yours. Ask. It is a win-win situation.
- Link to sites belonging to your organization's members.
- Link to sponsors and friends of your event.
- Link to social network sites like Facebook® and Twitter®.

TIP   Before you put a list of vendors, member organizations, sponsors, and other links on your site, try the links out to see if they are live. How many times have you tried websites only to find that "this page cannot be displayed" or "this site available for purchase" or some other message that lets you know that the site is not current? It still will happen. Change is inevitable, but at least you will have done what you could.

If you choose to build your own website

You may have some computer-savvy folks on your committee who can create a website for you or help you do it yourself. There are a plethora of hosting choices for inexpensive website building. Some may charge a monthly fee for hosting. Some may charge for a domain name. Some may not charge, but they will put advertising on your site that you don't have control over, making your site look busy and cluttered. Do some research. Ask other groups for recommendations. Look at sites from other groups in your community and see what you like.

When you have finished your site, the biggest challenge may be getting it recognized by the search engines. This doesn't happen automatically, and it takes time. Search engines send spiders crawling through sites looking for stuff they might add to their databases. They look for key words and tags.

Get lots of folks to go to your site. The more hits your site gets, the more obvious it becomes to the search engines. Get linked to sites that are already connected. You can do an internet search on *"How do I get search engines to find my website?"* and you will find advice.

Other Internet Promotion

It is becoming increasingly important to use other internet resources to promote your event as well. I heard the phrase "word of mouse" and thought it was really clever. What it means, of course, is that something was spread via the internet—with emails, social network sites, and, in the modern parlance, "It went viral."

Email

Email is the most common form of communicating back and forth with individuals on the internet. You can communicate with those whose addresses you know.

Blogs

A blog is either a type of website or part of a website. You can set up your own website to include a blog by using software such as WordPress (see Appendix, Books, Unique Resource Books). Blogs usually contain regular entries of commentary, sort of an online train-of-thought or diary. A famous one that comes to my mind is the basis of the movie *Julie & Julia* in which the heroine cooked her way through Julia Child's cookbook and recorded the experiences in a blog. Those reading the blog generally have an opportunity to respond, if you set it up that way. Blogs can be interactive.

Blogs could be used by your event to keep the public updated on performers or artists who are coming. They may be used to generate excitement about upcoming speakers. They combine text, photos, and perhaps even videos. They bring repeat traffic to your website, which is good.

Social Network Sites

Some social network sites are general—like Facebook and Twitter. Some are more focused with a particular following. There might be a site that will reach your intended audience. Do an internet search: check Wikipedia. Do your homework: ask around. They are generally not private, though some are restricted to members. The membership may include several million people, however. The public has access and can respond.

Before you associate your event with a certain site, be sure that it will be beneficial and not detrimental to your cause.

Part IV
Evaluation

...And then it begins again.
You gather feedback, look at what went well,
what you would do differently next time,
and what can be improved.

You have now come full cycle and are beginning again,
ready to make smart decisions about growth and move
with confidence into a bright future.

Chapters

20. Evaluation of Event Components

The evaluation process is very important and can be simple or elaborate. The more information you gather, the better off you will be when it comes to the planning for the following year.

Put together some guidelines and questions using the points in this chapter. Distribute this information to your committee prior to your evaluation meeting with them. The meeting will be more productive if the members have already given thought to the evaluation guidelines. The whole committee should meet to do the evaluation process. Their feedback is a good place to begin. The interaction of the members will lead to better insight.

The chairperson should consider all of the different components of the festival. All of the information gathered should be put into a composite form and kept in the binder for planning purposes. The information gleaned from the evaluation process will be helpful to chunk leaders next year as they begin to plan again.

This is a good time to bring your archive binder up to date. Include copies of publicity received, ads placed, a printed copy of what is on your website, agendas, minutes, invoices, contracts, vendor lists, chunk guides, and so on. Don't overlook evaluations from your vendors and entertainers.

The evaluation section follows the same pattern of organization as the event committee make-up in Chapter 3 and the timeline in Chapter 7. Categories are:

- General Overall
- Administrative
- Visual Theme
- Financial
- Logistical
- Main Course
- Getting the Word Out

Your experience has probably been that some categories went well, some were excellent, but others just limped along and were only adequate. How was the balance? Where will you have to beef up the leadership and volunteers to make a difference?

General Overall

At a minimum you should ask all of your volunteers and chunk leaders to tell you

- How their particular responsibilities went.
- Would they like to volunteer again next year and in what area?
- Their impression as to how the event went as a whole.
- What fell apart, and what could be improved?
- What were the strengths and what were the weaknesses of the event?
- Ask them to dream a little about what they would like to happen in next year's event.
- What would they wish the event to be like in five years and what steps should be taken to get it there?

Public attendance

What was the estimated attendance? How can you tell? Vendors like to know the numbers of people at events they are considering. Newspapers like to report how many came to an event. Event hosts like to feel good about attendance. None of them will be satisfied with, "There was a whole bunch of people there."

- For an event that sells tickets, you can look at the number of tickets sold or the seats filled. You get an idea, also, from the number of glasses used or programs handed out.
- Estimating crowd numbers at events with no central gate is very much an inexact science. If you are at a craft fair, people are moving all of the time, but not at the same speed. You can count the number of people passing through a particular section for thirty minutes. Then multiply that by the number of half hours that the event is open. If you count more than once and average the counts, you may be more accurate.

- If you know the square footage of your space, you can estimate by how tightly the people are packed in. Are they at arm's length from each other, are they shoulder to shoulder, or somewhere in between? This method works better for a concert where people congregate in one place at one time. Count at the peak of attendance.
- You may find a vendor or event worker with many years of experience at different events who will be able to give you a good idea of your attendance.
- When people figure the attendance at a large rally or political event, they might have photos taken from a blimp or from a satellite. Those counting divide the pictures into grids and count heads. This is interesting to know, but beyond our capabilities. Even for these high tech folks it is still a guesstimate.

You might also find it helpful to estimate how the different age groups were represented. Were there a lot of preschoolers? Families with children in strollers? Were there a lot of grade-school children or teens? Was the audience mostly young adult, middle-aged, or senior citizen? What else can you say about the makeup of the crowd?

How did the weather affect the event? Did you deal with the weather the best you could?

Administrative

List your goals for the event. For each goal, comment on how you did and how you can improve:

- Was it perceived by the public to be successful? Is it worth doing again?
- How did the event affect local businesses?
- What words of praise and gripes did you hear from the public?
- How did the venues work? Would you make any changes?
- Did your date work? Were there conflicting events?
- On the timeline, what changes do you need to make? Should some of the tasks be in a different place?
- Look at the office part of the process—how was the paperwork handled? How could it go more smoothly? What were the aggravating pieces of the puzzle?

Planning Process

Were the meetings effective? Was time well spent? Were the frequency, times and locations of meetings satisfactory? Were the committee members, staff, and volunteers kept well-informed? What activities suffered from lack of time and attention? How can you improve?

Budget, Keeping Records

Compare the proposed budget to what was actually taken in and spent. Make notes for following year. Look at the cost effectiveness of each component. Where should budget dollars be decreased and increased?

Volunteers

Were there enough? What areas needed more? Were volunteers pleased? How can we improve on finding volunteers? Were they well informed? Were tasks and people well matched?

Coordination with city, organizations or groups that partnered with you

Were the other partners involved pleased with the event? Did they work well with you? Did each organization pull its own weight?

Information Booth

Did it fulfill its functions well? Did they do a good job of handling raffle tickets, contest entries, and so on?

Medical Needs

Were there any incidents that required medical aid? Were they handled well? Were the supplies adequate and in the right place? Was the first aid booth staffed adequately? Could people find the booth easily?

Hospitality

Think about how vendors, volunteers, VIPs, entertainers, and the public were welcomed. Was the morning coffee on time? Were the resources available when they were needed? What comments did you hear? Were there any snafus with accommodations? Did registration go smoothly?

Visual Theme

Décor

Were you pleased with the decoration, ambience, and look of the event? What changes would you make? Was the decoration appropriate? Did set up and tear down go smoothly or should you simplify the décor? Do your labeling and directions need improvement to minimize problems of setting up?

Signage

Did it do its job? Did it get people to where they were supposed to be? On time? With the minimum of aggravation? Were the signs attractive and suitable for your theme? What can you use next year? What should be replaced or revamped?

Graphics / Design / Logo
Were you satisfied with them? What comments did you hear? Did they communicate what you were trying to do? Were there any frustrations in the process of creation and application? What do you need to change for next year?

Promotional Merchandise
Comment on the shirt design, the process, the sales, the size breakdown, the printer, the prices, your marketing, and the quality. Comment on the wine glasses or other merchandise, how they looked, how they were received. Comment on sales. Did you have a lot left over? Was it well worth the effort?

Program
Comment on its appearance, the content, the format. Was the printer easy to work with and priced right? Did you have to learn the hard way with extra charges for processes you knew nothing about, such as screening on photos? What could have made the production process go more smoothly? How was the program received by the public? Did it fulfill its function? Should anything be added or subtracted for next year? How could you improve? Did you have enough or too many programs?

Financial

Was the event financially successful? Where could we improve? Was the money handled properly? Did the starting cash drawers for each sales area have the change and the denominations of bills that worked best?

Sponsors
Comment on the sponsor and support solicitation process. Who might be recommended for next year? Were the sponsors happy with the results? Did your sponsor packets work well or did they fall short? How could we do a better job getting sponsors?

Program Ads
How did the ad-solicitation process go? Did the income from ads sold equal or surpass the cost of the program?

Logistics

Comment on the following.

- **Parking**
  Was there enough? Was it a hassle for the vendors, staff, and the public? How can the parking be improved? Did businesses in the area complain about traffic and parking? Was the signage helpful and adequate? Was the website helpful in helping people find parking?

- **Foot Traffic Flow through Event**
  Did the public move easily from one part to another? Were there areas that were neglected or too crowded? How could the strength of each area be improved?

- **Security**
  Were there any incidents during the day or night? Did you need more security? When? How was security perceived by the public? Was the security company used a good match for the event? Were they visible? Were their actions appropriate?

- **Garbage / Recycle Toters**
  Were there enough? Were they in the right places? Were they used properly? How can you encourage improvement?

- **Porta potties**
  Were there enough? Were they in the right places? Would you recommend the same company next year?

- **Technical Support**
  Were you satisfied with the technical support (sound system, electricity, lighting, and so on)?

- **Environmental Impact**
  How successful were you in greening your event? Was the public responsive to your attempts? Are you satisfied with your progress? What ideas can you put in place for the next event?

- **Set-up**
  Was everything in place at the right time? Did it go smoothly or were there hiccups in the system? What needs to be added or removed from the computer "stuff list"? Was there enough help? Did people complete their jobs?

- **Clean-Up**
  Was there enough help, or did it end up being the loyal few who did most of the work? Did it go smoothly? Why or why not? Was everything put away properly? Was everything that was borrowed returned?

Main Course

Look at the vendors, the entertainment, the reasons the public came. Were they pleased? Will they come again? How can you improve?

Vendors

Comment on the fees charged. Did the vendors comply satisfactorily with your credential requests? How can you avoid the hassle of last-minute document chasing? Did you have enough food vendors?

- Were they happy?
- Was the variety and quality of food sufficient?

Did you have enough merchandise vendors?

- Were they happy?
- Was the variety and quality sufficient?
- Did they do well enough to want to come back?
- Were there any vendors that you would not invite back?
- Name any vendors that you positively want back.
- Were there any comments regarding vendor parking?
- If you had trouble filling vendor spots, did you charge too much? Was there a competitive event that your target vendors went to instead?

Entertainment

Ask for comments on each performance or group:

- Would some have done better at a different time and stage?
- Would you invite the same performers again?
- Which were the best draws for the public?
- Were there some that the public ignored or didn't stay with until the end of the performance?
- Did the scheduling work well or did you fall behind?

Games for Children

How was participation from children? Which games did they go for? How was staffing in the area? Did the volunteers interact well with the children, or did they just put in their time? Jot down ideas for improvement. How were the prizes received?

Contests

Comment on each. Were entries plentiful? Did contestants enjoy the process? Did the process go smoothly? How were the prizes received? How can you improve next year? What were the comments from the judges on how the contests were handled? How can the entry form be improved?

Activities

Evaluate each separately. Comment on participation, staffing, décor, how smoothly each activity went, any entries or forms used, satisfaction and popularity.

Party, Dance, Dinner

Comment on the time chosen, the length, the location, the food, drink, and catering, the décor, the entertainment or band. Comment on the attendance, the flow, and the appeal. Was it cost effective?

Follow Up

Did each activity leader finish their evaluation? Did they complete notes that would make their activity go more smoothly the next year? Did they put away all of their equipment, signage, and décor? Did they bring their written records up-to-date and turn them in to a central location? Did they make notes for next year so they or their replacements could hit the ground running?

Getting the Word Out

Postcards, Bag Stuffers

Comment on how they were used. Were some wasted? Were they instrumental in increasing attendance? Were they attractive and informative? How can you improve?

Publicity and Advertising

Comment on press releases noting which papers and media outlets ran them. What kinds of activities attracted the attention of the press? What might you capitalize on for next year? What media were present at the event? Were any of your volunteers or staff interviewed by the press? What kind of free coverage did you get? Was there sufficient publicity? What ads did you pay for? Were they received well or noticed? Did they show up well? Were you satisfied with their placement in the newspaper sections and on the pages? What do you want to remember to ask your newspaper ad rep next time?

Poster and Poster Distribution

How could you improve on the poster design and printing process? Were there any frustrating steps? How could they work better? Did you have enough? Too many? Did they seem to do their job of getting people to come? Did you hear any comments about the poster? Were you satisfied with the distribution?

Website

Comment on the timeliness of updates and features, on the content, the appearance, and user-friendliness. Your website host can find you an amazing amount of information on how often your website was visited, what they looked at, when they visited, where they are located, how they got there—either directly, by an internet search or by a link from another site. Your web wizard can ask Google Analytics® or a similar program to print out a report with charts and all. Use this list of links you get from Google® to create a list of links you forge next year.

Afterward...

The two chapters that follow are really part of the evaluation process as well, but they get specific. Chapter 21 helps a committee think through the process when an event hasn't gone well. It is about discovering ways to fix it or to chalk it up to experience and move on. Chapter 22 helps a committee focus on growing an event, which may be bursting at the seams, possibly literally and figuratively.

After all of the evaluation points have been discussed, your information gathered, and everything has been wrapped up, you and your committee will likely be thinking about the next year. How can we increase attendance? How can we increase the funds we raise for our organization? What would you like to keep and what would you like to change? The dreaming and scheming begin here. Now that the pressure is off and the event is over, you have the leisure to think and to brainstorm for ideas. What can we do to keep the event fresh and exciting? How can we make it better?

You have gone full circle and are now ready to begin again. The vision comes first...

21. Why Events Fail: to Fix or to Move On

This chapter should be read before the event plans are well underway as well as after the event. Knowing what might go awry ahead of time may help you to avoid some problems and potential pitfalls altogether. While we all want our events to be successful, sometimes they aren't. (Life happens, and you know what they say about the best laid plans of mice and men.)

This section will look at overcoming difficulties and saving what might otherwise end up as a perceived failure. Some activities might be rescued if the leadership finds out in time to do something about them. If you are reacting after the event, you may be able to learn from the experience, do things differently, and be successful in the following year.

Some events just really don't work. Some events work well for a time, and then interest fizzles. Be honest in your evaluation, and try to look at the event from many different perspectives. With an open mind, listen to what people say. Turn down the filter in your head that says what you want to hear or what you think you should hear. Chalk the experience up to a learning opportunity, and move on.

Do not expect a start-up venture to make money or break even. Consider it as an investment in the future. You are laying the foundation.

Here are some reasons why events don't work.

1. The event was not a good match for the community or target audience.
   - For example, what might work in a university town may not fly in a town with a military base economy.
   - If the event appeals to a narrow spectrum of interest, it might need to be promoted in a larger region to attract the numbers needed for it to succeed.
   - Just because an event went well in one location doesn't mean it can be reproduced successfully in another.

2. Goals were unrealistic or were out of line with your activities:
   - Enough financial or people resources could not be found to pull off the event.
   - Planned activities had little to do with reaching the goals you set.

3. Dates chosen didn't work:
   - Did your date conflict with another event, or with a holiday?
   - Did vacations get in the way?

4. Expectations of the public were not met:
   - Or even worse than not being met, the public went from benign and uninterested to downright hostile.
   - Did the public feel misled about what they would experience or what it would cost?

5. Expectations of the hosting organization were not met:
   - It didn't make enough money to justify the amount of energy it took.
   - Boards of hosting organizations change. The people who were there when the event was proposed—and whose enthusiasm buoyed up the event at first—have been replaced, or the people have new projects to which they wish to give their energy.
   - The leadership of the organization lost enthusiasm for keeping the event fresh and exciting.
   - The event had "run its course".
   - Perhaps there is new leadership with different priorities at the top of the hosting organization.

6. Expectations of major sponsors were not met:
   - If they do not see results, or if they do not find the event worthy of attaching their name and reputation, they will drop out.
   - Sponsors may also be lost because of businesses closing or being bought by another company. You may lose sponsors when money is tight or when other projects compete for available resources. Some may be lost because of changes in personnel at the decision-making level.

- For whatever reason, your one large sponsor pulls out. To minimize the damage from this, court several smaller sponsors rather than one big one.

7. Expectations of vendors and others were not met:
   - If the event was not profitable enough, they will have little interest in coming again.
   - If they were led to expect unrealistic results, they will not be back.

8. The event did not make enough income:
   - Look at expenses. Did the venue and all of the permits and amenities eat up the profits?
   - Can costs be adjusted for another year?
   - Were there unexpected expenses, such as fencing off an outdoor venue, that were not figured in the budget?

9. Burn-out of leadership:
   - If the event has been running for several years, is the leadership getting burned out?
   - If the beginning leadership has retired, moved away, or pulled back, did someone step into the vacuum to take over the task?
   - Does new leadership share the vision of those who created the event?
   - Were there enough volunteers who were excited about the event to pull it off?
   - Did the worker bees feel like they were being taken for granted and not appreciated by the hosting organization?

10. The parent group never bought into the event wholeheartedly:
    - They were willing to support it as long as they weren't called upon to put a lot of effort into making it happen.
    - Very tellingly, they might refer to it as "Joe's" event, not their event.
    - They probably could not recite one goal of the event other than to attract people or to make money.
    - When "Joe" leaves, the event may fall apart—either with a desultory event that no one wants to repeat, or just die without any attempt to keep it going.

11. Committee failed to do the groundwork:
    - Some logistical problems were not addressed.
    - Parking was a problem.
    - Amenities were not available.
    - An unforeseen legal hurdle was not met.

- Police shut the event down because of perceived threat or danger. (This has happened when the promoter's choice of entertainment and bands conflicted with the experience of police in dealing with fans these bands attract.)
- Did the event activity leaders know what was expected of them?
- Were they given enough guidance and help?

12. Personalities and or politics got in the way:
- A diva (male or female) blew up, taking all of their friends who were helping away with them.
- A conflict between committee personnel and the hosting organization came to a head.
- A strong leader left, resulting in a power struggle that ate up energy with negativity.
- A person or group felt threatened by the event and sabotaged it.

13. Some leadership flaked. You may have options depending upon when you learn that the leadership is not going to follow through:
- How central to the event was this leader's portion?
- Could or did someone else take over?
- Could a particular activity be cancelled without disrupting the rest of the event?
- Could it be modified and simplified and still meet the expectations of the public and live up to your advertising?

14. Publicity and promotion were lacking:
- People's interest was not caught by what they saw and heard.
- Were your press releases ever published?
- In the editing process between the time the release was submitted by you to when it was published, was the focus of the release changed from what you intended? Were expectations changed either by what was left out or by comments added in the process?
- Did your posters and postcards get distributed in a timely manner, or was it a case of too little, too late?
- Did you target the right group of people with the right material with your publicity?
- Did you budget enough to get good promotion?
- Were your ads effective or easily overlooked?
- Was all of your ad information correct, or did your event get publicized for the wrong date, due to carelessness of a proofreader?

15. Weather did not cooperate:
- Severe storms, intense heat or cold, wind, or rain may have scuttled the event plans.

- A blizzard, a flood, or other "act of God" kept event from happening.
- If your event is dependent upon a crop and that crop fails, you are sunk—or at least swimming upstream.
- If weather has struck adversely at your event several years running, you might consider changing the date or changing the venue to one that is not as sensitive to the weather.
- The event based on wind, mentioned in the vision chapter, might have bombed totally if the weather during the event was unusually calm with absolutely no wind. Few of the activities, literally and figuratively, would have gotten off the ground.

16. Unavoidable "personal disasters" got in the way:
    - Illness of a major player, job loss, marital difficulties, sick children, relocation, a major volunteer who had plenty of time to organize took a paying job, a leader was in an accident.
    - Stress level of a major player caused health condition to flare up, leaving them unavailable, unreliable, or perhaps even disruptive of event moving forward.

17. Disaster happened:
    - There was an accident during the event with severe injuries. The public became leery and your insurance skyrocketed.
    - Your major entertainer became ill or injured and cancelled.
    - A heightened security alert caused attendance to be down and vendors and entertainers to cancel.
    - You were sued for infringement of someone's intellectual property. You had to take your planning back to the beginning.
    - The public's focus was on a national disaster; they were glued to their TV sets and not even thinking about your event.
    - There was a scandal involving leadership of the charity your event was raising funds for.
    - A flu epidemic happened to crest or have major impact on school, community, or event players.
    - And so on....

For many of these reasons, when you see failure looming and the event has not yet taken place, the committee or the major leadership needs to come together quickly and do some damage control. They need to prioritize, to decide what minimally must happen, and to work to see that it does. Some good ideas may be dropped, the schedule changed, and substitutions made. Sometimes the event just needs to be cancelled for that year, monies returned, and enticements designed to bring the players back the next year. How will the event be seen by the public if this happens?

If there has been a major disaster, cancellation might gain you public sympathy. The public cannot focus on frivolity and celebration if there is more serious work to be done. Conversely, it might be that if life gives you lemons, you have the opportunity to make lemonade. If your event was going to raise money for your organization, and your community experiences a major flood, hold the event, if possible, and donate the funds to the flood victims. The public perception of your organization as generous in time of need will benefit you with more support the next time around.

Of course, the reason you do give to the community is not for this public-relations benefit, but because you genuinely care for the place and the people. The event should be for your community, not the other way around. You are a part of the community, and when one part of it suffers, the whole is diminished and suffers even more.

22. Growing an Event

Where do you want your event to be in five years? The general overall evaluation process includes this question. What has to happen between now and then to reach that dream? What steps do you need to take in the coming years?

In the evaluation process you may decide that your event is ready to grow. If you are serious about growing it, you will put lots of energy and time into **Part III, Execution of the Plan.** You will become very familiar with all of the events in your wide region. In this wider area, what are the most popular entertainment, attractions, and activities? Do they fit in with your goals for your event? Would their variations help make your event unique? Talked about? Appealing to your audience?

- You will seek out the best entertainment, the best vendors, and the best activities. You will negotiate the biggest bang for your buck. You will make sure that your choice of entertainment draws well. You will keep the favorites and add new attractions.
- You will work to keep the event fresh, new, and exciting.
- You will see to it that your vendors do well and want to come back. The word will spread, and you will have vendors calling to see if they can come.

You will treat all of your vendors fairly and make it as pleasant and profitable as possible for them.

- You will promote and publicize your event smartly to get feet on the street, filled seats, and satisfied customers. If your vendors are prospering and your public feels that the event was worthwhile, they will stay longer, they will come back, and they will spread the word. You are well on your way to growing your event.

- You will work to ensure that your sponsors feel their investment has gone to a good cause. The resulting business they receive, or the amount of funds raised for a cause they hold dear, or the connection of their name with a popular, successful event will impress them.

- You will want to invite community leaders and influential folks to experience the event in a positive way. Invite the press and keep them informed.

> What are your strongest assets? Capitalize on them; put your time, money, and energy there. Strengthen any weaker portions of your event that are essential to your theme. Prune away the elements that don't augment your goals, that do not work well, and that you can live without.

Think about how you want your event to grow:

- **More creativity**. It is always a challenge to keep the event fresh and new. You want folks to look forward to new fun and to new experiences. You want them to come *every* year and not develop the attitude "Been there, done that."

- **Maintain event support from local business**. For a street fair, creative ways of getting people into the businesses and making them customers will help. Keeping businesses informed of event plans is tremendously important.

- **Physical space**. Is the event ready to grow to include more of the space available at the location? Add another street, add another building at the county fairgrounds, or add another room at the school?

- Do you need a **different location** to accommodate your activities and crowds and parking?

- **Time**. Do you want to expand from one to multiple days?

- **More activities**. Are more activities needed or desired? Do you want to expand in a certain area, add a new area, or refresh existing areas? Do you want to target an additional audience or just grow your same target audience? What will your choice of added activities accomplish?

- Can you think of a **new activity** that expands your audience? Will this new activity still enhance your goals or will it deflect from them?

- **Listen for ideas on improving your event** and ways of including more of the community. Talk to people. Talk to parents, to civic groups. Go to chamber mixers and begin a conversation asking for their comments, ideas, and dreams for their community.

- Think of your **community and what type of growth** you would like to see in the future. Can your event help advance this larger goal?

- **Budget considerations**. What are the budget ramifications of growing? Will you gain more income for your group or project? Will added expenses cut into your profit?

- **More vendors.** Do you have the physical space to accommodate them? Has your experience in securing vendors led you to believe you can fill the new space? Put more emphasis on a certain type of vendor—maybe you want to have more handcrafted merchandise. Perhaps you want to focus on one specific craft such as fused glass but keep the general craft area as well. You may wish to devote one area of vendors to children's items or crafts and add some hands-on activities. Perhaps you want more of your vendors to demonstrate their crafts.

- **More quality, same quantity**. Do you want to stay the same size, but grow in quality? Do you want to raise the bar on the excellence of vendors, bands, and entertainment?

- Do you want to increase the **number of local businesses and groups** that are involved in your event? Are you looking to maximize the local community potential?

- Are you looking to **partner with another group** or a professional promoter to aid you in your growth? What would this change about the leadership style, the creative control that you have, and your local participation? Would your bottom line be affected positively or negatively?

- **More logistical challenges**. What logistics will change as a result of your growth? Will bigger crowds mean a greater challenge for parking?

- **More attendance** or attendance from a wider region. Will your publicity team need to be expanded?

- What are the **volunteer and worker** ramifications of expanding? Will the dynamics of your committee change? Will you be able to find responsible, creative volunteers to take on the new challenges?

- Would this be a good time to **take the concept and reproduce it** in another place?

- Or **another time, same place**? Maybe your community could support two music events, two wine strolls, or two fun runs.
- Can you increase the **number of sponsors** so that you have more capital to improve the event? Will the changes you are looking at make it easier to get more sponsors?
- Think about the **beneficiaries of your fundraising**. Should you support the same causes the next time around? Could another cause be paired with your existing one in a way that both causes would benefit?
- Will the change result in **any negative aspects**?

Go back to your original vision, to the original brainstorming about what could happen at your event. Are any of these original ideas right for the new change? **Expand on the original vision**. Involve your committee in a new brainstorming session. Do some more searching on the internet. Look at similar events in other states. Do their activities spark ideas that will work for you? Lay out your goals and think about other avenues for reaching them.

Where do you want to be in five years?

23. Thank You and Appreciation

It is common courtesy to say, "Thank you!" when someone does something for you. If volunteers spend their time, money, and talent to make an event happen, they deserve to be recognized and to know that they are appreciated.

What form should this recognition take? What will your workers most appreciate? The form of recognition should be planned in advance. Some of these methods will need to be budgeted.

Here are some possibilities:

- Thank-you card sent to volunteers. Will you make a special one with graphics from your event? Will each card be personal or will everyone get the same?
- Thank-you letter to your donors and sponsors. Be sure to repeat your tax ID number so they can use the letter in their tax returns. This letter may make the difference as to whether they will consider your event for a donation next year.
- Listing in the organizational newsletter.
- Recognition at organization's meeting.
- Listing on the website.

- Recognition dinner for volunteers. Who gets invited? Will the invitation include a guest or spouse? Does a person need to rack up a certain number of hours before they are invited? Who will absorb the cost of the dinner?
- After-event party—"cast" party.
- Awards, certificates, plaques. Check to make sure names are spelled correctly. (Who is going to deliver the ones for those who were not present at the awards event?) Is this item budgeted?
- Ad in newspaper with names of volunteers. While such an ad will cost money, it may offset that by good will, good exposure, and by planting seeds for greater participation at next year's event.
- Should any volunteers be singled out for an honor like "Volunteer of the Year"? Who decides? Who will be disappointed because they were not chosen for the honor, but feel they are more deserving?
- How will you thank your vendors, your entertainers, your sponsors, your supporters? An email or note?

Run the list of those to be thanked by several people to make sure no one is overlooked.

Thank you to the readers

Thank you for reading and using this guide for the world of festival and event planning. If this book has been instrumental in sparking your ideas, organizing your thoughts, and creating an enjoyable community event, it has been very worthwhile. More power to you as you work with and for your community. Enjoy the process, treasure the friendships that you will make, and know that your efforts have made your community a better place to live. Glow in the satisfaction of a job well done!

Appendix

I. Green Festival Documents

Green Festival Vendor Categories and Quotas

Green Festival Vendor Categories and Quotas

 TIP The numbers after the categories represent the ideal number of a working wish-list. The numbers are potential vendors; there is no way that you will be able to fill all the slots. Set up the list in your computer with your own quotas, with lines and your wish list for each. As the slot is filled, write the name in the blank. Adapt the list to your own community and wishes. Include nonprofits and regional and state agencies.

Green vehicles

    Electric cars - 4

    1._____ *(Zap Motors)*

    2. _____ *(Chevy Volt)*

    3. _____

    4. _____

    Hybrid - 2   (Continue with lines as above.)

    Biodiesel - 1

    Solar-incorporated - 2

    Other alternative - 3

    Gasoline-powered, outstanding-mileage - 2

    Mass transit - 2

    Bicycles, other - 4

Household appliances—highly energy-efficient or alternative-energy use

    Refrigerators / freezers - 2

    Other - 2

Home heat, air

    Wind - 2

    Solar panels - 4

    Solar generator - 2

    Other - 3

Building green homes

    Contractors - 3

    Windows / insulation / gutters / other building - 6

Maintaining Green Homes
>Green household products - 3
>Green cleaning products - 2
>Businesses /corporations that manufacture green products - 2

Print
>Books / green / publisher - 3
>Books / used, " recycled" - 2
>Magazines / periodicals - 3
>Books, new - 2
>Children's magazines - 2

Other media - 2

Growing things
>Nurseries - 2
>Herbs/ specialty plants, seeds - 3
>Produce – local - 3
>Edible landscaping - 2
>Trees - 1
>Pest control - natural, green - 2

Food-related
>Slow food - 1
>Cookbooks - 1
>Natural, organic foods - 4
>Vegetarian - 2
>Other - 3
>Pet foods – natural - 2

Smarter use of water resources - 2

Air quality - 2

Recycling - 4

Conservation - 2

Natural fibers, clothing, textiles
>Cotton - 2
>Hemp - 2
>Wool - 2
>Silk - 2
>Recycled from soda bottles, etc - 2
>Linen - 2
>Adults' clothing - 2
>Children's clothing - 4

Other fiber-related
>Bedding - 1
>Home décor - 1
>Tote bags - 2

Children's items
>Baby / infant - 3
>Children's household items - 2

Toys - 3

Other - 2

Green nonprofit groups

Boy Scouts / Girl Scouts / 4-H - 4

Humanitarian - 3

Green - 3

Transportation - 3

Educational – children - 3

Educational – adults - 3

Health / exercise - 2

Seniors - 2

Garden - 3

Animal / domestic - 3

Wildlife - 5

Conservation - 2

Community development - 2

Green government agencies - 2

Cooperative games / education - 2

Peace promotion - 2

Green, ethical businesses - 4

Green, ethical advertising - 2

Green investment - 2

Fair trade goods - 4

Movers & shakers, and big-time players that should be involved - 4

1. _____ *(Opswatch Light & Power)*

2. _____ *(Opswatch Sanitary)*

3. _____ *(City of Opswatch)*

4. _____

Products, green, eco-friendly

Light bulbs - 2

Solar flashlights - 2

Rechargeable batteries - 1

Solar gadgets - 4

Toys - 3

Soaps, body, bath - 6

Animal products - 3

Candles (non-petroleum) - 2

Gardening / yard / outdoor décor / furniture - 3

Birdhouses / baths / other - 3

Arts / crafts - 4

Wood / other crafts - 2

Other - 5

Products for pets – 2

Office and business products

Paper - 2

Other - 4

Eco-travel

Visiting places that educate us about the world's natural treasures - 1

Visiting places using a green style rather than wasteful - 1

Wildlife appreciation / education - 2

Green hotels in region - 2

Cycling, hiking, enjoying outdoors — 4

Food vendors

Pre-packaged food vendors

Made in the USA - 4

Products made using green, eco-friendly manufacturing concepts. Criteria may include quality, local employers, products that don't have to travel massive distances, items made with pride locally.

New products - 3

(Ones that didn't exist ten years ago. Innovations because of new technology)

Other juried spots - 3

Guide for the Green Vendor Person

Guide for the Green Vendor Person

Green Festival, Opswatch, IZ

(This packet would include these items for the volunteer.)

- Database of potential green vendors.
- List of other events in our region that might be a source for vendors including craft fairs, home and garden shows, and business expos.
- A list of green vendor categories.
- Current vendor application packet.
- List of committee members, phone numbers, and responsibilities.

You will be working with these people

Ima Gogetter	(Food Vendor Person)
Effy Shunt	(Office Staff)
George Green	(Green Festival Chair)
Louisa Bright and Sam Early	(Street Bosses)

Guidelines for choosing vendors of green products at the Opswatch Green Festival
Think of these criteria:

- Natural, recycled, green, eco-friendly, organic.
- Not made from petroleum products, toxic or harsh chemicals.
- Conservation, more efficient, re-usable, child-safe, pet-safe.
- Merchandise that is more local. Part of an item's carbon footprint is the energy it takes to get it from the manufacturer to the consumer.
- Merchandise packaging that is minimal, reduced.
- Source of product, fair trade, corporate vision of stewardship

These are the tasks the *Green Vendor Chair* will do:

1. Seek out *green, eco-friendly vendors*. Ask everybody you know. Haunt the internet. Check the yellow pages. Go to as many events as you can. Peruse the list of green vendor categories and think of where you might find them.
2. Set up a *records system*. You will wish to keep track of who has gotten what information and their responses. Make notes about phone calls; keep copies of letters and emails. Set up a potential vendor binder and a binder for applications received. Keep vendors in alphabetical order so you can find them easily when the phone rings and somebody has a question.
3. Become familiar with the vendor packet. Most of your correspondence will be done by email where possible. Effy Shunt can scan a vendor packet and send it to you by email. You can attach it when you contact potential vendors by email. If you need them, envelopes and postage are available from Effy. She can also make copies for you.
   Vendors can also download the application packet from our website www.downtownopswatch.com. Tell them to click on applications.

4. Respond to any questions that a prospect might have. If you don't know the answer, ask George. If he doesn't know, work together with him to find the answer.

5. Screen applications as they come in. These may be some of your criteria:
   - Quality—would the public be interested enough to stop and look?
   - Does it fit in with our festival goals?
   - Are the items well priced?
   - Does it supplement what we have downtown, or does it duplicate what is already here?
   - Do we have variety and interest for the public? Do we have any popular draws?
   - Does the value as a vendor outshine any political negative overtones? (Green should not be controversial, but the potential is there, and we should be sensitive to it.)

6. Follow up on the applications that were sent out. See if there is any more information vendors need. The liability insurance that we are required to have by the city should not be a problem for most businesses. If they do not have it, ask Effy for a source. If the vendor fee is a problem for nonprofits, let George know. The committee may waive the fee.

7. Effy will check to make sure all returned applications have all of the required credentials and the check for the vendor fee. She will follow up on items still needed. She keeps the original and the documentation. You will get a copy of the application for your binder.

8. As chair of the green vendor chunk, you will be expected to attend the committee meetings and bring us up-to-date on vendors who have applied. The committee may also have suggestions about vendors to pursue.

9. At some point all of the people who are dealing with placement of vendors will get together. We will plug all of the green vendors, food vendors, entertainment stages, workshop areas, and the children's activities into the map.

10. After this meeting, an emailing will go out from Effy to vendors with acceptance letters and the assigned spaces. A map will be attached with directions on how to get where they belong and where they should park. Any last minute instructions will be given then also.

11. If you have any ideas for signage or ways to improve the vendor areas, please contact the appropriate committee person. If you have secured a very special vendor whom you think would be a good draw, draft a press release about them and forward it to the committee publicity person.

12. A day or so before the event you will work with a team to mark spaces. Effy will print out the list of vendors and their spaces for you and for the street bosses. You will chalk the vendor name on the sidewalk. If the weather threatens showers, print out vendor names on separate pieces of paper. Put these into page protectors and tape them into place early before the vendors arrive.

13. On the day of the event, be available bright and early (no later than 6:00 a.m.) to answer questions, to take care of the little problems that arise, and

to help it all run smoothly. The street bosses will help the vendors find their spots and be there throughout the day to help. Effy will have prepared little cards with committee cell phone numbers so we can keep in touch during the festival.

14.   Keep good records. This will help you or whomever is the chair next year to hit the ground running. Mark which vendors were the best, the nicest ones to deal with, the ones that festival-goers responded to the most, and any ones you would not invite back. Turn in your list of prospects, those who came, and ones you heard about that may be possibilities for next year.

15.   Fill out an evaluation form and pass it on to George. Send thank-you emails to the vendors who came and made the event a success. (Think positively!)

16.   We are all in this together, first to create a high-quality event for our community in a fun, meaningful, and satisfying way for those who come, and secondly, to make downtown Opswatch a better, more prosperous place to be. Do the best you can. Downtown folks are a good community and support each other. Feel free to get as many volunteers as you need to get the job done. The more the merrier. Get names, addresses, and phone numbers, and emails of your helpers so we can thank them.

George Green, Chairperson

Volunteer - Hold Harmless Agreement

Green Festival Volunteer Form
Hold Harmless Waiver, Assumption of Risk, and Release of Liability

I hereby waive, release and discharge any and all claims and damages for personal injury, death, or property damage which I/and or my minor child may sustain or which may occur as a result of my participation in the Event, Green Festival located in Downtown Opswatch. I understand and agree that:

1. This release is intended to absolve in advance the City and its officers, officials, employees, contractors, agents, and volunteers as well as Event Holder / Sponsor _____, its officers, officials, employees, and/or volunteers (collectively the "Released Parties"), from and against all liability arising out of or connected in any way with my participation in said Event;

2. Volunteering for said Event may be of a hazardous, strenuous, and physical nature and will involve interaction with other participants. Volunteering for said Event may involve risk of serious injury, disability, or death, or property damage and loss, which may result not only from volunteers, the Released Parties, or other's actions, inactions, or negligence or from the conditions of the facilities, equipment, or areas where said Event is being conducted;

3. Knowing the risks involved, I, nevertheless voluntarily request permission to volunteer for said Event and hereby assume any and all risks arising out of or connected in any way with my volunteering.

4. I hereby release, discharge, and absolve the Released Parties in advance from and against any and all liability, injury, damage, cost or expense, including litigation, arising out of or in connection with my volunteering for said Event, even though that liability, injury, or damage may arise out of the negligence or other legal fault of the Released Parties;

5. I and/or each minor child listed herein are in good health and have no physical condition which would prevent safe participation in said Event; I agree to immediately report to an Event official or City of Opswatch employee any unsafe condition observed by me and/or injury incurred by me and/or my minor child.

6. I understand that the Released Parties provide no medical insurance for treatment of illness or injury and that any cost of treatment will be at my expense. I understand that the use of emergency medical services may be required. I hereby release, discharge, and absolve the Released Parties from and against any and all liability, injury or damage arising out of or connected with the use of such medical services;

7. I understand and agree that this agreement is intended to be as broad and inclusive as permitted under IZ law, and that if any portion of this release and agreement is invalid, the remainder shall continue in full force and effect;

8. This release agreement shall be effective and binding upon myself, my heirs, next of kin, family, relatives, or assigns.

I HAVE CAREFULLY READ THIS RELEASE AGREEMENT AND FULLY UNDERSTAND ITS CONTENTS. I AM AWARE THAT THIS IS A RELEASE OF LIABILITY AND A CONTRACT BETWEEN ME AND THE CITY OF OPSWATCH. I VOLUNTARILY AGREE TO EACH OF THE TERMS AND PROVISIONS HEREIN AND SIGN THIS RELEASE AGREEMENT OF MY OWN FREE WILL.

PARTICIPANTS_____

_____

PARTICIPANT (OR PARENT / GUARDIAN) SIGNATURE _____

PARTICIPANT (OR PARENT / GUARDIAN) PRINTED NAME _____

DATE _____

Agenda – Last Minute Logistics Meeting

Green Festival, April 18, 2015 - Last Minute Logistics Meeting
Monday, April 13, 4:00 p.m., Downtown Office

Blanks are for people who are assigned to that task.
What is the Weather Forecast?
Street Closing
- Street Closed Signs - pick up and fill out_____ & _____
- Street Closed Signs - put out Wed. _____
- Barricades will be delivered on Tues.
- Close off streets @ 6:00 a.m. Sat. Leave opening into parking lots.
    - Opswatch and School, and McMeen and School _____ & _____
    - Oak & Church, and Oak & Library _____ & _____
    - Main at McMeen, Opswatch at McMeen _____ & _____
    - Pine at Library, Pine at Church _____ & _____

Set Up – General _____ & _____ & _____ & _____ & _____
Clean Up – General _____ & _____ & _____ & _____ & _____

Porta potties / Other Logistics
- Cone off porta potty spots when?
- Coordinate dropping off of porta potties. Lock them. Stow supplies.
- Unlock porta potties Sat. at 5:30 a.m.
- Cell phone cards for staff – make & distribute
- Make sure *volunteer hold harmless forms* are collected and put in binder
- Parking for vendors
- Parking for entertainers
- Roll out garbage & recycle toters _____ & _____ & _____
Cash drawers / Payments
- Beer booth
- T-shirt / Information booth – Who is responsible for?
- Checks cut for performers, etc.
Supplies needed – also, who is responsible for getting
- Cases of water
- Ice
- Duct tape
- Caution tape
- Clothesline for rainbow wheels
Street Bosses
- Church St. _____
- Library St. _____
- McMeen Ave. _____
- Opswatch Ave _____
- Question – Will there be coffee anywhere?
- Question – Will there be evaluation forms to distribute and pick up?

o   Have street bosses gotten vendor maps, directions for parking, etc and the message to stay around and solve problems on their street until at least noon?

Entertainer Logistics
- o   Meet Native American group _____
- o   Meet John Denver Tribute group _____
- o   Meet Elementary School Choir _____

Big Stuff to be moved
- o   Library St. – Info Booth – 2 pop ups, 2 tables, 4 chairs, shirt rack, shirts
- o   Beer booth – 2 pop ups, 2 tables, 4 chairs, ice chest, glasses
- o   Gazebo stage – sound system, A-frames
- o   Food court on Church – 3 tables, at least 10 chairs

Chunk Boxes
- o   Who puts together?
- o   When?
- o   Who gets them to their area?

Décor
- o   Rainbow wheels – ask Mark
- o   Ribbons and flowers around trees, poles – do NOT wind, don't put too high
- o   Baskets of flowers for gazebo stage?

Electricity –
- o   Gazebo stage
- o   Solar generators

Signage
- o   Help to put signage in place
- o   Vinyl banners
- o   No pets in food area
- o   Put out barricade covers w/ sponsor names
- o   Downtown event sign – at all cross streets
- o   T-shirt prices
- o   Schedule for Gazebo stage
- o   Schedule for Old First Church
- o   Schedule for Library and Community Center

Marking Vendor Spaces
- o   Who does and when?

Prizes
- o   Organize
- o   Solicit needed
- o   Label
- o   Put in chunk boxes

Information Booth
- o   Organize T-shirt and tote bag record sheets
- o   Staffing - Saturday

Set up _____ & _____

Work _____ & _____ & _____

Clean Up _____ & _____

Copies to be made
- o Plant ID game – adults
- o Plant ID game – kids
- o Into-stores activity forms
- o Programs
- o Vendor evaluation forms?
- o Incident report sheets
- o Volunteer Hold- Harmless Form

Hospitality – based at info booth
- o Water wagon
- o Sunscreen?
- o Ice
- o Water
- o First aid kit

Speakers
- o Press release info
- o Get information to web wizard

George – Stuff to watch out for
- o Cars parked on closed off streets after 6:00 a.m. They will need to be towed, and it takes a while.
- o Find out where the office wants vendors to park.
- o Find someone to put the barricade covers on.
- o Do you want to meet with the teen volunteers about doing the downtown décor with ribbons and flowers? Best time for this would be after school on Friday.
- o Sunscreen…or umbrellas… for staff at T-shirt booth and info booth.

II. Other Event Documents

You may create some of these documents on your own with help from your city, fire department, or police department. Some you may create using templates from your local arts council. You may also find templates on line.

Photo Release

Photo Release Form

Event Name _____

Name of participant _____

I give the Event Committee / Staff permission to use photographs and video recordings taken during the festival for all advertising purposes and other legitimate purposes, including, but not limited to: use in brochures, on the event or downtown website, and promotional literature for future events without compensating me.

Signature _____ Date _____

Print Name _____

Contact Information _____

Signature of parent or guardian (if under 18) _____ Date _____

Incident Report Form

Incident Report Form

Name of Event _____

Date of Incident _____Time _____

When completed, fax or deliver this to (Event Office, Information Booth, give contact information) immediately. Reported to (person) _____ at the time.

Person making report _____

Were you a witness? Yes   No   Your position in event _____

Nature of Activity where incident occurred _____

Exact Location _____

Weather conditions (if applicable) _____

Description in detail of what happened. (Who was involved, physical contact made, words said, gestures made, weapons involved, did the person seem to be under the influence, etc.) If vehicle was involved, attach information of owner, driver's license number, insurance information, and vehicle license number.

Witnesses (Use back if necessary.)

Name	Daytime Phone	Alternate phone
Name	Daytime Phone	Alternate phone

If incident was reported to police, list name / number of officer in charge

_____

Information on injured person or owner of damaged property
Name _____ Age _____

Address _____ Phone_____

Parent or Guardian (if under 18) _____

Describe injury or damage. What was the response? (first aid given, persons notified, etc.)

Silent Auction Forms

(Artist) Silent Auction Agreement Form

Visual artist participating in the silent auction will have two options regarding their donation of art to this event.

I. You can donate your item to the auction outright. This will qualify as a tax-deductible contribution to this event. Our tax ID number is _____.

2. You can choose to give 25% of the sale price of the art to the event. The artist will receive 75%.

Please complete the following when submitting your work.

Name _____

Address _____

Phone _____

I choose from above (circle)   Option 1   Option 2

Name of Item _____Medium _____

Value _____Starting Bid _____

Ending Bid and Sale Price _____

Signature _____ Date _____

This event cannot assume liability for any damage to the donated work. The artist assumes all risk and is responsible for any insurance desired.

For Office Use

The ending bid / sale price was _____.

For Option 2 - the amount of $_____ was delivered / mailed to the artist on date _____ by _____.

A thank you letter was sent on _____.

Silent Auction Bid Form

Silent Auction for (Name of Event) on (Date)

Item _____

Value _____

Starting Bid _____

Print legibly. Unreadable bids cannot be honored.

Name	Phone Number	BID
Lena Goodrich	*234-2345*	*$35*
Dorothy Smart	*456-3456*	*$38*

Art Show Agreement Form

Event Art Show / Contest Agreement

Thank you for participating in the (Event Name) Art Show

As a participant in the art show you agree to the following terms.

1. All art must be created by the artist.
2. Original work or prints may be submitted.
3. Art must be ready to hang or display. Art must be appropriate for a family event.
4. If art is sold, the artist will receive 80% and the event will receive 20% of the sale price.
5. Paying the sales tax will be the responsibility of the artist.
6. The event cannot assume any liability for loss or damage to any art work. All risk is assumed by the artist and he/she is responsible for any desired insurance.
7. All art must be delivered to (location) _____ on (dates _____ between the hours of _____.
8. All art must be picked up at the end of the event on (date) _____ by 5:00 p.m. Any art not picked up will incur a storage fee of $5.00 per day.

For further information contact _____ at (phone) _____.

Please complete the following:

Name _____

Address _____

Phone Number _____

Title of Work _____

Medium _____ Price _____

Signature _____

Guide for Taking Minutes

Guide for Minute-Taking at Meetings

The minutes of a meeting present in a clear, understandable, and legible way the record of what happened. They function as:

- An aid to the memory of those who were there
- An update for the members who were not present
- Working notes for those with responsibilities to do before the next meeting
- An aid to those who will later have the same committee responsibilities
- Confirmation that such action did or did not happen on a certain date should a question arise.

Good minutes help a committee complete its work efficiently and avoid needless rehashing of problems. They record policies that have been established to guide the committee in its work.

The chairperson may help the secretary by:

- Preparing and copying the agenda for members or having it visibly displayed
- Following the agenda and keeping the members from jumping from item to item and back again
- Asking to have motions re-read before a vote is taken to make certain they contain the sense of what the motion-maker is saying
- Sitting near enough to the secretary to facilitate communication
- Instructing the secretary when any unusual items are to be included— something that would not ordinarily be recorded

The secretary should have the minutes done while fresh in the mind—within a week of the meeting. People work from their minutes. They need the minutes in time to complete their assigned tasks. It doesn't help a committee to distribute minutes at the following meeting and let people discover there was a task that they should have completed by then. You also waste meeting time by folks reading minutes.

Minutes should be emailed or distributed to the members as soon as possible. A copy should be filed in the appropriate permanent binder record.

General rules for minutes.

These are pretty formal and based on *Robert's Rules of Order*. You can adapt them to your need and custom depending on your group. (I have underlined what I consider to be essentials.) While the committee of the whole might use the formality, chunk groups and subcommittees probably don't need to.

If you are a nonprofit corporation, follow the legal requirements for meeting minutes from the rules under your incorporation. If your group uses public funds, you may be required to adhere to more formal rules in your meetings and also required to post agendas before meetings. Find out and proceed accordingly.

Minutes should include the following:

1.   The kind of meeting (regular, special, team, chunk).
2.   <u>Name of group.</u>
3.   <u>Date and place of meeting.</u>
4.   Those present, absent, and excused. (<u>A sign-in sheet may be sufficient.</u>) Note any guests or staff present. In the body of minutes, note latecomers' arrival and time. This is helpful in case there is a question over who was present for a particular debate. For the same reason, note anyone who was excused to leave early and when they left.
5.   Approval of minutes of previous meeting.
6.   If applicable, there should be a treasurer's report which may include the receipts, disbursements, and beginning and ending balance. There may also be a budget report with last year's figures, this year's budget, and status to date.
7.   All communications received since the last meeting and action taken on them. For example, "referred to another group," "chair directed to write a response," etc.
8.   If the agenda is followed properly, the minutes will be in order and coordinated to those items.
9.   <u>Every motion put before the group should be recorded and whether it passes or fails.</u>
10.   <u>For any action taken, note who is responsible to communicate it or organize it to make it happen. Specify name and when action is to be accomplished or reported on.</u>
11.   <u>For actions that take funds, specify where money is to come from.</u>
12.   Reports of subcommittees should be received and any actions on them recorded.
13.   The secretary should preserve any papers for which the group is responsible and file them properly.
14.   The minutes should include the <u>date, time, and location of the next meeting.</u>
15.   They should be signed by the person preparing them.

It is customary to record only what was done at a meeting, not what was said. The secretary should never make any personal reflections on what was said or done in the minutes. But if the committee is best served by including the pros and cons regarding a particular decision, opinions of members, or the synopsis of a discussion, the chair may instruct that these be included. It is sometimes helpful to a committee.

III. Resources

I have selected these few books and websites to jumpstart your search for helpful, good-quality resources:

- Many of the topics have numerous books written on the subject. Use the resources I have listed to help you find more.
- Check authors included in this list for other books they may have written on the same or similar subjects.
- Some of the titles are older and may be out of print. They might still be in your library system or available through an interlibrary loan from a larger regional library system. They might also be found in used book stores and on www.Amazon.com.
- The one constant thing about life is that it changes. Even though the websites included were live at the time this book was published, they may have since disappeared into cyberspace. Use the topics to do an internet search for timely information.
- Do library, book store, and internet searches for sites on these topics.

a. Books

Books on Festival and Event Planning

Caputo, Kathryn. *How to Produce a Successful Crafts Show*.
(Mechanicsburg, PA: Stackpole Books, 1997). This little book does a comprehensive job of leading the reader through the steps of putting on a craft show. Both the crafter and the customer viewpoints are included.

Coons, Patti. *Gala! The Special Event Planner for Professionals and Volunteers.*
(Herndon, VA: Capital Books, Inc., 1999). The strengths of this brief, introductory book are its focus on luncheon-type events, timelines, and media relations. It does not include vendors, craft booths, and activities for children. It has very little about sponsors, budgets, income, and expenses.

Diehl, Daniel and Mark P. Donnelly. *Medieval Celebrations: Your Guide to Planning and Hosting Spectacular Feasts, Parties, Weddings, and Renaissance Fairs,* 2nd ed.
(Mechanicsburg, PA: Stackpole Books, 2011). Well done and helpful, this book gives all of the information you need to plan medieval holidays, weddings, and feasts. It includes recipes, manners, advice and patterns for costumes, décor, and even songs, dances, and games. Many color illustrations augment the text.

Freedman, Harry and Karen Feldman. *Black Tie Optional: A Complete Special Events Resource for Nonprofit Organizations,* 2nd ed. (Hoboken, NJ: John Wiley & Sons, Inc., 2007). This book is aimed at professionals and volunteers who plan special events as fundraisers. A good variety of sample events is included. Timelines, budget outlines, and help for finding and working with volunteers are given. If you want celebrities at your event, you would do well reading the advice in this book.

Kilkenny, Shannon. *The Complete Guide to Successful Event Planning,* 2nd ed. (Ocala, FL: Atlantic Publishing Group, Inc., 2011). Kilkenny's book asks good questions and is well organized. Advice is included for more formal events, business events, and those events where attendees come from long distances and meet in hotels. Many check lists and timelines are provided both in the text and on the accompanying CD.

Wolf, Paulette, and Jodi Wolf. *Event Planning Made Easy; 7 Simple Steps to Making Your Business or Private Event a Huge Success*, (New York: McGraw-Hill, 2005). This book is set up in a way that could be helpful to novice small-event planners. Though its focus is corporate events, weddings, private celebrations, and fundraiser galas, all of the basics of planning are here. The events the authors have in mind are large, with catered meals, celebrities and big name entertainment, and big budgets.

Books on Activities for Fundraising; School Fundraising

Bray, Ilona. *Effective Fundraising for Nonprofits: Real-World Strategies That Work,* 3rd ed. (Berkeley, CA: Nolo, 2008).   This resource includes a section on special events, but rather than on planning or producing the event, the focus is how the special event can raise money. Reading this book will provoke thought and will give you heads-up on cautions related to fundraising. It will be valuable to the event leadership.

Bray, Ilona. *The Volunteers' Guide to Fundraising; Raise Money for Your School, Team, Library, or Community Group.* (Berkeley: Nolo, 2011). This book gives excellent guidance for the fundraising aspects of an event. Bray's knowledge of nonprofits, corporations, and legal structures make this book an important reference book. She has chapters on fundraising dinners, home and garden tours, auctions, benefit concerts and lectures, and walkathons and other sporting events.

Corcoran, Jack. *School Carnival Guide: How to Run a School Carnival for Fun and Profit.* (Winder, GA: Alpaca Press, 2011). I have not seen this book, but I include it here because it is touted as being the most complete guide to running a school carnival fundraiser. Jack Corcoran has over 20 years experience in helping PTAs and PTOs run school carnivals.

DeSoto, Carole. *For Fun and Funds; Creative Fund-Raising Ideas for Your Organization._*(West Nyack, NY: Parker Publishing Co, 1983). This book contains more than 160 activities for raising money. Help is also given for putting on an event and publicizing it. It is an older book, but the ideas are still good.

Sandlin, Eileen Figure and Richard Helweg. *199 Fun and Effective Fundraising Events for Nonprofit Organizations*. (Ocala, FL: Atlantic Publishing Company, 2010). This book is full of fundraising ideas which are briefly described. The degree of difficulty for completing each activity is charted.

Festival Décor Topics

Higham, Cindy. *Snowflakes for All Seasons: 72 Fold & Cut Paper Snowflakes*. (Layton, UT: Gibbs Smith, 2004). This book has directions and patterns for making streamers of flowers, bunnies, kites, and birds. They are all done with the technique used for traditional snowflakes and streamers, but are tailored to any holiday or theme.

Miyai, Yukiko. *Clay Art for Special Occasions*. (Waipahu, HI: Island Heritage Publishing, 2009). Beautiful decorations, mostly flowers made from polymer clay are the focus of this resource. The techniques might be adapted to other mediums.

Reeder, Dan. *Papier-Mache Monsters: Turn Trinkets and Trash into Magnificent Monstrosities*. (Salt Lake City, UT: Gibbs Smith, 2009). This is a marvelous book on the process of making papier-mâché dragons and other creatures. Using the techniques in this full-color book, décor could be made to fit almost every theme. He has written other books on papier-mâché also. Check out another book of Dan Reeder's, *Dragonmaker's Handbook*. He also has a website with videos where you can watch him making dragons and other critters from start to finish in time-lapse photography. www.gourmetpapermache.com.

Books That Are Good Resources for Children's Events

Kilby, Janice Eaton and Deborah Morgenthal and Terry Taylor. *The Book of Wizard Craft*. (New York, NY: Lark Books, 2001).
Kilby, Janice Eaton and Terry Taylor. *The Book of Wizard Parties*. (New York, NY: Lark Books, 2002). The above two books are marvelous resources for crafts, activities, and atmosphere for children's fantasy events.

Pence, Shari Ann. *Games Galore for Children's Parties and More: 80 Fun Games and Activities for Parties, Classrooms, Youth Groups, Carnivals, Company Picnics, Rainy Days and Special Occasions*, 2nd ed., (Funcastle Books, 2005). This book contains a good mix of active and quiet games and activities. Safety is emphasized. Most games are non-competitive.

Ragsdale, Susan and Ann Saylor. *Great Group Games: 175 Boredom-Busting, Zero-Prep Team Builders for All Ages.* (Minneapolis, MN: Search Institute Press, 2007). Lesson learning, cooperation, building community, and developing trust are not-so-subtle by-products of these activities.

Warner, Penny. *Kids' Outdoor Parties* (Children's Party Planning Books). (Minnetonka, MN: Meadowbrook Press, 1999). This resource provides outdoor party themes for children. Ideas for games, decorations, activities and food might be adapted for other events involving children. The same author has also written *Kids' Party Games and Activities* (Minnetonka, MN: Meadowbrook Press, 1993).

Unique Resource Books

Editors of Chase's Calendar of Events. *Chase's Calendar of Events: The Ultimate Go-To-Guide for Special Days, Weeks and Months*. (New York, NY: McGraw Hill). This reference is published annually. Use it for inspiration. It includes websites to browse, and could be a good source of ideas to augment your theme.

Fitzgerald, Barb. *Food Booth: The Entrepreneur's Complete Guide to the Food Concession Business,* 2nd ed. (Cornelius, OR: Carnival Press, 2011). This book is aimed at those who want to set up a food booth, not the event producer who might be looking for food vendors. However, it provides interesting insight and might give hints to working well with food vendors.

Grunfeld, Frederic V. *Games of the World: How to Make Them, How to Play Them, How They Came to Be.* (New York, NY: Ballantine, 1982). This resource with plenty of photos and drawings does exactly what the title says. Use it for inspiration for activities at your event. Excellent resource book.

Gryczan, Matthew L. *Carnival Secrets: How to Win at Carnival Games, Which Games to Avoid, How to Make Your Own Games*. (Grand Rapids, MI: Zenith Press, 1988, 3rd printing in 2008). More than 35 games are described in this book. This resource is included here, not so you can win at these games, but to give you ideas on constructing fair, fun, and novel games designed for your event.

Majure, Janet. *Teach Yourself Visually WordPress*. (Indianapolis, IN: Visual [Wiley Publishing], 2010). This is one of many books on using WordPress, which is a popular, free, downloadable software used for setting up blogs. Check for others on WordPress, as well as the subjects of blogging platforms or blogging software.

Mancuso, Anthony. *How to Form a Nonprofit Corporation*, 9th ed. (Berkeley, CA: Nolo, 2008) This resource gives a step-by-step guide to forming a nonprofit corporation and avoiding the pitfalls.

Palmer, Helen. *The Enneagram: Understanding Yourself and the Others In Your Life*. (New York, NY: Harper & Row, 1988). This is one of many books written on the subject. You can also find more by visiting www.enneagraminstitute.com or by checking Wikipedia "The Enneagram of Personality".

Riggs, Adam. *Critter Costuming: Making Mascots and Fabricating Fursuits*. (San Jose, CA: Ibexa Press, 2004).

b. Periodicals

The following are periodicals, even though they are listed by their websites. Check your local bookstores and libraries for copies.

www.renaissancemagazine.com
Magazine for Renaissance history and information. Includes a link to Renaissance and Medieval fairs.

www.faeriemagazine.com
Magazine for those intrigued with lore, music, and art inspired by the world of fairies. Includes a link to fairy-related festivals.

www.sunshineartist.com
www.craftsreport.com
These are magazines aimed at craftspeople and artists. They also list events.

c. Websites

Sites for Long-standing Festivals.

Look for ideas on organization, activities, and creative inspiration for your event.

www.anokahalloween.com
Website for the Anoka Halloween celebration and parade. Anoka, MN, proclaimed the "Halloween Capital of the World", has carried on this family-friendly festival since 1920.

www.gilroygarlicfestival.com
Based on a garlic theme, this celebration in Gilroy, CA, has arts & crafts, entertainment, and cooking demonstrations and competitions. It has raised millions of dollars for local charities.

www.huckleberryfestival.com
More than 30 years running, the Huckleberry Festival, Trout Creek, MT, is held in August. It is put on by volunteers and features food vendors with huckleberries in ice cream cones, pizza, cheesecake, drinks, and atop Polish dogs. There are also more than 100 arts and crafts vendors, a huckleberry pancake breakfast, entertainment, a dessert contest, fun runs, a pageant, children's activities and more.

www.kvmr.org/celticfestival
This is a Celtic music festival put on by a radio station in Grass Valley, CA. Vendors, world-class Celtic musicians, costumes, living history, and demonstrations make up this growing festival.

www.makerfaire.com
Touted as the "world's largest do-it-yourself festival", this event invites families to make, create, learn, invent, play, recycle and be inspired by celebrating arts, crafts, engineering, food, music, science and technology. It is held in Detroit, New York, and the San Francisco Bay Area every year.

www.shrewfaire.com
This is the website for the Shrewsbury Renaissance Faire in Kings Valley, OR. It includes a compendium from the *Shrewsbury Villager Guide* teaching participants how to speak, dress, act, and behave as a Renaissance person.

www.solfest.org
The Solar Living Institute puts on this annual, green-technology fair in September. (Go to the 'About' tab, then click on Solfest. They have also produced the Moonfest.) Solfest has workshops, demonstrations, vendors, speakers, activities, music, and much more.

www.stjamescourtartshow.com
This Louisville, KY, fair held in October showcases a rich cultural and artistic legacy with more than 700 artists.

www.storytellingcenter.net
The National Storytelling Festival is held in October in Jonesborough, TN. Accomplished storytellers provide stories of childhood, celebrating different cultures, and venturing into the realm of imagination.

www.winter-carnival.com
Capitalizing on Minnesota's frigid winters, this festival provides indoor and outdoor fun. Among its activities are ice-carving competitions and golf on ice.

Unusual and Creative Events That Caught My Attention

www.chickenshow.com
The Wayne Chicken Show is held in July in Wayne, NE. Volunteers at this show work hard to keep the event "cheep" for everyone. They make money by selling "cluck-tibles" (T-shirts, and other memorabilia). They tout "egg-citing" games like egg roulette, which is a real crack-up to watch.

www.heronfestival.org
Held in April at Clear Lake State Park, Kelseyville, CA, this educational festival celebrates the nesting of the plentiful great blue herons. Families enjoy bird and nature walks, an omelet brunch, speakers, children's activities, and pontoon boat tours.

www.festivalofowls.com
The International Festival of Owls, held in March in Houston, MN, was begun as "hatch-day" party for a great horned owl and has blossomed into a three-day festival for adults and children. It has intriguing activities like an owl-faced pancake breakfast, a program on owls in literature, pellet discussions, and an owl prowl. This is a real hoot.

www.kitefestival.com/kite-festival
Held in August in Long Beach, WA, this week-long kite festival draws spectators and kite fliers from all over the world. There are many competitions including special categories for children and seniors.

www.woollyworm.com
The Woolly Worm Festival is a truly innovative festival held in October in Banner Elk, NC. About 20,000 folks attend this event with craft vendors and woolly worm races. They claim 1000 worm trainers. This has been an annual event for more than 30 years.

Sites for Organizations Specializing in a Particular Type of Event

www.asgf.org
The goal of The **Association of Scottish Games and Festivals** (ASGF) is to provide its members with information, ideas, and resources on producing Highland Games in the United States.

www.dmrenfaire.com
Des Moines, IA, Renaissance Faire. The site includes a short history on the development and construction of the permanent fair location.

www.gradnight.org
Grad nights were started for the purpose of keeping graduates safe and sober and having a night of spectacular fun. This site includes an extensive manual for planning grad nights.

www.guildofstgeorge.com
This website has been included to show how a guild is organized. It is an example of a guild whose purpose is to recreate living history from Elizabethan times.

www.renfaire.com
On this site you can find out about Renaissance, medieval, and pirate fairs. Hundreds of fairs are listed. Lots of helpful information is given about educating folks about Renaissance history and fairs.

www.sca.org
Society for Creative Anachronism (SCA)
The SCA is an international organization dedicated to researching and re-creating the arts and skills of pre-17th-century Europe. Their website will have information on activities and membership.

Sites to Find Events and Vendors, or Where Your Event Can Be Listed

www.artscraftsshowbusiness.com
This is the site for the publication of art and craft shows, street fairs, festivals, and so on. It has both an east coast and a west coast division. It is published quarterly by subscription. Sample listings are given on the website.

www.craftlister.com
On this website you can find events within a certain distance of a zip code and within a time period.

www.craftmasternews.com
This site reviews and evaluates over 1000 fairs in the western U.S. By subscribing to their quarterly magazine, you have access to these reviews and a large, diverse number of events. By clicking on a state, you have access to an event calendar without a subscription. The site is also linked to the eastern U.S. counterpart.

www.eastcoastartisan.com
East Coast Artisan was formerly the Craft Digest. It lists upcoming events, lists show promoters, has some artist profiles, and gives reviews on craft books. It covers the area from Maine to Virginia.

www.festivalnet.com
Here is a site that helps you search events by month, and within specific mileages from your zip code. While it gives you enough information to find about an event, even more information is available to subscribers.

www.festivals.com
Another site to find out about events in your area or across the USA.

www.festivalsandevents.com
On this site you will be able to list your event, see other events by state, and find resources to help locate vendors and entertainers. There are also helpful articles on planning an event.

www.topeventsusa.com
This website gives a listing of many of top, popular festivals in the USA. You can search by state or by type of event. The site lists their choice for the "Top 20 Festivals".

Performance Rights Organizations

ASCAP - American Society of Composers, Authors, and Publishers. www.ascap.com

BMI – Broadcast Music, Inc. www.bmi.com

SOCAN – Society of Composers, Authors, and Music Publishers of Canada. www.socan.ca

Sites That Give Help on Various Topics

www.AlleyCatScratch.com
This is a site for those who need help in creating costumes. The site began with a love for fantasy costumes and movie costumes, especially those from *The Lord of the Rings*. It includes tips for elaborate intricate costumes, as well as help for a parent whose child tells him the night before that he needs a costume for school. The site claims over 1500 pages of costume tips and sewing information.

www.dryiceinfo.com/fog.htm
Here is a website link giving information on safe handling of dry ice and how to achieve different special effects using dry ice.

www.gcb.state.mn.us/ConductRaffle.htm
This link to the Minnesota Gambling Control Board states what raffle games are legal in Minnesota and gives instructions on how several different games are to be conducted. They even tell you how to set up cow plop bingo (though they have a different name for it). They also tell you types of games that are not allowed and the reasons why they are not. Use this site to give you new ideas on creating raffles suited to your target audience.

www.paradefloats.wordpress.com
Many parade float ideas are found on this site.

www.parentbooster.org
This is an organization that will help its members navigate through the legal jungle of school booster clubs and keep them in compliance with the IRS. Their website has interesting and helpful information.

www.preservationnation.org/main-street
The Main Street Program is under the National Trust for Historic Preservation. Its tag line is "Helping people protect, enhance, and enjoy the places that matter to them". Helping revitalize historic downtowns is a priority. Promotion through special events is one way of reaching their goal. Browse through the site for a variety of resources.

www.squidoo.com/PaperMacheArmature
This site gives step-by-step help for creating large sculptures out of papier-mâché.

Commercial Sites with Help or Products for Greening an Event

www.cleangreenbags.com
www.earthwisebags.com
www.reusethisbag.com
These above sites may be checked for reusable tote bags.

www.earthwarebiodegradables.com

Earthware Biodegradables is a source for Earth-friendly alternatives to the petroleum-based plastic knives, forks, and spoons typically used in to-go food service.

www.earth-to-go.com
This company makes biodegradable containers and cutlery from potatoes.

www.tree-free.com
Tree-Free Greetings, Inc. is a greeting card company with a commitment to the environment. They use soy–based inks and paper made from sustainable resources such as sugar cane. Tree-Free paper saves trees, energy, and has a low carbon footprint. They have hundreds of wonderful designs.

Sites for Resources to Enhance and Help Produce Your Event

www.aervoe.com
Marking products (for example, spray cans of marking chalk), safety, traffic control and outdoor products. While the site is set up for larger consumers, you may find items that here that are available at your local hardware store.

www.badgeaminit.com
Carries buttons and button-making equipment and supplies.

www.carnivalsavers.com
Carnival games and prizes. Has free carnival game ideas.

www.dillonimporting.com
Toys, novelties, prizes. This was the source for the Medieval Fantasy Festival—large Rat-Tat-Toe rats, squoosh rats, and rubber rats for hurling.

www.doverpublications.com
Dover Publications, Inc. 31 East 2nd St., Mineola, NY 11501-3582 (800) 223-3130
Dover publishes a plethora of useful books including clip-art and graphics books. Many graphics are copyright free for your projects.

www.egggame.com
This is a game using a round board and a spinning egg. Educators use it to teach cooperation and communication. The website tells about the curriculum. It may be "egg-zactly" what your event needs.

www.folkmanis.com
Folkmanis is a company that manufactures hand puppets. They are innovative, well-made, well-priced, and designed to work well on your hand. They have many animals, fantasy creatures, and character puppets.

www.kitebuilder.com
Website for kites and kite-making supplies. Has an on-line catalog.

www.contemporarydrama.com or www.ChristianPlaysandMusicals.com
Meriwether Publishing Ltd., P.O. Box 7710, Colorado Springs, CO   80933-7710.
(800) 937-5297.   Click on the Meriwether link for how-to books on theater,
including titles on banners, costuming, mime, and stagecraft.

www.orientaltrading.com
Party favors, toys, prizes, games, novelties, décor.

www.trumeter.com
There are several types of measuring wheels that will make the job easier than
messing with a tape measure. The one that we used is called a Mini Measure Maxx,
made by the Trumeter Co. It was suggested for use in offices, factories, and short
distances. Look on their site under *distance-measuring products*, and then click on
indoor measuring wheels. We found our wheel at a local hardware store.

d. Favorite Events

As I talked with people during the course of writing this book, I asked them to name
some of their favorite events. This list has been compiled from their favorites. It
includes huge, commercial events as well as small, educational ones.

Anoka Halloween Parade and Festival, Anoka, MN
www.anokahalloween.com
BAEER Fair (Bay Area Environmental Education Resource Fair), San Rafael, CA
www.baeerfair.org
Davis Whole Earth Festival, Davis, CA
wef.ucdavis.edu
Dickens Faire, San Francisco, CA
www.dickensfair.com
Dragon Con, Atlanta, GA
www.dragoncon.org
Fairy Festival at Spoutwood Farm, Glen Rock, PA
www.spoutwood.org/fairie-festival
Festival of Trees, Sandy, UT
www.festivaloftreesutah.org
Hot August Nights, Reno, NV
www.hotaugustnights.net
Irish Day, Murphys, CA
www.murphysirishdays.org
Kinetic Sculpture Race, Baltimore, MD
www.kineticbaltimore.com
KVMR Celtic Music Festival, Grass Valley, CA
www.kvmr.org/celticfestival
Lompoc Flower Festival, Lompoc, CA
www.flowerfestival.org
Maine Fiber Frolic, Windsor, ME

www.fiberfrolic.com

Maker Faire, S F Bay Area, Detroit, or New York

www.makerfaire.com

Maryland Renaissance Festival, Annapolis, MD

www.rennfest.com

Northern California Pirate Festival, Vallejo, CA

www.norcalpiratefestival.com.

Pear Fair in Courtland, CA

www.pearfair.org

Pelican Island Wildlife Festival, Sebastian, FL

www.pelicanislandfriends.org

Pirates in Paradise, Key West, FL

www.piratesinparadise.com

Shrewsbury Renaissance Faire, OR

www.shrewfaire.com

Southeastern Wildlife Exposition, Charleston, SC

www.sewe.com

Sonoma Jazz Festival, Sonoma, CA

www.sonomajazz.org

Sonora Celtic Fair, CA

www.sonoracelticfaire.com

Stockton Asparagus Festival, Stockton, CA

www.asparagusfest.com

Sweet Pea Festival, Bozeman, MT

www.sweetpeafestival.org

Valhalla Renaissance Fair, South Lake Tahoe, CA

www.valhallafaire.com

Veiled Prophet Fair, St. Louis, MO

www.vpparade.org

IV. Glossary - Event Terms and Jargon

Acronym or Initialism - A "word" formed with the initial letters of words: examples of these are PIN number (personal identification number) and PSA (public service announcement).

Ad sell sheet - A handout sheet designed to make selling a program ad easier and to provide accurate information to the buyer. It includes a short summary about the event, all of the specifics for the ad, a sketch of the comparative size, and the placement of the ad on the page. It lists the costs for each ad size and any additional services such as screening photos.

ADA - *Americans with Disabilities Act.* For event purposes it deals with accessibility to restrooms, public spaces, and parking.

Advertising - In the context of this book, it is promotion that you pay money for, such as an ad in a newspaper.

ASCAP and BMI - *American Society of Composers, Authors and Publishers*, and *Broadcast Music Incorporated*. These are performance rights organizations. They license the work of writers (songwriters, usually), and pay royalties to the copyright owners. Technically, any time any licensed music is played in public, it is subject to royalty payments.

Back Line - This refers to the instruments and accoutrements that the musicians don't want to haul with them. They want the event to provide them. Typically these are bulky, heavy items like drum sets and bass amplifiers. These needs would be spelled out in the rider requirements.

Barricades - A-frame contraptions or other stand-alone structures that are used to block off streets closed to traffic or areas where the public is not allowed.

Carbon footprint - The amount of CO_2 or greenhouse gasses left behind as a result of a particular activity. The total carbon footprint will be not only that from the activity itself, but all that is involved from the beginning to end. If you serve a community dinner, your carbon footprint will depend on the choices of food you have, where they were grown, how they were grown, how they traveled to you, how they are prepared and with what kind of energy, what they are eaten with, and how the waste is treated.

Chunk - In this book a *chunk* is a particular segment of the event committee's work that must be tackled. In a more formal setting it might be called a subcommittee.

Contract - Agreement between the event and the entertainer. A basic contract will deal with the where, when, load-in time, and compensation details. Parties agree to follow this firmly.

Core Committee - Usually consists of the event chairperson and the chunk or sub-committee chairs. It functions somewhat like an executive committee. It often provides a sounding board for new ideas.

Cover Music - As opposed to original music played by the composer, cover music has been previously recorded by someone else. When a pianist plays songs made popular by someone else, he is playing cover music.

Demonstrator - Someone who is demonstrating a skill or craft such as wood-carving or archery. Depending on which is appropriate, they might be either classified as entertainment or a merchandise vendor. Events with a living history section will likely have demonstrators showing old-time skills.

Facility - In this book it refers to a building or inside venue for an event.

Fair Trade - Fair trade goods are those grown by people who earn a minimum wage and have health and safety standards. Fair trade goods are usually exports from developing countries to developed countries. They include such items as handicrafts, coffee, tea, and so on.

Goals - These are the big ideas, the purposes that are the foundation or the mission statement of your event.

Gobo - Device placed over a theatrical light to project shapes or patterns. According to Wikipedia the name is derived from **GO**es **B**efore **O**ptics.

Greywater tank - Large tank, usually available from the porta potty rental company. Greywater is dishwater, water and ice from drink coolers, and hand-washing water. Food vendors will dump their greywater in the tank rather than haul it back home or pour it out where you do not want it.

Guild - Group of people who share interest in a particular historical period, aspect of that period, or in a particular skill. They meet to discuss, learn, and to share their enthusiasm by providing educational opportunities for the public.

Hat show - A show where entertainers "pass the hat" among the audience at the end to get money for their performances.

In-kind - Support given by a donor or sponsor that is not in cash form, but in the form of product (examples: prizes, snacks, bottled water) or service (examples: advertising space, graphic design work).

to **Jury Vendors** – The process of choosing which vendor applications you will accept at your event, usually done by a small group of folks who have criteria in mind and who will choose only the best and most appropriate for their event. In this context, "jury" does not mean a twelve-person panel as in a criminal trial. A **jury fee** is a small amount charged by established events to applicants seeking to be included into a highly competitive market.

Logistics - The art of getting things to the right place, needs met in plenty of time, and all with as little hassle as possible. Well-organized logistic choices are what make the event go smoothly behind and in front of the scenes. They include all of the housekeeping details.

Objectives - These are fairly specific actions that you have decided are the ways you will meet your event goals. Usually measurable, they may change often as your planning and evaluation dictate.

Parent Group - If your group is putting on an event under the auspices of a larger, formal group such as a nonprofit corporation, that organization is the parent group. You report to the parent group and work under their direction.

Pop-up - In this book it is used as a generic term to refer to canopies and tents that vendors bring with them or that house event functions like an information booth or first aid booth.

Press Release - An article written by event personnel and submitted to media outlets, such as newspapers, TV and radio stations. It includes who, what, where, when, and why information. It also gives the contact for further information and questions. Press releases are published at no cost by the media on a space and time availability.

Promotion - In this book promotion is the *total* picture that includes all of the activities and marketing designed to stimulate the public's interest in the event.

PSA (public service announcement) - Radio and television stations are required by the FCC to show that they serve in the public interest. One way they do this is to air PSAs about health, safety issues, and events—often from nonprofit organizations.

Publicity - In this book publicity refers to all of the promotion that you do not pay for. Press releases, feature articles in a newspaper, being included on various calendars in the community, and public service announcements are examples of publicity.

Ratapult - Competitive event designed by the Medieval Fantasy Festival, Vacaville, CA. In this event, costumed, toy, stuffed rat puppets were launched from trebuchets and catapults.

Rider Requirements - Negotiable and required details about amenities and hospitality added to a contract. Sometimes this is a wish list from the musicians.

Seller's permit - Vendors get this from whomever handles the sales tax for their state. Most states issue one as sellers are required to collect sales tax and remit it to the state.

Set (in music) - A set is a group of songs or pieces about 45 minutes long. A set is usually followed by a 15-minute break. Times are negotiable.

Set-up, Tear-down - Set-up is the physical action of putting up all of the barricades, pop-ups, booths, stages, décor, and all of what it takes to get ready for the event. Tear-down is getting it all put away at the end.

Site - In this book a site is the outdoor venue for an event. City parks, streets, playgrounds, and fields would be sites.

Sponsor menu - A list of items and goodies designed to entice a sponsor to support your event. "If you sponsor us at this level, you will receive...."

State Standards in Education - These are standards set by your state. They are designed to cover all of the skills, concepts, and knowledge that are expected at each grade level.

Template - Sample form or document which an event can use as a model to design their own. Several samples or templates are included in the Appendix.

Toters - Bins or cans for garbage and for recycling. In some localities composting bins may be needed.

Trebuchet - (TRE-boo-shay) a type of medieval siege engine used for throwing huge rocks, dead cows, and other demoralizing items. A type of catapult, it has a pivoting arm. The payload is placed in a sling attached to one end of the arm. A counterweight is attached to the other end. When the counterweight is dropped, the arm moves up, and the sling lets go of its load which is launched a good distance.

Vendor - In this book it means someone who buys exhibit space to sell food, arts and crafts, or other merchandise. Vendor fees are one source of income for events.

Venue - The location where your event will happen.

VIP - Stands for "very important person". I know, we *all* are important, but practical considerations may call for special treatment of some individuals within the context of your event.

Index

W

Author and Illustrator

Betty Lucke brings her experiences as a pastor, elementary school teacher, and retail business owner to this *Festival Planning Guide*. Betty is a graduate of Macalester College, St. Paul, MN, and of Princeton Theological Seminary, Princeton, NJ. She has worked extensively in education, group leadership, organization, planning, and with volunteers. She has worked on many special events, including the Medieval Fantasy Festival, which she envisioned and with volunteers brought to life for its glorious seven-year run. She lives in Northern California with her husband, Rick, and their Welsh Terrier, Hobbit.

If you would like
more information, more resources,
to order more books,
or to contact the author,
visit www.festivalplanningguide.com.